Contemporary Debates in American Reform Judaism

Conflicting Visions

DANA EVAN KAPLAN
Editor

Routledge
New York and London

Published in 2001 by
Routledge
29 West 35th Street
New York, NY 10001

Published in Great Britain by
Routledge
11 New Fetter Lane
London EC4P 4EE

Routledge is an imprint of the Taylor & Francis Group

Library of Congress Cataloging-in-Publication Data

Contemporary debates in American reform Judaism : conflicting visions / edited by Dana Evan Kaplan.
    p. cm.
  Includes bibliographical references and index.
  ISBN 0-415-92628-9 — ISBN 0-415-92629-7 (pbk.)
    1. Reform Judaism—United States.   I. Kaplan, Dana Evan.
BM197.C6 2000
296.8'341'0973—dc21

00-036895

43859443

Contents

Dedicated to the memory of Rabbi Alexander M. Schindler
— *Born October 4, 1925 - 16 Tishri 5686 died November 15, 2000 - 17 Heshvan*
5761

Past President of the Union of American Hebrew Congregations
— *1973 - 1996*

A man of vision, compassion, and courage who — like Moses — led us
through many a desert toward a land of promise.

Dedicated to the memory of Rabbi Alexander M. Schindler
— *Born October 4, 1925 - 16 Tishri 5686 died November 15, 2000 - 17 Heshvan
5761*

Past President of the Union of American Hebrew Congregations
— *1973 - 1996*

A man of vision, compassion, and courage who — like Moses — led us
through many a desert toward a land of promise.

Foreword

MARTIN E. MARTY

Contemporary Debates in American Reform Judaism is a set of arguments that, one hopes, will inspire a set of conversations.

Here is the difference between arguments and conversation, say experts in rhetoric who have compared the two: Arguments begin with the rhetoricians in possession of answers, conflicting truths that they set out to defend. In the end someone has convinced, converted, defeated, or exiled the other. Truth prevails, or at least holds the field for the moment until another challenge comes along. Conversations begin with the rhetoricians posing questions, pursuing truth toward ends uncertain through means not predetermined. No one ever says, "I sure won *that* conversation." Conversations have something of a game character, to be played out on their own terms and for sheer enjoyment. Or they may be useful instruments for expanding imaginations: "I never thought of that before, until you brought it up that way."

Vital societies need both argument and conversation. There can be no republic without argument, since conflicting interests have to represent themselves, seek justice, and, one hopes, pursue the common good in uncommon ways.

Similarly, there can be no vital societies, no associations, no "peoples," no fellowships without argument. Argument contributes to self-examination and purification. It challenges us to show our best face, put our best foot forward, and make a better proposal for the future.

Contemporary Debates in American Reform Judaism is argument on such terms. There are in the pages to follow some rather bitter, often profound self-examinations as authors probe their own commitments and the records of the partisan interests they represent. Similarly, there are some critical assaults on others, attacks based on diverse interpretations of the history of Reform Judaism, accompanied by some often drastic suggestions about the future of the movement. This bystander found his pulse racing at times; he could only picture what will be going on in the minds of those for whom the future of Reform Judaism is of more than passing importance.

Contemporary Debates in American Reform Judaism will fail in its purpose, however, if it ends as an entertainment, a display of argumentative powers. This is not the literary equivalent of professional wrestling, with its posturing and rigged outcomes. The book should be useful to those who really do not know where Reform Judaism is, should be, is going, and should go. They will have questions: "What is the best course?" "How should we regard intermarriage?" "Is there a future for Reform—indeed, for Judaism—in a world often described as secular, pluralist, given to 'spiritual' quests apart from community?" "What would be good outcomes, and how do we pursue them?"

I do not need to anticipate the arguments defended in the chapters to follow. Dana Evan Kaplan has done that with accurate, succinct summaries designed to whet the reader's appetite. Let me make just a few observations.

First, the agenda set forth here bears some resemblance to that proposed in the middle of the twentieth century, when some of us non-Jews first eavesdropped on the conversations and arguments that animated life in a new national situation. That situation was sometimes described as "Judeo-Christian," an invention of the times, or "Protestant-Catholic-Jewish" America, also a coinage of mid-century years. Before World War II Judaism was quite remote from the experience of most non-Jews. But World War II, the deghettoization that came with suburbanization, and other forces meant the virtual end of the Catholic ghetto and the Jewish ghetto, leaving us with the inner-city, predominantly black ghetto. It also revealed how the Protestant majority, usually male, always white, had thought it was speaking for the America that it dominated culturally, when it was but one voice among the many.

Between 1945 and 1967 Reform and Conservative Judaism, the two brands most of us came to know as other-than-remote, nonexotic, asked many of the questions that get revisited in this book. They had to do with synagogue attendance, the liveliness of community, the education of the young, and the fear that Judaism-without-boundaries would disappear but Judaism-with-high-boundaries would be beside the point in pluralist America.

What is astonishing to today's reader is the general absence in such discussions of the role that the birth of Israel in 1948 was to play in American Jewish life. Even more, the Holocaust had not yet been made central in Jewish consciousness. The Six-Day War, which American Jews experienced as a threat to the survival of Israel, changed all that. Israel and the Holocaust became the central themes of the agenda.

Most of the authors of this volume—Ephraim Tabory aside—have spent less energy on Israel and the Holocaust and have returned to questions about Reform and, at least implicitly, Conservative and Orthodox Judaism. More of them seem worried about life in a culture that is too open, too friendly; compare this to discussions half a century earlier about life in a culture that was too closed and unfriendly. Behind it all there is a haunting issue: will American Judaism survive? The question is not whether Jews will disappear—that will not happen for generations, even with high intermarriage rates. But will they be so diffused, so individualized, so unobservant that there will no longer be much of a sense of Jewish peoplehood? And if there is to be a people, what will characterize it, hold it together, and give it impulse toward various futures?

I know that my mention of survival instead of Israel-plus-Holocaust as a theme throughout this book will give ammunition to enemies of Reform Judaism or to some Reform Jews who have no way of defining Jewish faith(s) and people(s) apart from the determining events code-named "Israel" and "Holocaust." Rather, I would say that this generation has internalized the positives of the former and struggled with the negatives of the latter to the point that they do not have to be talked about in every conversation, written about on every page.

But survival is not a very noble theme, is it? I have a friend who rather bracingly observes when the subject comes up, "If we don't survive, we don't do anything else, either." I am happy to note that this book is about the "anything elses" of Reform Judaism. What will belief, practice, observance, and causes look like in reformed Reform?

I often remind non-Jews who wonder why so many Jews care about peoplehood that there are fewer Jews in the whole world than there are members of the largest single Protestant denomination (out of some two hundred) in the United States, the Southern Baptist Convention. I don't have to remind them that the Southern Baptist Convention is making moves to lower the number of Jews of the Covenant by "Baptistizing" them. But Reform is not, finally, about numbers. It is about the life of Jews and Judaism itself.

The second look-ahead for me is to note the differences and similarities between the Reform Jewish course and that of today's Catholicism and mainstream Protestantism. It is easy to be a traditionalist Catholic, an Orthodox Jew, a fundamentalist Protestant. Not that the practices of those three are not strenuous, rigorous, or demanding; it can be inconvenient to hold to beliefs that seem eccentric, even weird, to outsiders. But modernity and now postmodernity do not lack people ready to engage in all kinds of difficult practices (look at the zeal with which some people pursue the market) or in holding strange beliefs (observe the success of New Age bookstores). What is difficult is to present a faith and a way of life that are relatively unsheltered from others in the larger culture and yet possess distinctiveness.

What the distinctiveness should be becomes the theme of both the historical and forward-looking chapters in this book. What follows is discussion about issues that concern, or should concern, all Reform Jews, most other Jews, majorities of religious Americans, and many beyond those three circles. After they have read *Contemporary Debates in American Reform Judaism*, I hope to overhear some of them, at least, conversing about what they took from these arguments.

Introduction

Conflicting Visions of the Reform Movement in the United States Today

DANA EVAN KAPLAN

Contemporary Debates in American Reform Judaism: Conflicting Visions is a ground-breaking collection of essays that takes a hard look at the Reform movement today in the United States of America. Most demographers believe that the Reform movement is presently the largest American Jewish denomination, and it may be the group that will have the most decisive impact on the future of the Jewish community. Yet relatively little has been published on this fascinating and quickly changing religious entity. From the preface by Martin Marty to the Afterword by Gunther Plaut this volume is an attempt to begin addressing this lacuna.

The Reform movement has generated tremendous energy in recent years. Those who attend the movement's biennial conferences come away in awe of how enthusiastic so many Reform Jews are today. Eric Yoffie, the president of the Union of American Hebrew Congregations (UAHC), the Reform congregational body, says, "The Reform movement is large, sprawling, fast-growing, and diverse; for all of its problems, there are many pockets of enthusiasm, excitement, creativity, and deep commitment."[1] Yoffie himself deserves a great deal of the credit for being able to channel the excitement that is out there into the building of one of the most vibrant, liberal religious movements in America today. In December 1999 he told five thousand delegates at the UAHC Biennial Convention held in Orlando, Florida, that they were creating "a new Reform revolution." Building on the Jewish literacy initiative he inaugurated at the previous biennial, Yoffie proclaimed a "revolution" in worship to bring Reform Jews back to the synagogue. For those in attendance the spirit of worship was already restored. Thirteen-year-old Julia Bloch of Larchmont, New York, described her impressions: "Five thousand Jews were reciting prayers aloud. Some stood, some sat, some prayed in Hebrew, some in English, some chanted, some spoke, some belted, some muttered. But it was the sound of five thousand Jews praying. And there, for that moment, the room felt holy."[2]

There is a new seriousness about God and holiness, and there is a move to integrate spiritual feelings into concrete ritual observances. Reform Jews are reading more about Judaism, and they are studying the Torah, the Talmud, the Midrash, and other traditional religious texts. New types of people are coming into Reform congregations, which has injected a bold excitement into Reform Jewish life. Yet as Yoffie suggests, the movement has difficulties as well. Some of these problems are "teething" issues that are affecting the movement as it grows. Others are related to the relationship between Reform Jews and the rest of the Jewish people. Finally, there are challenges that the Reform movement faces along with all other American liberal religious groupings. Many of the authors in this volume analyze where those problems come from and how they can be addressed.

One of the unique characteristics of this collection is that it combines a historical perspective with contemporary debate. Many collections, as well as single-author volumes, tend to focus exclusively on history, theology, or sociology. This book attempts to look at issues from several of these perspectives and then applies those ideas to the situation today. If an author refers to the various platforms or statements of principle passed in 1855 or 1869 or 1885, we want to understand what those platforms said, and what influence they have on us today. If an author refers to Abraham Geiger of Germany or Kaufmann Kohler of the United States, we want to know not only what those thinkers said on Reform Judaism then, but also what that can teach us about Reform Judaism today.

American Jews: Adaptationists Rather than Rejectionists

One of the basic premises of Reform Judaism is that the Jewish religion can be adjusted to fit the changing needs of people in modern society. This is true despite the fact that there is a great deal of difference in how the elite of the movement understands this concept as opposed to how most of the laity understands it. However, the basic point is that Reform Judaism allows and even encourages Jews to adapt to changing social conditions as it corresponds to the adaptionist approach of the American Jewish community. As political scientist Charles Liebman has noted, American Jews are "adaptationists rather than radical."[3] Jews will adapt their Judaism as best they can to fit in with the expectations of pluralistic American society, as they understand those expectations. This is a "consumer orientation" based on individualism combined with a strong resistance to authority. Most American Jews will not be radical, which in this context would mean refusing to go along with what they perceive to be the American way of life.

There are, of course, exceptions to this rule. Between 6 and 10 percent of

American Jews practice Orthodox Judaism. Depending on how one understands adaptation, at least some of the Orthodox groups are radical rather than adaptationist. As a consequence, the American Jewish community is increasingly splitting into two factions: the rejectionist Orthodox, on one hand, and the non-Orthodox, on the other. Those in the modern Orthodox movement are in the peculiar position of trying to maintain some level of affiliation with both sides, a task that will become increasingly difficult in the coming years. The vast majority of American Jews will adopt nonjudgmental attitudes about broad social and cultural norms. If the society as a whole is accepting new standards of behavior, such as the fact that many young couples are now living together before marriage, most American Jews will accept these standards as well.

Similarly, as American society becomes more accepting of gay and lesbian relationships, so too will most Jews accept this new reality. This acceptance includes even the rabbinate. For example, Congregation Beth Israel of West Hartford, Connecticut, published an article in its July 1999 newsletter to introduce their new assistant rabbi, a lesbian. They simply wrote in the very first paragraph, "Over the next few months, we hope that everyone will have the opportunity to meet Rabbi [Elissa] Kohen, Missy Sachs, her partner, and Bailey, their dog, and welcome them into our community."[4] Imagine such a development in our grandparents' days! The same is true with the increasing acceptability of divorce and, most important for the purposes of our discussion here, increasing intermarriage between different ethnic and religious groups.

As Liebman states, "They do not adopt the radical stance, which would argue that if the cultural environment is inimical to Jewish norms and values, Jews must either change that environment or withdraw from it. They do not even ask the kinds of questions which might lead to a radical posture."[5] Whereas someone who believes in radical religion will see God as having revealed divine truth to humankind, and will believe that this truth is available to those who seek it out, the adaptationist will view the Jewish religion as a way of life that is changeable according to the nature of the society in which Jews live and their individual place in that society.

The Reform movement is by far the most adaptationist of the three major denominations of American Judaism. Therefore, Reform becomes increasingly attractive to American Jews who have acculturated to the point where their values reflect American values, or perhaps more accurately, the values espoused by certain middle- and upper-middle-class substrata within American society. The fact that American Jews are accepting rather than rejecting of the values of society is one of the main factors that have moved many of them in the direction of Reform congregations in their local communities. Because one of the core beliefs of Reform Judaism is that the autonomy of the individual is the final arbiter of religious decisions, this affiliation thus frees the individual to follow the currents of society rather than the obligatory legal structure of traditional

Judaism that compels specific behaviors. Was this how the Reform movement always saw things, or is this personalistic approach a direct influence from contemporary society? Much of the conflict over where the Reform movement should go originates in disputes over how to view the place from where American Reform Judaism came. But let us start with a description of where the Reform movement is today.

The Competitive "Religious Economy" in the United States

Contemporary Debates in American Reform Judaism begins with a sociological analysis of Reform Jews and Judaism in the United States based on the 1990 National Jewish Population Survey (NJPS). Bernard M. Lazerwitz and Ephraim Tabory of Bar Ilan University give a detailed picture of where Reform Jews were and how they compared to other American Jews, particularly their "ideological neighbors," Conservative Jews. Research has shown that religious involvement in the United States is much higher than in Europe. One reason for this may be the pluralistic nature of American society. This creates a "religious economy" in which movements have to compete with one another to attract new adherents, as well as to hold the ones they already have.

Lazerwitz and Tabory argue that the United States is a particularly "competitive market" for Jewish synagogue affiliation. Most American Jews will follow those religious traditions that can be made to fit in with the norms of American society, while they are likely to discontinue practices that seem to overtly emphasize their minority status in the country. The Reform movement's approach to religious tradition is based on the principle of choice, and this approach makes it possible for Reform Jews to link their secular and religious lives together in a consistent structure. However, the desire to accommodate themselves to the American rhythm of life puts tremendous pressure on Reform Jews to be less rather than more ritually observant.

Lazerwitz and Tabory go through different categories describing how Reform Jews feel about issues and, perhaps more important, how they practice; they then attempt to explain the implications of their findings. I decided to put this essay at the very beginning of the collection because it gives an excellent overview of where the Reform movement is today, and it can help the reader place some of the arguments made in other essays into the context of broader trends affecting American Reform Judaism.

Congregation and Community amid a Rapidly Shifting Religious Population

One of the major questions facing the Reform movement is how it will change religiously in the coming years. Many of the essays in this collection deal with the move away from Classical Reform and toward "tradition." Beyond the adoption of certain previously ignored ceremonies, what does this mean for the type of Judaism that will be practiced? How will American religious trends impact on American Reform Judaism?

Richard Cimino attempts to answer this question. Cimino, the editor of *Religion Watch* and coauthor of a popular book on American religious trends, argues that Reform's liberalizations give it the ability to emphasize those elements of Judaism that will be most relevant to twenty-first-century "seekers."[6] He further argues that Reform has successfully accommodated itself to the perceived needs of its members, as well as "newcomers." He points out that even policies and statements that might superficially be understood as representing a move away from "the marketplace," such as the 1999 *Statement of Principles for Reform Judaism*, can be understood as a way of responding to the desire on the part of assimilated American Jews to find existential meaning; thus, these policies and statements are consistent with a market approach.

Cimino believes that American Judaism is successfully responding to the growing awareness that the "civil Jewish religion" is not providing the basis for a strong Jewish identity, seeing evidence of this in the rebirth of interest in spirituality. Reform is enlarging its repertoire, and this is allowing a much larger number of people to find spiritual meaning and religious satisfaction within the Reform movement. Nevertheless, rational-choice theory suggests that the fact that the Reform movement is so liberal may mean that it will have trouble retaining many of those whom it attracts. As personal religious choice continues to become more important, the Reform movement will need to continue to adapt to dramatically changing trends in order to retain the loyalty of those born Jewish and to attract a maximal number of those who are seeking a meaningful religious community.

Lewis Friedland expands on Cimino's comments concerning the fragile nature of the Reform Jewish community in a rapidly changing society, stating that in the United States today community in general is under extraordinary pressure. He suggests that most thriving religious communities are either those that are linked to esoteric forms of spirituality or those that have rejected the challenges of modernity through a willed return to tradition. The Reform movement, Friedland argues, finds itself caught in the middle. The Reform synagogue functions as a service organization in which the members pay a yearly fee and in exchange receive "a cafeteria of choices." This is necessary under the circumstances but is hardly enough, because although members coexist in time and space, they have no binding commitments to each other or to a higher cause. Friedland argues that the Reform synagogue can transcend the mediocrity of being only a service organization by reconstructing itself as a center of modern Jewish renewal. This requires a resacralization of religious life, a process that will require the renewed commitment on the part of a substantial percentage of the congregants. This resacralization process can be facilitated through a critical reengagement through the larger civic community.

A Low Level of Participation

Perhaps as a result of the impact of individualism, most Reform congregations can attract only an infinitesimally small percentage of their members to attend services. The fact that it now seems widely accepted that most congregants will not attend synagogue may be the concrete expression of the belief that most Jews no longer feel that synagogue attendance is obligatory or even meritorious.

Further, tradition is no longer viewed as a commitment that one must undertake as a sacred responsibility to one's family. Rather, religiosity is to be pursued because of the spirituality that is inherent in it. Many American Jews feel that the synagogue, including the Reform synagogue, has failed to nurture their spiritual side, and it relies instead on an individual's desire to connect with his or her historical faith. For many Americans there is no longer any sense of an obligation to connect with one's historical religious tradition, and this leaves many feeling bored by the Reform worship services and uninterested in becoming more involved in Reform congregational activities. The Jewish Renewal movement has been the most successful Jewish denomination to capture and harness this spiritual urge. The Reform movement, however, has been slow to copy what has worked for Jewish Renewal, and it remains uncertain if the Reform movement is open to serious evaluation and change.

In recent years, many nondenominational, fundamentalist Christian groups have gained momentum and increased their influence and activity. This has not been true of most of the liberal religious movements, however. For example, the 2.6-million-member Presbyterian Church (USA) reports that it has been losing members since 1960.[7] As a liberal religious denomination, the Reform movement is thus in a highly vulnerable situation as well. Despite the fact that there has been a great deal of religious energy generated in certain sectors of the movement, there is still considerable apathy among the rank-and-file members, and this apathy can easily turn to alienation and eventual disaffiliation.

The Role of the Rabbi in the Selection of a Congregation

One of the most important areas to look at is how people choose a denomination and a congregation. Many of those in the Northeast and Midwest live in stable communities where their parents and grandparents were members of the same synagogues they currently belong to, a pattern that does not hold true for the newer Jewish communities of the Sunbelt.

After World War II large numbers of Jews left the Northeast and Midwest, many moving to California and Florida. More recently, increasing numbers of Jews have been moving to cities such as Denver, Las Vegas, and Phoenix. We decided to look at one sample case, that of Palm Beach County in Florida. Palm Beach County has a Jewish population of over 220,000, making it the sixth largest Jewish community in the United States. Yet only 18.2 percent of all Jewish households in South Palm Beach County are affiliated with a synagogue. What is going on there? And how typical is it of the United States? Joel L. Levine, who has served as a rabbi in Palm Beach County for over two decades, attempts to answer these questions.

One of his most interesting arguments is that the most important factor in synagogue affiliation in that community is "the quality of the rabbi." This is in marked contrast to my personal observations in the Midwest, where it seemed to me that most often people belong to the synagogue to which their parents belonged. If they switch synagogues, they would switch primarily as a result of moving further out into the suburbs and wanting a synagogue that was closer to their home. This is not the case in regions of the country with higher migration rates.

Levine also discusses other reasons that people join or do not join congregations. Florida typifies many of the trends that are becoming more prevalent in American Jewish life: internal migration, affluence, disaffiliation, intermarriage, and the quest for spirituality. The bottom line is that most Jews will join congregations if and only if they are convinced that the temple has something meaningful to offer them.

Reform Judaism as a Consistent Theological System

It is critical to understand where the movement came from in order to fully comprehend where Reform Judaism is today and where it may go in the coming years. The next several chapters explore this. Jacob Neusner of Bard College argues that in the nineteenth century, the major Reform Jewish theologians believed that their vision of religion represented the Judaism that all Jews—and non-Jews as well—should embrace and practice. Neusner argues that these thinkers had a "remarkable certainty" that what they believed was the religious truth. Therefore, Reform did not represent itself as one brand of Judaism among many, and no Reform theologian suggested that it was up to the individual to choose whatever theology was to his or her taste. Neusner argues that this religious confidence contrasts with the complete failure of nerve that he believes has caused Reform to move toward greater tradition.

Neusner's argument helps us to frame the debate that runs throughout the rest of the collection. Those influenced by Classical Reform, such as Harold Silver and Jay Brickman, argue that as the Reform movement has moved away from and indeed rejected the Classical formulation, it has diminished its own power to attract and hold the congregational member. Others such as Arnold Wolf argue almost the precise opposite. All of the authors are concerned with the transmission of Jewish tradition from generation to generation. We start this section with a debate over belief because what Reform Judaism represents itself as believing will undoubtedly have a substantial impact on its ability to meet the challenges of the twenty-first century.

The Legacy of Classical Reform Judaism

Classical Reform Judaism was the form of Reform Judaism that developed in the United States in the late nineteenth century. Exemplified by the 1885 Pittsburgh Platform (formally known as the Declaration of Principles), Classical Reform Judaism minimized ritual and emphasized universalism. While much research remains to be done on the nuances of the Classical Reform period, the following statement in the 1885 Pittsburgh Platform typifies the general approach: "We hold that all such Mosaic and rabbinical laws as regulate diet, priestly purity and dress originated in ages and under the influence of ideas altogether foreign to our present mental and spiritual state. They fail to impress the modern Jew with a spirit of priestly holiness; their observance in our days is apt rather to obstruct than to further modern spiritual elevation."

By the 1930s there were signs that at least some of the Reform movement's leaders were feeling the need for a return to tradition. Classical Reform Judaism had been developed during a period of heady optimism, but at virtually the same time pogroms were becoming a serious threat to the Jews of Eastern Europe. By 1881 the flood of East European Jewish immigration to the United States had begun. By the time of the rise to power of the Nazi party in Germany in 1933, it was impossible to see the world as an idyllic place where Jew and Gentile could continue to work side by side to make the world a better place and to bring justice and peace in the spirit of the prophets to all. Rather, there seemed to be a dire need for a Jewish homeland that could absorb the huge number of Jews who faced prejudice, persecution, and even death. While almost no one imagined the enormity of the tragedy that would befall European Jewry, the possible risks facing millions of Jews were very apparent.

In response to the changing political environment, the Reform movement began to embrace political Zionism and more generally to move away from a definition of Judaism that minimized the role of peoplehood in Jewish self-definition. Reform rabbis continued to speak of Ethical Monotheism, which stressed that the Jewish belief in one God would lead to the highest ethical behavior, as well as a devotion to a prophetic Judaism that would motivate Jews to fight for the rights of the downtrodden.

Following World War II large numbers of American Jews left the urban ghettos of New York, Philadelphia, and Chicago for the suburbs that were springing up. The movement that benefited the most from the process of suburbanization during the Eisenhower 1950s was the Conservative movement. Conservative

Judaism appealed to the now-Americanized East European immigrants, and even more so to their children, because it appeared to allow for the adaptation to American society that was considered so important. At the same time it was substantially more traditional than the Reform movement. Yet the Reform movement gained membership from the suburbanization trend as well. In 1940 the UAHC had 265 congregations with 59,000 units. By 1955 there were 520 congregations with 255,000 units. By the end of the 1990s the UAHC had more than 875 congregations, with between 1.2 million and 1.5 million individual members.

Several of our essays describe the tension between the old and the new. Rabbi Harold Silver of Beth Israel Congregation in West Hartford, Connecticut, describes his personal career track and his impressions of a large Classical Reform temple in the 1950s. Silver observes that the "Jewishness" of the congregants became "paper-thin" or "virtually nonexistent." Thus a return to tradition became a necessity.

One of the strongest advocates of such a return is Arnold Jacob Wolf, rabbi emeritus of KAM Isaiah Israel of Chicago. Wolf states that the 1885 Pittsburgh Platform was produced by rabbis who were "mostly fine scholars in the noble tradition of Abraham Geiger, but they were very poor theologians." His argument is that not only were they naive, but they were incoherent. Kaufmann Kohler and Emil Hirsch formulated a theological platform filled with misconceptions that has led to the Reform "pick-and-choose" Judaism of today. Wolf is one of the bluntest writers that I have ever read. When he writes, "Our fathers and we have sinned, but repentance is always possible," we understand immediately that he is condemning much of what was done in the name of Reform Judaism in the United States over the last 150 years. However, he does not leave us completely up in the air. In this volume he describes the type of Reform Judaism that can be created and that can provide the basis for both pluralism and a meaningful religious commitment.

Defending Classical Reform—The Religious Version of Classic Coke™

Arnold Wolf refers to the 1885 Pittsburgh Platform as "Reform's original sin." Along these lines, many Reform rabbis have jumped on the bandwagon of the "return to tradition" and are pushing for a sort of Reform that incorporates much more traditional ceremony than had previously been acceptable. Not everyone is pleased with this trend. Jay Brickman, rabbi emeritus at Congregation Sinai in Milwaukee, Wisconsin, argues that the new Pittsburgh Platform passed by the Central Conference of American Rabbis (CCAR) in Pittsburgh in May 1999 may turn out to be the religious equivalent of the *Classic Coke*™ debacle: As the reader may recall, Coca-Cola Enterprises, Inc., thought that increasing numbers of consumers wanted a sweeter, more Pepsi-like cola drink, but *New Coke*™ was greeted with tremendous protest from loyal Coca-Cola drinkers who did not want the traditional recipe tampered with. Brickman argues that the end result of the new platform may very well be the same as what happened to Coca-Cola Enterprises, Inc.

Brickman describes how churches in Wisconsin are filled to overflowing on Sunday mornings and compares this to the sparsely attended services of the local Reform temples. He suggests that the fact that most of the service is in Hebrew is one of the big "turnoffs" for many congregants. The fact that the services are "replete with traditional gestures" may also unsettle many. Brickman argues that in contrast to the traditional Jewish service that he sees as lacking appeal in contemporary America, the Protestant worship format has proved to be extremely popular. Assuming this fact to be true, he asks, "Why have we not avidly pursued a like procedure?" Brickman answers the question by saying that at one time the Reform movement did exactly that. He argues that this vision of Classical Reform Judaism is what motivated the founders of the movement. "The present manifestation of Reform Judaism bears so small a resemblance to the vision of our movement's founders . . . [that] it might be more equitable to leave the title Reform with us [who remain loyal to Classical Reform] and find a new appellation (such as neo-Orthodox) for the present manifestation."

American Orthodox Responses

While some of the authors in this collection have attacked the recent trend in the Reform movement toward greater tradition, one would expect Orthodox rabbis to applaud this move. Orthodox rabbi Aryeh Spero writes about what he describes as the "two hundred years' war," suggesting that many Orthodox Jews have not fully understood that the Reform movement of today is very, very different from the German Reform Judaism of the early nineteenth century or the Classical Reform Judaism in late-nineteenth-century America.

Spero describes a number of battles that the Orthodox have had with the Reform movement over the past two centuries, arguing that some are no longer relevant, while others have become exceedingly serious. Spero argues that many of the sociological objections that Orthodoxy had regarding Reform have "lost their ability to object" as a result of the changes that have occurred in all sectors of the Jewish community. He argues that many *haredim* have refused to acknowledge "the salutary accomplishments of Reform" under any circumstances. Spero suggests that the fear of assimilation may be driving much of the *haredi* attitude rather than the actual halachah. He condemns "strident ideology" and "fanaticism" that "saddles the ideologue with holier-than-thou tribal characteristics."

Like Brickman, Spero uses the analogy of *Coca-Cola*™. But rather than using Brickman's point that consumers rebelled when Coca-Cola Enterprises, Inc., tried to replace "Coke" with *New Coke*™, Spero argues that if Coca-Cola Enterprises, Inc., were to use Pepsi syrup for making *Coca-Cola*™, the product would no longer be "Coke" even though the label would so read. "New Age spiritualism, avant-garde cultural notions, scriptural interpretations befitting Karaites, and radical leftist ideology, even when cloaked in lofty-sounding prophetic garb, remain what they are—not Torah."

Proactive Conversion and an Aggressive Outreach Approach

Alexander Schindler, the former president of the UAHC, argues that the Reform movement should embrace outreach and expand it even more than it has. Schindler explains that when he launched the Reform movement's Outreach campaign in the 1970s, he envisioned it not merely as a response to the increasing intermarriage rate. In fact, he believes that any Outreach program that is limited to the non-Jewish spouses of Jewish partners "is an affront to them." By this he means that such a limited Outreach campaign inevitably casts doubt on their integrity because it implies that such individuals could not have chosen Judaism on its merits but rather did so only to please their partner. Instead Schindler states that he envisioned Outreach as a long-range effort to present Judaism as a religious resource for a world in dire need of spiritual inspiration.

The last few decades have been very tumultuous years for the Reform movement. In particular, the movement has been deeply affected by the tremendous rise in the intermarriage rate, which the NJPS calculated to be 52 percent of all marriages between 1985 and 1990. While others dispute this figure, all agree that the intermarriage rate has risen dramatically since the early 1960s and is much higher than it ever was before. This 52 percent figure became the focal point for what many described as a "crisis" among American Jews.

The Reform movement has been affected by this trend more so than either the Conservative or the Orthodox movements because Reform Jews are more acculturated and less ritually observant. This is also due to the fact that those who intermarry are likely to look to Reform Judaism as a solution for their desire for religious affiliation—if they are interested in Judaism at all. Largely in response to this developing trend, the CCAR passed the patrilineal descent resolution, formally known as *The Status of Children of Mixed Marriages,* which accepts the children of Jewish fathers and non-Jewish mothers as Jewish if they are raised as Jews and undergo significant public religious acts of identification.

Will Patrilineal Descent Become a "First Class Disaster"?

Many see this as a radical break with the past and a potentially divisive decision that will split the Jewish people into two. Steven Bayme, of the American Jewish Committee, argues that the patrilineal descent resolution places the personal interest of individuals over the collective welfare of the Jewish people as a whole. Bayme states that while it is perfectly understandable that individuals will try to pursue their own interests, "for Jewish leadership to pursue personal rather than collective agendas and aspirations will result in short-term gains and satisfactions but long-term failures." Many of the leaders of the Reform movement believe he is mistaken.

Current UAHC president Eric Yoffie argues for the importance of Outreach. The author explains how Outreach came about, and what the consequences of the early campaign were. Like Schindler, Yoffie outlines some of the objections to Outreach and explains why in his view these critics are not correct. He also discusses the theological principles underlying Outreach, something that is so important for a policy that is frequently seen as an attempt to place a Band-Aid on the hemorrhaging caused by extremely high intermarriage rates. Using his theological understanding of the religious concepts underlying Outreach, Yoffie proposes that certain limitations be placed on the ritual participation of the non-Jewish spouse in the synagogue. He believes that Outreach begins with the premise that Jews have a unique destiny, and that you do not draw people in by erasing boundaries; therefore, a Reform movement that advocates Outreach is sending a clear message that being a Reform Jew means deepening one's love of God and taking seriously the practice of Judaism as a way of life.

The dramatic increase in intermarriages has generated opportunities for Outreach. Many rabbis first encounter mixed married couples when such couples call the temple to inquire whether the rabbi would be willing to officiate at an intermarriage ceremony. According to recent studies, at least 40 percent of the American Reform rabbinate is willing to officiate at such ceremonies under certain conditions. Rabbi Hillel Cohn of Congregation Emanu El in San Bernardino, California, explains how he views this issue and why he changed his original position and will now officiate at the marriage of such couples. Since this is perhaps the most controversial issue within the Reform movement, Cohn's radical departure from tradition must be understood and taken seriously. While the tradition obviously would proscribe such a ceremony, the American religious environment is one in which barriers are being broken down and identity distinctions are being blurred.

The Impact of Changing Sex Roles on the Reform Movement

Women have been taking on a far greater role in all facets of American religious life over the past thirty years than they were allowed to in previous generations. This trend, a direct consequence of the feminist movement, has had a dramatic impact on every aspect of American life. Reform Judaism has been able to respond quickly and actively to changing sex role expectations, allowing women to assume responsibility for all aspects of the religious and communal life of individual congregations and the movement as a whole. Karla Goldman, of the Hebrew Union College–Jewish Institute of Religion (HUC-JIR) in Cincinnati, discusses the role of women in Reform Judaism. She argues that despite the clear male orientation of Hebrew Union College throughout most of its history, the question of gender equality was always present, "raising challenges that still speak to the present moment's assumption of gender equality and apparent acceptance of female religious leadership."

Rabbi Denise Eger, the founding rabbi of Congregation Kol Ami in West Hollywood, California, writes that Reform Judaism has already contributed to a number of different revolutions in terms of how Jews look at their tradition, and that one of these revolutions has been the welcoming of gays and lesbians into the Jewish community and Jewish religious life. Eger describes the background and history of this process as it unfolded in the 1970s and 1980s. She discusses how the major institutions of the Reform movement responded to this challenge, and outlines the role of the individual congregations in this dramatic transformation.

Eger gives a fascinating insider perspective on the same-sex marriage officiation resolution that was passed by the CCAR at its Greensboro, North Carolina, Conference in March 2000. A resolution on this subject was originally scheduled to be voted on two years earlier in Anaheim but was delayed due to opposition from those who feared that it would irreparably damage the prospects of the Reform movement in Israel. Even the Greensboro resolution was a compromise text—a reflection of the incredibly controversial nature of the subject. The final resolution acknowledges those rabbis who will not perform such ceremonies along with those who will, and it drops the term "marriage" in favor of "same-gender unions." Nevertheless, many traditionalists condemned the resolution. Rabbi Rafael Grossman, former president of the Rabbinical Council of America (RCA), states that in his view gay commitment " . . . goes to the very root of Jewish morality, in the sense of defining what is moral behavior. To give sanction to something like this breaks the moral fiber of Judaism. Why would they do this?"[8]

Hinda Seif, of the University of California at Davis, presents an ethnographic study of bisexual women who have reembraced their Jewish heritage. Her study reveals the fascinating practice of constructing multiple interpretations of religious understanding through the creation of new midrashim, as well as the adaptation of various home rituals to suit the unique needs of this often-neglected Jewish subgroup. Jewish female bisexuals have returned to Judaism by creating a new understanding of the traditional Jewish family and have built strong emotional connections to each other in ways that have implications for all Reform Jews.

I had originally suggested that bisexuality was an area of increasing importance to the Reform movement, but Eric Yoffie wrote me that in his view this is " . . . simply untrue. Reform Judaism is proud of its outreach to gay and lesbian Jews, and has asserted that loving, permanent homosexual relationships are an indisputable reality in which 'kedushah'—holiness—can be present. However, the distinction between homosexuality and bisexuality is an important one. Bisexuality raises very different issues, and I am aware of no Reform group or leader who suggests that Reform Judaism sanctions bisexual behavior."[9]

The Importance of Good Leadership for the Future of the Movement

Samuel Joseph of HUC-JIR in Cincinnati, places the discussion of the future of Reform Judaism in the context of the transformation that he believes the Reform synagogue must undergo. He describes the changes in society that have had a tremendous influence on Reform Jews and their congregations, stating that synagogues do not exist in a vacuum. Joseph argues that if the American Reform synagogue continues to do business as usual and function as it has operated over the past several decades, there will be a continual decline in the level of participation and that of affiliation.

Joseph proposes a model of a learning congregation that he believes is essential for building successful synagogues. Congregations must engage people in shared learning, and there must be a willingness and the capacity to challenge the assumptions and the cultural regularities in the congregation. Perhaps most important, people must make a time commitment to reflect and to learn. Joseph shares an example from his hypothetical Temple Shir Chadash.

He also analyzes the dynamics of synagogue boards, discussing the example of Congregation Emanuel in San Francisco. This congregation was recently reported on the front page of *The Forward* as an example of a "synaplex" congregation, meaning that every Friday night there are several different services, just as in a cineplex several different movies are offered at any one time. Joseph argues that in spite of the stereotype of such boards as being very aggressive, the opposite is actually true. This is because people want the operation of the congregation to run smoothly; they want to avoid dissent and certainly conflict. That may be why these boards are composed of people who seem to think in similar ways. A dominant way of thinking develops, and either people fit in with that emerging culture or they do not. If they do not, they very well may not stay on the board.

The Impact of Israeli Religious Policies on American Reform Judaism

Ephraim Tabory gives us a perspective on how the Israeli attitude toward Reform Judaism affects the American Reform movement and American Reform Judaism. Tabory argues that most American Reform Jews are apathetic about what happens in Israel, which may be one of the biggest reasons that the Reform leadership has found it difficult to mobilize their laity to pressure the Israeli government for change. Tabory argues, however, that even if there is a general indifference toward Israel, there may be a considerably greater interest in how Israel relates to the Jewish identity of Reform Jews and the Jewish identity of their children and grandchildren. As more and more Reform Jews are married to people who were not born as Jews, the Orthodox monopoly on the definition of

Jewishness in the state of Israel for the purposes of marriage has the potential to generate a response much stronger than almost any other issue. This is because Orthodox rabbis and their adherents do not recognize Reform converts as Jewish. They do not recognize the children of such converts as Jewish and will continue not to recognize the children of a Jewish father and a non-Jewish mother as Jewish despite the Reform movement's patrilineal descent resolution of 1983.

Tabory suggests that Israel's seeming rejection of the authenticity of Reform Judaism has the potential to lead American Reform Jews to question whether the state of Israel legitimately represents the Jewish people. As the American Reform Jewish community becomes more and more nonhalachic, not only in its observance but also in its definition of Jewish identity, the gap between American Jews and Israel may grow wider and wider. The issue of patrilineal descent is probably the single most important reason for this.

Visions for the Future

The collection closes with articles that refer to the future of the Reform movement. Alfred Gottschalk, former chancellor of HUC-JIR, gives his vision for a Reform Judaism that needs to be "courageous and not timorous." Gottschalk argues, "We are past the age of the 'hush-hush Jew,' the apologist and the assimilationist." Gottschalk argues that the challenge of helping the many Jews-by-choice understand the concept of Jewish peoplehood is one of the central challenges facing the Reform movement. He also predicts that the Reform movement will grow in Israel.

Gottschalk is very honest about the state of Reform Judaism today. He writes, "This is a time of great gestation," suggesting that Reform "is grappling with issues . . . reaching into the very essence of Judaism's capacity to survive modernity and postmodernity." Gottschalk is openly hostile to New Age influences on Reform Judaism. He writes that many New Age religious movements "make no pretense of seeking past validation for contemporary ideas or beliefs." Yet he argues that the 1999 Pittsburgh "Platform," which he refers to as the recent "debacle," was relatively unaffected by the great enthusiasm for New Age ideas. He does not believe that favoring rabbinic modalities rather than prophetic modalities is necessarily the best way to solidify Reform Judaic authenticity.

There are thus many challenges facing the Reform movement today and in the coming years. How well it can respond will determine to a large degree the quality as well as the quantity of American Judaism. The central question is how liberal Judaism can thrive or even survive in an American society that is based to such a degree on individualism. We hope that the reader may begin to formulate his or her own ideas on how to answer this important question while reading through this collection. The book concludes with words of inspiration by Sheldon Zimmerman, the president of HUC-JIR. Zimmerman argues, "We have succeeded beyond any legitimate expectations" as Americans but that "the old anchors, that which rooted us, are no longer." Zimmerman explains what it is that makes the Reform Jew unique and what it is that characterizes the Reform approach to *kedushah*, holiness. And that search for holiness is the real goal of religion. May we succeed in our search, and may we help to bring a sense of holiness to the entire world.

Notes

1. Communication from Eric H. Yoffie to the editor, April 27, 2000.
2. No Author, "The Orlando Biennial Album," *Reform Judaism* (Spring 2000): 37.
3. Charles S. Liebman, "Religious Trends among American and Israeli Jews," in *Terms of Survival: The Jewish World Since 1945*, ed. Robert S. Wistrich (London: Routledge, 1995), 299–300.
4. "We Warmly Welcome Our New Rabbi Elissa Kohen!" *Congregation Beth Israel Newsletter*, July 1999, 4; author's interview with Elissa Kohn, April 14, 2000.
5. Liebman, "Religious Trends," 299–300.
6. Richard Cimino and Don Lattin, *Shopping for Faith: American Religion in the New Millennium* (San Francisco: Jossey-Bass, 1998).
7. Jim Jones, "Fidelity Clause Retained," *Christianity Today*, August 9, 1999, 16.
8. J. I. Goldberg, "Continental Divide," *The Jewish Journal* (Los Angeles), April 7, 2000, 6.
9. Communication from Eric H. Yoffie to the editor, April 27, 2000.

Where We Are Today

1

A Religious and Social Profile of Reform Judaism in the United States

BERNARD M. LAZERWITZ and EPHRAIM TABORY

This chapter presents a social and religious profile of Reform Jews in American society. The depiction of Reform Jews is enriched by contrasting these persons with their "ideological neighbors"—Conservative-denomination-preferring Jews, as well as those Jews who maintain that they have no denominational preference.

This study of American Jews also considers the overall American religious environment. America's Christian population is quite religious. The work of Stark and Iannaccone (1994) shows that religious involvement is much higher in the United States than in Europe, due in part to the much looser church-state relations in the United States. In the pluralistic society of the United States, Stark and Iannaccone claim, religious institutions compete with one another, and this leads to more vibrant religious movements that are responsive to the needs of the religious "market." Religious attendance, they say, is lower in Europe than in the United States, because state religions, lacking real competition, become lax over time, lazy and unresponsive to the needs of their public. The result is that the public ceases to be attracted to the remaining religious product.[1]

The United States involves a particularly competitive market for Jewish synagogue affiliation. Jews in the United States are a small minority group and now account for less than 3 percent of the American population. The more-liberal Conservative and Reform denominations account for the overwhelming number (79 percent) of Jewish adults who prefer a Jewish religious movement.[2] By 1990, the more traditional Orthodox denomination, which requires rather strict compliance with Jewish religious law, accounted for just 6 percent of

America's Jewish adults. Sklare, Lazerwitz, and colleagues argue that American Jews by and large continue those religious traditions that readily fit in with American society and curtail those practices that highlight their minority status in American society.[3]

Various Jewish historical practices have been scaled back, if not totally abolished, by the Conservative denomination, and this is all the more so for the Reform denomination. The Reform approach to religious tradition allows its adherents to link their religious and secular American lives to a great degree. We find that the minority status of the Jews in the United States and their desire to accommodate to American life leads Reform adherents to be less ritually observant. Synagogue attendance aside, we expect to find relatively lax observance of the accepted forms of Jewish involvement, when using other Jewish denominations as a standard.

Before moving on to our depiction of Reform Jewry, we provide an overview of our data sources. The final sections of the paper will be devoted to our analysis of data, and the implications of the data for the Reform movement.

Data Sources

The characteristics of those Jews who prefer the various Jewish denominations were ascertained in the National Jewish Population Surveys of 1971 and 1990. (These two surveys will be referred to as 1971 NJPS and 1990 NJPS.) The 1971 NJPS data were obtained from randomly selected household respondents obtained by a combination of samples from local Jewish federation lists and a complex, multistage, disproportionately stratified, area cluster sample design for Jewish housing units not on federation lists. The 1971 survey yielded 5,790 interviews at a 79 percent response rate. The 1990 NJPS sample was obtained by selecting residences from among all United States residential telephones through random-digit dialing (RDD). This process obtained a probability sample of households, using a screening interview, in which at least one resident was then Jewish or had a Jewish parent. Within these households, one sample Jewish respondent was selected by the next-birthday method of respondent selection.[4]

The 1990 survey obtained 1,905 Jewish interviews through the use of a two-stage interviewing procedure that first screened all telephone sample respondents for eligibility. Respondents were later contacted for the actual interview. The response rate for the initial screening interview was 63 percent; the response rate among those screened and actually interviewed in the second stage was 68 percent, for a combined (0.63 × 0.68) rate of 43 percent. (After clarification of final eligibility, the final response rate was nearly 50 percent.)

The goal of probability surveys is to enable one to generalize from sample findings to the population that has been sampled. Our concern is with the adult

Jewish population of the United States. To ensure comparability between the two surveys, we have adopted the definition of an adult used in the 1971 survey: anyone twenty years of age or older.

Since there are varying numbers of Jewish adults in sampled households, it is necessary to adjust or weight the statistics derived from respondent answers to survey questions by the number of Jewish adults in a sampled household. This compensates for the fact that some households have more Jews in them than others. That is, since only one Jewish adult in a given household has been interviewed, a potential respondent in a household with two Jewish adults is more likely to be interviewed (one chance in two) than, for example, somebody in a household of three adult Jews (one chance in three).[5]

In each survey respondents were asked the following question with regard to their Jewish denominational preferences: "Referring to Jewish religious denominations, do you consider yourself to be Conservative, Orthodox, Reform, Reconstructionist, or something else?" Respondents who declared they were "just Jewish," secular Jews, or in any case not Orthodox, Conservative, Reform, Reconstructionist, or traditionalist, were classified into a fourth code category: those with no denominational preference.

Analysis of the 1971 survey showed that important insights into the nature of denominational identification are gained by dividing those with a given preference into those who are synagogue members and those who are not synagogue members.[6] We do that here as well. Given the focus of this chapter, on Reform Jews and how they differ from the other major American Jewish denominations, the presentations here will be limited to Reform and Conservative Jews and to those Jews without a denominational preference. Accordingly, the 1971 NJPS yielded 2,432 Conservative respondents, 1,911 Reform respondents, and 811 no-preference respondents. The 1990 NJPS yielded 762 Conservative, 743 Reform, and 286 no-preference respondents.

Evidence

Between 1971 and 1990 only the Reform denomination showed an increase in its proportion of the American Jewish adult population. Between these survey years the Orthodox denomination declined by 5 percent and the Conservative denomination declined by 2 percent, while the Reform denomination increased by 6 percent, going from 33 percent to 39 percent of the American Jewish adult population.

An increase in the number of Jewish adults who claim a Reform preference is in itself not an adequate indicator of the dynamics of the Reform movement. The increase in Reform adult preference was not accompanied by an increase in Reform synagogue membership (see Table 1). While the other two Jewish denominations registered an increase in the percentage of their adult adherents who claimed synagogue membership, the Reform denomination registered a decrease. The data in Table 1 indicate that between 1971 and 1990, the proportion of Orthodox and Conservative adults claiming synagogue membership increased from 66 percent to 72 percent and from 57 percent to 59 percent, respectively. However, the proportion of Reform adults decreased from 51 percent to 43 percent.

Education

Synagogue members have considerably more Jewish education than those respondents who are not members (Table 2). The ranking of these categories indicates that Conservative synagogue members have considerably more Jewish education than the others. Reform members rank between the Conservative members and the Conservative nonmembers. Reform nonmembers and the no-preference respondents are equivalent and also have the lowest rankings on Jewish education.

Religiosity

Overall, the pattern of education in Table 2 is also found with regard to frequency of synagogue attendance (Table 3). Members of Conservative synagogues are the most frequent attenders, followed by Reform members, who fall just about midway between Conservative members and Conservative nonmembers. Reform nonmembers and the no-preference respondents bring up the rear on attendance. However, Reform nonmembers are more clustered than are no-preference respondents.

The information in Table 4 moves us out of the synagogue and into respondents' homes. Items a through c cover major annual home religious practices. Items d and e deal with weekly and daily religious practices.

Table 1

Percentage of Jewish Adult Synagogue Memberships by Denominational Preference, 1971 and 1990

	Synagogue Membership	
Denomination	1971	1990
Orthodox	66%	72%
Conservative	57%	59%
Reform	51%	43%

Source: This table is derived from Lazerwitz et al., Table 3.2.

Table 2

Received Eight Years or More of Jewish Education by Adult Jewish Denominational Preferences, 1990 NJPS

| | Denominational Groups | | | | |
| | Conservative | | Reform | | No-Preference |
	Member	Nonmember	Member	Nonmember	Nonmember
8 years or more of Jewish education	59%	33%	39%	20%	19%

Source: This table is derived from Lazerwitz et al. Table 3.6.

Table 3

Synagogue Attendance by Adult Jewish Denominational Preferences, 1990 NJPS

| | Denominational Groups | | | | |
| Synagogue Attendance | Conservative | | Reform | | No-Preference |
Frequency	Member	Nonmember	Member	Nonmember	Nonmember
None	1%	21%	4%	25%	46%
1–2 times per year	17%	45%	26%	53%	46%
3–9 times per year	30%	21%	33%	18%	3%
10–12 times per year	22%	6%	19%	2%	3%
13 or more times per year	30%	7%	18%	2%	2%

Table 4

Home Religious Practices by Adult Jewish Denominational Preferences, 1990 NJPS

| | Denominational Groups | | | | |
| Home Religious | Conservative | | Reform | | No-Preference |
Practices	Member	Nonmember	Member	Nonmember	Nonmember
a. Always attends seder	85%	59%	77%	48%	24%
b. Always lights Hanukkah candles	88%	57%	76%	46%	24%
c. Fasted on Yom Kippur	87%	60%	64%	44%	15%
d. Lit Friday night candles at home	24%	10%	11%	3%	3%
e. Has separate dairy and meat dishes	32%	13%	5%	3%	4%

The annual religious practices of participating in a Passover seder, lighting candles during Hanukkah, and fasting on Yom Kippur again produce a Conservative member lead, followed by the Reform members and then Conservative nonmembers. These three categories are followed by Reform nonmembers and, at a considerable distance, the no-preference category.

A considerable change appears with regard to items d and e, which are performed much more frequently throughout the year. On these variables Reform members either come quite close to the Conservative nonmembers or fall below them. These two items have less of a role in Reform ritual than in Conservative ritual. In the Reform denomination, Friday night candles may be lit in the synagogue service, not necessarily at home, and observance of the traditional laws of kashrut is a low-priority, voluntary act for Reform adherents.

If, following Reform practice, a ritual is given home emphasis, then synagogue membership plays an important role in increasing its observance. A rank order emerges in which Conservative synagogue members lead, followed by Reform members. Conservative nonmembers follow closely. Reform nonmembers lag further behind. They are followed by the no-preference category.

This ranking of Conservative members, Reform members, Conservative nonmembers, Reform nonmembers, and a no-preference group also appears for synagogue attendance. When a ritual is not important for the Reform denomination, Reform members fall to the level, or lower, of the Conservative nonmembers, while Reform nonmembers and the no-preference categories fall to nearly zero and are like each other.

Community Activity

On the whole this ranking of Conservative members, Reform members, Conservative nonmembers, Reform nonmembers, and a no-preference group reappears for activity in Jewish voluntary associations (Table 5). However, with regard to activity in general community voluntary associations (item b), a new pattern emerges. Synagogue membership is quite influential for the members of either Conservative or Reform synagogues on activity in general community voluntary associations. These two groups are the most active ones, and they are quite close to each other. Unexpectedly, the respondents who have neither a denominational preference nor a synagogue membership follow right behind the two membership groups. The other two nonmember groups closely resemble each other and come last on general community voluntary association activity.

Ethnicity

Table 6 explores the ethnic aspect of number of Jewish friends. Here the pattern is for the Conservative category to be first. This category is followed by the

Table 5

Activity in Voluntary Associations by Adult Jewish Denominational Preferences, 1990 NJPS

| | Denominational Groups | | | | |
| | Conservative | | Reform | | No-Preference |
Voluntary Association Activity	Member	Nonmember	Member	Nonmember	Nonmember
a. Number of Jewish voluntary associations					
0	41%	74%	54%	79%	90%
1	24%	18%	20%	14%	8%
2	13%	4%	16%	4%	2%
3+	22%	4%	10%	3%	0%
b. Number of general community voluntary associations					
0	43%	55%	34%	52%	48%
1	14%	18%	23%	16%	14%
2	13%	10%	16%	12%	11%
3+	30%	17%	27%	20%	27%

Table 6

Jewish Friends by Adult Jewish Denominational Preferences, 1990 NJPS

| | Denominational Groups | | | | |
| | Conservative | | Reform | | No-Preference |
Number of Jewish Friends	Member	Nonmember	Member	Nonmember	Nonmember
None	2%	5%	3%	6%	12%
Some	31%	45%	51%	64%	63%
Most or all	67%	50%	46%	30%	25%

Reform, and at the end comes the no-preference category. Membership impact is shown by the leads the Conservative and Reform members have over their nonmembers.

Visits to Israel

Table 7 examines trips to Israel. By now it is readily apparent that the pattern is for the Conservative members to lead, followed by the two similar groups of

---

Table 7

Trips to Israel by Adult Jewish Denominational Preferences, 1990 NJPS

Number of trips to Israel	Denominational Groups				
	Conservative		Reform		No-Preference
	Member	*Nonmember*	*Member*	*Nonmember*	*Nonmember*
0	49%	71%	73%	81%	83%
1	28%	17%	18%	13%	11%
2+	23%	12%	9%	6%	6%

Conservative nonmembers and Reform members. Last comes the similar groups of Reform nonmembers and the no-preference category. Of these groups, only the Conservative members have a considerable proportion (51 percent) who have made the trip to Israel.

Political Orientation

Table 8 looks into political liberalism, and indicates a pattern reversal. The most liberal group, by far, is the no-preference category. Next in rank are the Reform nonmembers. The two membership groups are equivalent and third in rank order, with the Conservative nonmembers following in the rear of all the others.

Synagogue Attendance

Table 9 examines American religious attendance. It is quickly seen that, at best, the religious attendance of the Conservative denomination is similar to that of the group of liberal Protestant denominations. The rate of religious services attendance in the Reform denomination is considerably below that of even liberal Protestant denominations. From the viewpoint of American religious life, the Reform denomination's adherents stand out with their relatively low frequency of attendance at religious services.

Retaining Their Children

One of the strengths of the Reform denomination is its success in retaining those persons who were raised in the denomination. Reading the percentages of Table 10 vertically indicates that 79 percent of those raised as Reform Jews retain this identification as adults. A mere 9 percent of those raised as Reform Jews have become Conservative, and just 12 percent now have no preference. Even 16 percent of adults who were raised as Orthodox Jews have become Reform. Obviously Reform Judaism has aided its institutional growth by attracting a considerable number from the Conservative denomination.

Table 8

Adults Who Feel Politically Liberal by Denomination and Synagogue Membership, 1990 NJPS

	Denominational Groups				
	Conservative		Reform		No-Preference
	Member	Nonmember	Member	Nonmember	Nonmember
Politically Liberal	40%	34%	39%	44%	56%

Source: This table is derived from Lazerwitz et al., Table 3.7.

Table 9

Comparing Protestants, Catholics, and Jews by Religious Attendance

Religious Group (Adults)	Never	1–2 times per year	3–11 times per year	Monthly	13+ times per year
Protestants					
Fundamentalist	11%	19%	11%	7%	52%
Moderate	15%	22%	14%	9%	40%
Liberal	22%	27%	14%	8%	29%
Catholics	12%	19%	11%	7%	51%
Jews (1990 NJPS)					
Conservative	9%	29%	26%	16%	20%
Reform	16%	42%	24%	9%	9%

Source: This table is derived from Lazerwitz et al., Table 3.9.

Table 10

Childhood Denomination by Current Preference for All Adult Jewish Respondents, 1990 NJPS

	Was Raised			
Is Now	Orthodox	Conservative	Reform	No-Preference
Conservative	52%	62%	9%	20%
Reform	16%	28%	79%	28%
No preference	8%	9%	12%	47%

Source: This table is derived from Lazerwitz et al., Table 5.2.

Table 11 shows that the "recruits" to Reform are somewhat more traditionally inclined than are those persons who were raised within the denomination. (The majority of those entering the Reform denomination from the Conservative denomination are less traditionally inclined than those they leave behind.) Overall the potential impact of the characteristics of these new adherents is to move the Reform denomination in a more traditional direction.

Intermarriage

Table 12 introduces the issue of intermarriage among all the adult adherents of the denominations. For all married respondents, intermarriage is associated with denomination and synagogue membership. Intermarriage increases as one goes from Conservative to Reform to no preference, and it also increases as one goes from the member to the nonmember category. The major difference between members and nonmembers is the convert-in category. Most instances of conversion to Judaism are associated with synagogue membership.

Table 13 pictures intermarriage among those respondents married between 1971 and 1990. (A disadvantage of this restriction in time is that there are not enough cases of intermarriage to permit a breakdown by synagogue membership.) The dramatic change is the growth in intermarriage. During this period only 44 percent of the marriages among Reform adherents were between two Jewish individuals or involved a convert to Judaism. The majority of Reform Jewish children are now raised in families with parents of two different faith backgrounds.

Table 11

Religious and Community Involvement Characteristics for Denominational Stayers and Switchers, 1990 NJPS

Denominational Changing	Often attends Synagogue	Home Religious Practices[a]	Jewish Primary Groups[b]	Jewish Organizational Activity[c]	Is Synagogue Member
Remained Conservative	15%	39%	45%	43%	57%
Conservative to Reform	11%	15%	26%	39%	49%
Remained Reform	6%	10%	19%	27%	36%

Source: This table is derived from Lazerwitz et al., Table 5.5.

Key: [a] Shabbat candles; Hanukkah candles; kosher homes

[b] Most friends Jewish; neighborhood Jewish; opposes intermarriage

[c] Member of several Jewish organizations; works 20 hours a month or more for Jewish organizations; donates money to Jewish organizations

Table 12

Intermarriage Types by Current Denomination and Synagogue Membership, 1990 NJPS

Denomination-Synagogue Member	Both Spouses Born into Jewish Families	One Spouse Convert-in	One Spouse Jewish, One Spouse Christian	One Spouse Jewish, One Spouse "Other" or "None"
Conservative				
Member	88%	8%	3%	1%
Nonmember	72%	4%	15%	9%
Reform				
Member	66%	24%	7%	3%
Nonmember	55%	8%	29%	8%
No preference				
Nonmember	38%	1%	41%	20%

Source: This table is derived from Lazerwitz et al., Table 6.3.

Table 13

Family Types for Jewish Marriages of 1970 to 1990 by Denominational Preference, 1990 NJPS

Denomination	Both Spouses Born into Jewish Families	One Spouse Convert-in	One Spouse Jewish, One Spouse Christian	One Spouse Jewish, One Spouse "Other" or "None"
Conservative	54%	9%	24%	13%
Reform	30%	14%	43%	13%
None	15%	3%	55%	27%

Source: This table is derived from Lazerwitz et al., Table 6.6.

Table 14 pictures the type of Jewish involvement for the different 1971–1990 family types. (Again, the lack of a sufficient number of cases prevents the breakdown of converts by denomination.) On the whole, convert-in marriages, in which most of the converts become Reform, are synagogue members—almost 80 percent of them. They are also fairly frequent synagogue attenders. In fact, they report more synagogue attendance than families with both spouses born Jewish. Furthermore, their synagogue attendance level

Table 14

Jewish Involvement of Jews Married between 1970 and 1990 by Type of Marriage, 1990 NJPS

Jewish Involvement	Both Spouses Born into Jewish Families		All Convert-in Marriages	Heterogeneous Marriages		
	Conservative	Reform		Conservative	Reform	None
Synagogue member						
Yes	64%	50%	78%	22%	19%	3%
No	36%	50%	22%	78%	81%	97%
Jewish organization activity index						
High	54%	44%	43%	12%	15%	7%
Moderate	36%	28%	34%	30%	31%	25%
Low	10%	28%	23%	58%	54%	68%
Jewish Primary Group Involvement Index						
High	64%	39%	27%	4%	3%	2%
Moderate	26%	34%	36%	15%	16%	8%
Low	10%	27%	37%	81%	81%	90%
Synagogue attendance						
12 or more times per year	42%	19%	50%	8%	11%	2%
3–11 times per year	30%	33%	27%	27%	16%	6%
1–2 times per year	23%	37%	15%	45%	54%	54%
0 times per year	5%	11%	8%	20%	19%	38%
n (couples)	107	86	62	74	158	125

Source: This table is derived from Lazerwitz et al., Table 6.7.

reaches that given in Table 9 for the moderate Protestant denominations and Roman Catholics.

The activity in Jewish organizations of the convert-in marriages is equivalent to that of Reform Jewish families where both spouses were born Jewish. However, the convert-in marriages display a sizable decrease in involvement in Jewish primary groups.

As would be expected, the heterogeneous marriages show far less involvement. The persons who enter into these marriages are seldom synagogue members; they seldom, if at all, attend synagogue. They seldom are involved in Jewish organizations, and they have a low level of Jewish primary group involvement. These findings apply for both the Conservative- and Reform-preferring heterogeneous marriages.

The rate at which a non-Jewish spouse converts is higher when the husband is Jewish and the wife is not Jewish than it is when it is the wife who is Jewish and the husband is not Jewish. This was previously noted by Mayer.[7] Among the two groups with sizable numbers of converts, 67 percent of the converts to Conservative Judaism and 71 percent of the converts to Reform Judaism are women.

The Influence of Jewish Community Size

We turn to another issue that may influence the ability of Jews in the United States to perpetuate their heritage, namely, the influence of Jewish community size. We now examine the degree to which respondents who prefer the Reform denomination and who live in Jewish communities of varying sizes have different degrees of Jewish primary group involvement. The analysis for this table controls for demographic and socioeconomic factors as well as for Jewish community size. The dependent variables are the respondent's score on an intermarriage scale and the number of close friends who are Jewish. A measure of friendship with Jews is included for contrast, as it is another aspect of the permeability of the boundaries between Reform Jews and non-Jews in an open society.

The concentration of the various Jewish denominations differs noticeably in Jewish communities of different sizes. For example, 71 percent of the Orthodox respondents live in the larger Jewish communities of the metropolitan areas of New York City, Los Angeles, Miami, Chicago, Philadelphia, Boston, and Washington, D.C. Sixty-six percent of Conservative respondents live in these areas, as do 57 percent of Reform respondents and 60 percent of those with no denominational preference. The number of Orthodox and Conservative respondents and of those with no preference in the smaller Jewish communities is too few to permit statistical analysis involving community size and other variables. For Reform Jews only (and then just barely so) are the numbers in communities of all sizes sufficient for statistical analysis.

Forty-nine percent of Reform synagogue members and 62 percent of Reform Jews who are not synagogue members are concentrated in the larger metropolitan areas. Table 15 shows the results of a multiple regression analysis for Reform Jews in which synagogue members are differentiated from nonmembers. The results indicate that for Reform Jews, the larger the Jewish population, the lower the intermarriage mean score and the larger the average number of close Jewish friends. In Jewish communities with a population of fewer than 40,000 there is an increase in the intermarriage mean scores and a decrease for Reform Jews in the number of close friends who are Jewish. In short, the boundaries between the primary associations of marriage and friendship are stronger among Reform Jews in larger than in smaller communities.

Table 15

Number of Close Friends and Intermarriage Score by Jewish Community Size for Reform Jews, NJPS 1990

| | Reform Jews | | | |
| | Synagogue Members | | Not Synagogue Members | |
Jewish Community Size	No Close Friends Jewish	Score on Intermarriage Scale	No Close Friends Jewish	Score on Intermarriage Scale
1 million plus (NYC metro area)	3.6	1.2	3.3	1.9
Around 500,000 (Los Angeles and Miami metro areas)	3.6	1.5	3.3	2.1
200,000–300,000 (Chicago, Philadelphia, Boston, Washington D.C. metro areas)	3.6	1.5	3.1	2.1
40,000–150,000 (11 Jewish communities)	3.5	1.0	3.1	2.4
15,000–39,999 (18 Jewish communities)	3.2	1.7	2.7	3.5
3,000–14,999	3.3	1.7	2.9	2.3
Under 3,000	3.1	1.9	2.5	3.7

Source: This table is derived from Lazerwitz et al., Table 6.10.

In the larger communities Reform Jews maintain considerable involvement in Jewish primary groups. Indeed, in communities of 200,000 or more Jews, 75 percent of Reform synagogue members are in homogeneous marriages (both spouses are Jewish), while only 57 percent are in homogeneous marriages in communities of fewer than 200,000 Jews. Among Reform Jews who are not synagogue members, the corresponding figures are 66 percent in the larger communities and 50 percent in smaller communities. Similarly, among members of Reform synagogues who live in the larger Jewish communities 54 percent report that all or almost all of their closest friends are Jewish, while in the smaller communities (fewer than 200,000 Jews) only 40 percent do so. Among Reform Jews who are not synagogue members the corresponding figures are 38 percent and 18 percent.

Summary

In this chapter we have seen that while Reform Jewry has grown as a religious preference, it is attracting a decreased proportion of its adherents into synagogue membership. This finding takes on added significance when we note the additional finding regarding the importance of synagogue membership. The influential context of synagogue membership is what gives Reform Jewry its religious life.

Becoming members of a synagogue raises the religious characteristics of Reform Jewry to a much higher level, a level that approaches that reached by those who join more traditional Conservative synagogues. This includes synagogue attendance, attendance at Passover seders, lighting Hanukkah candles, and fasting on Yom Kippur. It does not include traditional items of religious behavior that have been dropped by the Reform denomination, such as the laws of kashrut.

Merely preferring the Reform denomination without a synagogue membership does raise the religious involvement of this group over that of the no-denominational-preference-no-membership group that typically is at the bottom of all Jewish matters. The strong impact of synagogue membership again appears for activity in Jewish voluntary associations. Synagogue members are much more active than are those who merely prefer the same denomination.

When the ethnic aspect of friends and orientation toward Israel factors are examined, Reform denomination adherents move toward the low end of the scale—toward the levels of the no-preference category. This holds for Jewish friends (Table 6) and for trips to Israel (Table 7). It also appears for the broader indices of Jewish primary groups and ties to Israel analyzed by Lazerwitz and colleagues.[8]

With regard to activity in general community voluntary associations, the no-preference category just about ties the two membership groups. The nonmember

groups are equivalent to each other and fall below the other three. A fairly similar pattern appears on the politically liberal scale. The no-denominational-preference group is the most politically liberal. This category ranks much higher than
the adherents of the two denominations, with the Reform nonmember group
somewhat ahead of the two membership groups.

The Reform denomination has the strongest retaining capacity of all the
denominations. It also has been receiving two different sets of "recruits." One set
includes a considerable number of new Reform adherents who come from the
Conservative denomination and are more traditionally oriented. The other source
derives from intermarried couples, especially couples in which the wives are converts to Reform Judaism.

In fact, the number of families with a convert into Reform Judaism or families formed by couples with two different religious backgrounds—one being a
preference for Reform and the other retaining a non-Jewish background—is so
great that these patterns now constitute the majority of Reform families. This
mixed religious background is even more prevalent among Reform nonmembers, who also have fewer converts-in. Typically, the convert to Reform Judaism
is a woman. When Reform families have a convert-in, they do join a Reform synagogue in considerable percentages and become religiously active.

We note that Reform Jews are less inclined to attend religious services than are
American Christians. While Americans as a whole are regarded as a religious people, Reform Jews do not indicate that they are a religious people in the traditional
sense.[9] In fact, they differ greatly from the American pattern of high religiosity.

Finally, it comes as no surprise to find that Reform Jews are widely scattered
throughout the United States. The result of this is that these persons live in what
might be called more isolated Jewish conditions, in addition to having small
Jewish numbers with whom to interact.

Implications

Our academic analysis of the Reform denomination carries implications for the
future direction of the movement. We suggest some of the parameters that the
denomination might consider in charting its future course.

Synagogue Membership

The data clearly indicate major differences between those Jews who belong to a
Reform congregation and those who merely prefer the Reform denomination but
do not actually belong. Those who belong manifest a much more vibrant Jewish
life than those who do not belong. We recognize that the nature of this relationship is not unidirectional. Membership alone does not lead to a more vibrant
Jewish life. Indeed, it may be that those who more strongly identify as Jews decide

to join the synagogue. It is logical to argue that there is a mutual relationship, and that synagogue membership in itself does have some independent impact on Jewish identity. Our interpretation of the data indicates that movement leaders who wish to increase the commitment of Reform Jews would be well advised to take steps to increase congregational membership.

We posit a series of hurdles that one has to cross in order to decide to join a congregation. These may include ideological barriers and religious feelings. They may include the attitudes of significant others. We suggest some steps that might have an impact on membership.

Synagogue Membership Fees

Membership fees that keep people from joining are leading to a loss of Jewish life. We recognize that synagogues need the fees that members pay in order to cover their operational costs, and yet we would recommend that everything be done to keep these fees to a minimum, especially for young families just beginning their foray into the economic system. Given the high mobility of American Jews, the initial membership fees paid as "building fees" might be waived for those who already paid such fees to a different synagogue. Moving is a time when people seek out community. At the same time it is the period when it is easiest to be relieved of social pressures to join a synagogue, given the fact that movers are often cut off from significant social networks. Given that moving involves substantial expenses, synagogue membership fees may be seen as one item that can be put off to a later date—a date that may never come.

Membership Programs

We would also recommend conducting programs that appeal to potential members as well as to those who are already members. Of course, many synagogues do just that, but more still needs to be done. Members should be encouraged to seek out new members. Strangers should be warmly welcomed. This does not happen by itself. Arrangements have to be made to greet new persons and interact with them. This interaction should be not only for that meeting, but also a part of a follow-up in the days to come. Our imagination in making suggestions is no greater than that of others; the point we make is that membership has such an impact that everything must be done to get nonmembers to join.

Jewish Education

Jewish education also has a demonstrable impact. There is a need for more ingenuity in creating an effective educational system for Reform children and adult members. The current Reform Jewish education system requires considerable augmentation. Such an augmentation must consist not only of more hours or

days of the week devoted to classroom work, but also an extended informal education system consisting of strong youth movements, summer camps, weekend
gatherings, trips to Israel, and similar approaches.

It is not our place to recommend the specific contents of the educational curriculum. It does seem to us, though, that knowledge of Hebrew is an important
factor in Jewish education, and we note that this was a topic included in the set
of principles by the Reform movement in 1999 (see the "Rituals" section below).

Non-Jewish Interest in Reform Judaism

Reform Judaism and Reform Jews are engaged in a historic population exchange
with the surrounding non-Jewish population. This is a social fact, regardless of
one's opinion of this exchange. Given this, it is important to have a continuing
program aimed at the proper indoctrination and presentation of Reform Judaism
to non-Jews. This is especially so since the evidence indicates that soon a
majority of Reform families will have religiously mixed backgrounds. Indeed, the
entire Reform congregation and local Reform community ought to be brought
into this activity. We leave it to the clergy and educators in the Reform movement to determine the specific nature of the indoctrination. The point is to get
people actively involved in their Judaism and thereby enhance the likelihood of
Jewish continuity.

Zionism and Israel

Despite the obstacles put in the way of Reform Judaism and Reform Jews
in Israel, and perhaps specifically because of them, we suggest that it is important
for the American Reform Jewish population to develop and maintain involvement
with Israel.[10] The role and importance of the state of Israel and its Jewish population must be explained to American Reform Jews, especially with regard to
Reform Judaism's historical orientation toward the Zionist movement. Identification with Israel can help galvanize the Reform community. At present the relationship of most Reform Jews to Israel is precarious.

Overcoming Social Isolation

With a sizable proportion of Reform Jews living in relative isolation from other
Jews, it is important for the Reform denomination to link together its small-town
Jewish congregations and to encourage Jewish programming on an intercongre-
gational basis. Social events can be held on an areawide basis; religious services
can periodically be held in the same manner.

In the larger Jewish communities the same sort of programming can be held
on a metropolitan basis. For either large or small Jewish communities the benefits of lessened isolation from other Jews can be considerable.

Rituals

Observance of religious rituals has an impact on Jewish identity, and it is therefore with interest that we note the principles adopted by the Central Conference of American Rabbis (CCAR) in May 1999.[11] The principles, adopted by a vote of 324 to 68, opened the door to increased use of traditional rituals, such as wearing skullcaps, keeping kosher, and praying in Hebrew, that were basically abolished by the movement more than 145 years ago. With reference to the statement of principles, Rabbi Paul J. Menitoff, executive vice president and professional head of the CCAR, said that "when so many individuals are striving for religious meaning, moral purpose and a sense of community, it is important that we have a modern set of principles that define and invite commentary on Reform Jewish belief and practice."[12]

Developments regarding the way Reform congregations and Reform Jews react to this statement bear watching. There are theoreticians who argue that more rigid religious requirements are beneficial for religious organizations, and that such requirements and demands explain the success of more-conservative denominations without recourse to assumptions of irrationality. Iannaccone, for example, argues that strictness makes organizations stronger because it reduces free riding.[13] Members who lack commitment are screened out, and participation among those who remain is stimulated. The CCAR statement of principles indicates the sensitivity of movement leaders to the need to find a balance between increased commitment and the principle of maintaining an open-door policy for a wide variety of Jews with different religious and spiritual needs.

Notes

1. Rodney Stark and Laurence Iannaccone, "A Supply Side Reinterpretation of the 'Secularization' of Europe," *Journal for the Scientific Study of Religion* 33 (1994): 230–52.
2. Bernard Lazerwitz, Alan Winter, Arnold Dashefsky, and Ephraim Tabory, *Jewish Choices: American Jewish Denominationalism* (Albany: State University of New York Press, 1998), 40.
3. Marshall Sklare, *Conservative Judaism: An American Religious Movement* (New York: Schocken, 1972); Lazerwitz et al., *Jewish Choices*, 142.
4. See Charles Salmon and John Nichols, "The Next-Birthday Method of Respondent Selection," *Public Opinion Quarterly* 47 (1983): 270–76.
5. For more information on the design characteristics of these two surveys, see Lazerwitz et al., *Jewish Choices*.
6. Bernard Lazerwitz, "Past and Future Trends in the Size of American Jewish Denominations," *Journal of Reform Judaism* 26 (1979): 77–82; Bernard Lazerwitz and Michael I. Harrison, "American Jewish Denominations: A Social and Religious Profile," *American Sociological Review* 44 (1979): 656–66.

7. Egon Mayer, *Love and Tradition: Marriages between Jews and Christians* (New York: Plenum, 1985), 230.

8. Lazerwitz et al., *Jewish Choices*, Table 3.6.

9. See Stark and Iannaccone, "A Supply Side Reinterpretation."

10. Ephraim Tabory, *Reform Judaism in Israel: Progress and Prospects* (New York: Institute on American Jewish–Israel Relations and the Argov Center of Bar Ilan University, 1998).

11. Central Conference of American Rabbis, *A Statement of Principles for Reform Judaism Adopted at the 1999 Pittsburgh Convention,* May 1999, http://ccarnet.org/platforms/principles.html.

12. See http://ccarnet.org/platforms/principles.html.

13. Laurence R. Iannaccone, "Why Strict Churches Are Strong," *American Journal of Sociology* 99 (1994): 1180–211.

2

Reform Judaism and Modern American Community

LEWIS A. FRIEDLAND

I write this essay as a lifelong Reform Jew, as a sociologist (although I do not specialize in religion), and as one who has thought a bit about the nature of community in the United States and my place in it. Indeed, my interest in writing on Reform Judaism and community is a deeply personal one. Although I was raised in a devout Reform Jewish family, the son of two congregation presidents, and served as a former youth group president, as an adult I feel distanced from the Reform community. Although I am a member of a temple and attend services more regularly than some, I remain deeply troubled about whether I will be able to pass my faith on to my own son, who is studying for his bar mitzvah as I write this. To try to make some sense of this dilemma, I have wrestled with the question of why I have had such trouble recommitting to the Judaism of my parents while at the same time finding it difficult to leave.

As a sociologist, my starting point is the more general problem of community in America today. A robust sociological discussion has been raging for almost two decades concerning whether communities of every kind are in decline, and if so, what the causes might be. It seems evident that the possibilities for Jewish community are linked to the more general fate of community in the United States, and this is even more true for the possibility of the Reform Jewish community. The fate of the Reform Jewish community in the United States is inextricably intertwined with the particular problem of the American middle class. Understanding the more general sociological forces at work on American community can at least help us define the boundaries of our particular problems as Reform Jews.

If community in general is under extraordinary pressure, grasping the possibility of religious communities poses particular difficulties. Those religious communities that are thriving in the United States today tend to fall into two groups. The first are those tied to a generalized search for spiritual identity linked to esoteric forms of religion. For Jews in particular this group comprises those who have embraced Buddhism or drifted toward various forms of Eastern or New Age religion. The second thriving group rejects the challenges of modern community through a willed return to tradition, a closing off from the modern world. In the Christian world these are the evangelicals and charismatics, whose churches have been growing at the expense of mainline churches. In the Jewish world, they are the growing Orthodox communities.[1]

Reform Jews find themselves in the middle, caught between an American community in crisis and a religious bifurcation between a general search for spirituality, on one hand, and a return to tradition, on the other. This peculiar location does not bode well for the Reform tradition. As I will suggest in my conclusion, however, there is some hope for the possibility for a modern Judaism that receives tradition critically and engages in the difficult work of rebuilding community. It is here that our best hope lies.

Community in America

The problem of community runs deep in American life and is intertwined with American religion. From its inception as a colony of England America was conceived as a new Eden, a city on the hill for the rest of the world. The Puritan divines saw America as a moral beacon in civic form, a new Jerusalem. At the same time Americans themselves began to escape from these constraining moral communities, as they pushed beyond the eastern seaboard into the ever-expanding western frontier. The peculiar structure of American community evolved as an attempt to resolve this tension between moral constraint and the desire to escape it.[2]

American modernity poses particular problems for the preservation of community. Robert Bellah and his coauthors of the modern sociological classic *Habits of the Heart* argue that community is made particularly difficult in the United States because individualism, "the first language in which Americans tend to think about their lives, values independence above all else."[3] They identify two forms of individualism, utilitarianism and expressive individualism; neither is unique to the American experience, but both take more extreme form here. The core of utilitarianism is the belief that in a society in which everyone vigorously pursues his or her own interest, the social good will automatically emerge. Expressive individualism, in contrast, stresses the exploration of self-identity and the search for authenticity above all else. Bellah argues that these two seemingly contradictory impulses, the first leading to the pursuit of self-interest, the second to hedonism and consumerism, are resolved in a society oriented toward consumption as the primary standard of "the good."

Nonetheless, this individualism has been sustainable in the United States only because of broader moral understandings, rooted in community and voluntary association, or in Bellah's terms, commitment, community, and citizenship. In *Habits* these are gathered under the rubric of "civic membership," understood as the intersection of personal identity with social identity. Civic membership is in crisis, reflected in "temptations and pressures to disengage from the larger society" by every significant social group.[4]

Other commentators have held that there is a crisis of social capital, the network of civic associations and trust that sustains community life. This argument is summarized in Robert Putnam's now-famous phrase that we as a nation are "bowling alone."[5]

The interpersonal dimension of this crisis is the loss of civic consciousness more generally and of a sense of generalized obligation to the rest of society. This is coupled with a tendency to withdraw into the private realm of the family, which, more and more, is oriented toward consumption and personal satisfaction. This leads to a loss of solidarity, not only with those "like us," relatives, neighbors and those nearby, but even more so with those more distant socially, economically, and culturally.

Religion and Community

What does this crisis of community mean for religion in the United States? One of the earliest commentators, Alexis de Tocqueville, saw a close link between religion and community in a democratic society.[6] Religion, he believed, restrained the impulses of utilitarianism from their tendency toward greed in isolated individualism and helped channel the expressive individualist urge toward a sense of common obligation. He also saw that under the conditions of the Enlightenment, religious belief declined, and that therefore religion was under the greatest pressure in democratic societies.

This pressure cuts deeply into the commitment of individuals to any group larger than the family, leaving a fissure that is particularly dangerous for religious faith. Two of America's leading religious sociologists, Stark and Glock, have argued that both organizationally and theologically, the heart of religion is commitment.[7] Historically, the primary concern of all religious institutions has been to lead people to faith, and the continued existence of any religion would seem to depend on accomplishing this task. The obvious corollary question, of course, is: commitment to what? For Jews historically, this commitment has been to God, to Torah, and to the Jewish people. In a moment we return to the specifically religious elements of commitment, but first let us turn to the problem of the Jewish people.

Jewish cultural identity in the modern world cannot be maintained indefinitely as a simple attachment to nostalgia, whether in the form of food, Jewish humor, or safely sanitized images of shtetl life. Nor, as Michael Goldberg argues starkly[8] and Arnold Eisen more gently,[9] can the remembrance of the Holocaust be the foundation of Jewish cultural memory more generally. The building of a specifically Jewish identity in America has historically rested on the tension between Jews and the outside world, a tension built on our own religious beliefs, anti-Semitic exclusion, or our immigrant outsider status. Indeed, Bellah argues that ethnic identity in general is supportable only as religious identity: "Religion provides an essential mediation between the ethnic group and the larger culture of the modern world."[10]

What happens when the ethnic group no longer needs religion to mediate between itself and the larger culture? This is a problem for Jews in general, but, as should be obvious, it is heightened for Reform Jews, those most likely to be integrated into the larger culture. This culture, as we have argued, generates both an environment of consumerism that is corrosive to community and an ideology of individualism. Individualism, in turn, leads simultaneously to immersion in the larger world of utility and interest fed by consumerism, and to private separation from community in the search for authentic personal identity. Neither path leads to community or ethnic identity.

Before returning to the prospects for building a Reform Jewish community in the face of a larger, corrosive culture, we look briefly at the specifically religious challenge that the reception of tradition poses for modern Jews.

Judaism and Contemporary Community

Traditional Judaism holds that the Jewish people are bound by the covenant with God, and our faithfulness to the covenant determines our course as a people. Historically this faith was reinforced by two forces binding together the Jewish community. Externally force or the threat of force in the Diaspora bound us together against the outside world. Internally we were bound together by halachah, the law that interpreted the covenant after the destruction of the Temple. Modern Jews in the United States are no longer bound by either the threat of external force or the halachic code. Our relation to covenant is freely chosen, and this freedom of choice extends, of course, to whether we decide to remain active members of a living Jewish community at all.

Creating this complex, modern relationship to covenant poses an extraordinary challenge (as the many rabbis and Jewish educators struggling with this daily know far better than I). A covenant is *binding*, a restriction of choice. If external, willed by God and the closed community, this restriction is a fact of life, not to be fundamentally questioned. A freely chosen covenant, on the other hand, implies an acceptance of the rules by which one agrees to be bound. As we have seen, modern Americans of all religions have resisted the restriction of personal choice in the interest of a larger vision of the good. The peculiar challenge of Reform Judaism, then, is to persuade its members, and those who might be members, why the acceptance of the covenant is necessary in the American spirit of the voluntary community.

One of the most perceptive commentators on this modern Jewish dilemma, Arnold Eisen, has argued that despite growing rates of out-group marriage and declining participation in Jewish life, there is a contrary tendency, an ingathering of Jews who have chosen the limits that receiving tradition imposes. Following the general line of argument of *Habits of the Heart,* Eisen says the source of this return is that "Judaism offers precisely what many in America have lost thanks to the freedoms and choices conferred by modernity: integral *community* and *meaning* profound enough to live by." The strategy implied is precisely the rebuilding of contemporary community through "reimagining the tradition in ways that speak profoundly to the minds and hearts of American Jews as they actually are. The point is to *fashion a community* that helps Jews live rightly and live well without abandoning full participation in American society, and to *describe a Judaism* that assists their quest for wholeness and transcendence."

Eisen's vision of this quest and how we might achieve it resist summary, but here are the central ideas. First, tradition is received through *learning,* our own and that of our children. Jewish learning in America must be broad and deep. Second, tradition (including learning) cannot take place outside of *community,* in the first place Jewish community but also the wider world. The Jewish commitment to justice moves us outside of our own community; our ethics are grounded through dialogue with others. Both require partners outside of ourselves. Third, traditions and communities demand *rituals,* sacred and separate times and spaces through which we reaffirm our commitments. Fourth, tradition and community also require a *language and grammar,* both literal and figurative. Fifth, and finally, Jews must wrestle with *God.* Eisen follows Buber in holding that the Jewish approach to God is through Torah, and that the way to begin for modern Jews may be with the suspension of the question of belief. Nevertheless, the encounter with God is central to Judaism, and they cannot be separated.[11]

This vision embraces the ideal of many communities involved in "multiple tables at which Torah is studied." Eisen's certainly looks to the outer world, as both the *olam* in need of *tikkun* and as the environment of modernity in which all Jews must live. But his vision is predominantly inward-looking, a vision of Jewish renewal through a turning back to Torah. On the whole it is a vision that I embrace. However, I want to raise a few questions before returning to the question of the relation of the Reform Jewish community to the larger American community.

Taking Hold of Torah tries to carve out a precarious position between modernity and tradition. While Eisen does not call for a withdrawal from the world, he asks us to draw a boundary around our community, to create an imaginary *eruv,* the traditional extension of the realm of the family out into the community as a whole. Eisen's boundary is plural and imaginary, not fixed, geographic, and legal. It moves with us through multiple contexts of modern life. It is nonexclusive. We might imagine it as a series of overlapping circles constituted by different communities rather than one circle bounding the sacred space of the Jewish people. It is a genuinely religious response to the challenge of American secularism, attempting to voluntarily reconstitute a sacred space, linking us back to the notion of a voluntarily binding covenant. It is a humble vision, not a prophetic one, but a call to action nonetheless.

As I wrestled with the ideas of *Taking Hold of Torah* I found myself hoping that they would break through for me, that I would find myself accepting Eisen's vision, but I could not. I was left with my paradox: a Jew tied to my community, able neither to leave nor to believe. In wrestling with Eisen, I was forced to rethink what my own vision of a Jewish community might be, and its relation to the wider world.

The Synagogue and Civic Life

At this point, we have come full circle. We have argued that community in the United States has been eroded over a long period of time, buffeted by the twin forces of market utilitarianism and expressive individualism. These individualist forces have been held together by a countervailing tendency toward civic voluntarism, but this is also now eroding. The decline of civic volunteerism is particularly ominous for congregational religion in America, which has both reinforced and depended on it. The binding force of religion is commitment, and traditional commitment is strengthened by exclusion from the mainstream. For Jews (and others) this exclusion has meant that ethnic and religious identities overlap.

As Jews have been integrated into the larger, modern culture, dominated by consumerism and individualism, commitment to both ethnicity and religion has waned. This is particularly true for modern Jews, of course, who both make up the entire Reform movement and are the group from whom Reform draws its potential recruits. One important response to this crisis of modern Judaism is Eisen's call for a modern reception of tradition. This depends on a form of freely willed, self-binding commitment. The sources of motivation for such a commitment are found in the desire for meaning and community that is widespread among American Jews (and others).

It may be that Eisen is right. Perhaps the centrifugal force of the desire for meaning is sufficient to pull modern Jews toward the type of voluntary community necessary to sustain a freely willed covenant. While I find his vision compelling, however, I think that there is an alternative, better perhaps a variation, that takes our identity as modern Americans as seriously as our identity as modern Jews. This requires asking what the conditions are for the rebuilding of a larger civic community that can sustain the rebuilding of Jewish community, and what the relations are between the two. This is a question of emphasis, but a significant one. The central responsibility for Jews in Eisen's vision is the rebuilding of Jewish community, not through ignoring the world outside but indeed by acknowledging and engaging it. It is a reasonable argument that asks how it is possible for us to be engaged as Jews in the rebuilding of the larger American community if we allow our Jewish identity to slip away. In the conclusion of this essay, I reframe this question slightly to ask how we can rebuild our identity as modern Jews without the revitalization of civic community in America.

The starting point for answering this question is the voluntary association and its role in civic life. The Reform synagogue, whatever its Jewish content, is also a voluntary association, first and foremost. This is its inner organizational structure. It is governed by the laws of nonprofit organizations in the United States and is subject to their sociological regularities as well. A vast literature has explored the career of nonprofit organizations in the United States, and I cannot hope to summarize it here. Rather, I draw freely to make a few general statements. The Reform synagogue cannot transcend its "organizational ecology," the environment in which it competes with other organizations, Jewish and secular, and from which it recruits its membership. Many environments compete for the time of Reform Jews: cultural institutions such as shopping malls and television; professional ambitions for status and market success in education and career; secular organizations, both professional and community; Jewish civic organizations, not the least of which are Jewish Community Centers, federations, and those oriented toward Israel; and finally Jewish religious organizations, including other modern denominations (especially Reconstructionism and Conservatism). Clearly the Reform synagogue cannot transcend or control these environments, *but it can, within limits, choose its orientation toward them.* At a minimum it can be self-conscious about what kind of organization it wishes to build. Here there are at least three alternatives.

First, the Reform synagogue can continue on the traditional postwar course of many mainstream congregations, attempting to be a service organization. Pay a basic membership fee and then receive a cafeteria of choices: some High Holy Days services to start, followed by some (generally marginal and ineffective) religious school, a bar or bat mitzvah when it is time, pastoral services for the sick, burial services for the dead, and family mitzvah services for the living. Members coexist in time and space but barely know each other and almost never have binding commitments to each other. This is the model of my current synagogue, to which I return in a moment, a model that Eisen skillfully and critically dissects, and the institution from which many Jews, especially younger Jews of the baby boom generation and younger, are turning away from in droves.

Second, the Reform synagogue can, following Eisen, reconstruct itself as a center of modern Jewish renewal. This involves the willed rebuilding of the Jewish community as a community of freely chosen commitment. It requires a moving away from the service model toward one of the *reconstruction of a community of meaning*. This, in turn, means a resacralization of religious life, no mean task in the wake of the disenchantment of the modern world. It means the redrawing of the modern *eruv* to create a sacred space as well as the rededication to Torah, Jewish learning, and the education of our children, which is to say, our survival. I believe this is a necessary task but not a sufficient one.

Third, the Reform synagogue can build on the second model through a critical reengagement with the larger civic community. This means framing engagement at the center of synagogue life, within *tikkun olam,* the healing of the world, not as a secondary consequence of an imperative for mitzvah. The difference may seem too subtle at first. The received model of mitzvah or *tzedakah* is one of charity. This is, of course, not the actual meaning of either but is the meaning that they have come to take on in the contemporary Jewish understanding of civic action. Charity, as we know, involves doing things for others as objects of our goodwill. The rebuilding of civic community involves doing for ourselves *with* others; it demands a rethinking of the foundations of both our larger eroding civic community and our congregational communities.[12]

Within congregations the concept of rebuilding civic life challenges us in two ways. First, it demands that congregants take responsibility for ourselves and our congregations, breaking the model of service provider and client. This is difficult, of course. It is a call for more demanding, active congregations that challenge their members not only to get involved, but to take responsibility for defining the congregation and its goals. This will in turn require a major transformation of synagogue life, one that is envisioned, for example, in the Synagogue 2000 project. This means a rethinking of all of the structures of participation within the synagogue: the relations of rabbi to board and board to congregation; the participatory structure of committees, decision making, and communication; and the choices that congregants make about the teaching of our children and our forms of prayer and song.[13]

Second, the rebuilding of congregation challenges us to engage responsibly with the communities around us. This is more and more difficult as middle-class Jews withdraw from the city to the suburb, rendering the problems of civic life as those of someone else, "the city," rather than problems that we share as part of a common lifeworld. While Jews may still be less likely to retreat into closed, gated communities, the geographic separation of Jews in the suburbs creates a break in our ability to imagine a shared fate with others. When we cannot imagine a shared community, we cannot see the connections between our lives and others. One of the most hopeful responses to this break is the emerging network of Jewish community-action movements. At least sixteen cities, including Los Angeles, Oakland, New York, Washington, Boston, Chicago, and Minneapolis, have formed local networks to engage in activities of *tikkun*. In Minneapolis, for example, Jewish Community Action (JCA) has addressed, in tangible civic actions, issues of welfare reform, the cutting off of food stamps for immigrants, and affordable housing. JCA is partnering with Public Achievement, a youth network, to help Jewish youth find their way to "public work" that builds on the commonwealth of the entire community. It is not surprising that a leading Reform congregation, Temple Israel, has been at the forefront of JCA activities, helping to sponsor a Sukkot conference on the problem of housing and to build interfaith coalitions.[14]

Such activities are not new, of course, nor do they offer any sort of panacea to the problems of meaning or community. However, failing to reach out to others—withdrawing behind the walls of the suburbs, resting content with the service model of congregational life, abdicating leadership to the rabbi and board—poses grave risks for the health of Reform Jewish congregations.

My own congregation offers a sad example of the possible fate should we ignore this warning. Once a vibrant, leading presence in Milwaukee, the congregation gradually gave up control to a single charismatic rabbi who, in turn, controlled our board for many years. The congregation became a hollowed-out shell, a service station. When a grandiose plan was floated to maintain two synagogues, one in the city and one in the suburbs, no one seriously questioned its feasibility until it was too late, after the new facility was built. A new board finally took control of the congregation, audited the books, and realized that having two facilities was not sustainable. It then chose to treat congregants as shareholders in a business rather than as members of a shared community. It exercised its legal power against a divided congregation and voted to close the urban facility, the last Reform synagogue in the city of Milwaukee, leaving a congregation in tatters. A new rabbi is working hard to rebuild community, help the congregation restore trust, and reinfuse spiritual meaning into the daily life of the synagogue, but his task is greatly complicated by the collapse of civic association within.

While this example is extreme, it is based on what happens when the real tendencies of civic collapse play themselves out. There is no guarantee that participation in the reinvention of civic life can help resolve the paradoxical position of Reform Jews who want to sustain community inside our congregations. But in the absence of the rebuilding of community inside our walls in order to reengage the community outside, we can be all but certain that our unique place in the modern American world will continue to shrink, perhaps to the vanishing point.

Notes

1. Robert Wuthnow, *Experimentation in American Religion: The New Mysticisms and their Implications for the Churches* (Berkeley: University of California Press, 1978); Robert Wuthnow, *Rediscovering the Sacred: Perspectives on Religion in Contemporary Society* (Grand Rapids, Mich.: W. B. Eerdmans, 1992); Robert Wuthnow, *Sharing the Journey: Support Groups and America's New Quest for Community* (New York: Free Press, 1994). For the most important macrosociological overview of the relations between society and religion, see Robert Wuthnow, *The Restructuring of American Religion: Society and Faith since World War II: Studies in Church and State* (Princeton, N.J.: Princeton University Press, 1988).
2. Sacvan Bercovitch, *The American Jeremiad* (Madison: University of Wisconsin Press, 1978); Robert N. Bellah, *The Broken Covenant: American Civil Religion in Time of Trial* (Chicago: University of Chicago Press, 1992).
3. Robert Bellah, Richard Madsen, William M. Sullivan, Ann Swidler, and Steven M. Tipton, *Habits of the Heart: Individualism and Commitment in American Life* (Berkeley and Los Angeles: University of California Press, 1996), viii.
4. Ibid., xi.
5. Robert D. Putnam, "Bowling Alone: America's Declining Social Capital," *Journal of Democracy* 6 (1995): 65–78; Robert Putnam, "The Strange Disappearance of Civic America," *The American Prospect* 24 (1996). For an overview of the civic crisis and emerging solutions, see Carmen J. Sirianni and Lewis A. Friedland, *Civic Innovation in America* (Berkeley and Los Angeles: University of California Press, 2000).
6. Alexis de Tocqueville, *Democracy in America,* trans. George Lawrence (New York: Harper and Row, 1969), 447–48.
7. Rodney Stark and Charles Y. Clock, *American Piety: The Nature of Religious Commitment* (Berkeley and Los Angeles: University of California Press, 1968), 1.
8. Michael Goldberg, *Why Should Jews Survive? Looking Past the Holocaust toward a Jewish Future* (New York: Oxford University Press, 1995).
9. Arnold Eisen, *Taking Hold of Torah: Jewish Commitment and Community in America* (Bloomington: Indiana University Press, 1997).
10. Bellah, *Broken Covenant,* 108.
11. Eisen, *Taking Hold,* 31–34.
12. For an analysis of the difference between charity and civic action, see John McKnight, *The Careless Society: Community and Its Counterfeits* (New York: Basic Books, 1995).
13. For Synagogue 2000, see www.S2K.org.
14. For the Minneapolis project, see www.jewishcommunityaction.org.

3

Reform Judaism in the Spiritual Marketplace

RICHARD CIMINO

It has become acceptable, almost trendy, to view many aspects of American life through the metaphor of the marketplace. Religion has not been exempt from this consumerist perspective. For many Americans religion and spirituality have been divorced from their institutional moorings. While Americans have always balanced religious commitment and individualism, some observers view the 1960s and the growing individualism and distrust of traditional institutions as intensifying what critic Harold Bloom calls this "American religion." Whereas forty years ago one would find spiritual sustenance and inspiration in churches, synagogues, and other congregations, today religious seeking can take place in the vast spirituality sections in bookstores, on the Internet, or even within corporations trying to harness spiritual practices to boost productivity.

As religion has taken on more disembodied forms, it can be packaged and repackaged for consumers. If one doesn't like a particular feature of a religion, it can be jettisoned and the other, more attractive, components can be highlighted and adopted. Spiritual experiences, which tend to be less divisive than doctrine and more market-friendly, also figure highly in contemporary forms of religious seeking and finding.

How will Reform Judaism fare in such an environment? A cursory overview of developments in this branch of American Judaism suggests that its history of adapting and adjusting to American society provides it with a ready-made stall in the spiritual marketplace. Reform's liberalization of the Jewish tradition gives it the ability to emphasize and offer those elements of Judaism that would be most relevant to believers and seekers. Greater freedom in observance and the overturning of matrilineal descent in establishing Jewish identity are two prime examples of how Reform has sought to accommodate itself to felt needs of its members and newcomers. Even the 1999 denominational statement endorsing traditional ritual and observances can be interpreted as a way of meeting the spiritual needs of assimilated Jews who now hunger for meaning after a long exile in secularism.

Rehabilitating Spirituality and Tradition

Realizing that success, social action, and the survival and stability of Israel do not provide a strong Jewish identity, American Jews are expressing a new interest in beliefs and spirituality. By rehabilitating and refashioning traditions and rituals that have historically marked Judaism, Reform is enlarging its repertoire, providing a large number of American Jews with access to spiritual resources that they once would have had to find in Conservative and Orthodox precincts. For instance, a renewed observance of the Sabbath (a trend that is also evident among mainstream Christians) is obviously a return to tradition for Reform Jews, but such retrievals from the past often have a modern sheen to them. Sabbath observance becomes for some not so much a duty to perform in obedience to God as much as a lifestyle choice that provides practitioners with a zone of sanctity and sanity in a hectic and materialistic world.

The same can be said for the resurgence of interest in Jewish mysticism. The Kabbalah and other sources of Jewish mysticism are repackaged for seekers (Jewish and non-Jewish) who have little regard for the traditional rubrics and theology that historically have undergirded these teachings. Thus Jewish healing finds itself as one entree on the menu of a whole range of holistic and New Age health techniques.

With its new openness to rituals and spirituality, Reform is in a position to draw seekers and keep members who themselves have experienced a spiritual awakening. It is not at all unusual to find members of Reform synagogues who were first drawn back to some form of spiritual concern and practice through New Age and Eastern religions, only to discover later that the same insights and benefits, if not more, can be found by retracing the roots of one's own tradition. As one rabbi and former Buddhist teacher said in *Shopping for Faith*, a book this author cowrote with Don Lattin, "Authentic Judaism was originally presented as a deep spiritual path. But the presentation of Judaism most people in America received was a denatured and despiritualized version. We have to rediscover the sense of spirituality that was lost in Judaism."[1]

Another effect of consumerism on religion is the way people try to mix and match different kinds of beliefs and practices. A major example of mix-and-match spirituality is the trend of many American Jews who are active in their synagogues and observant while also taking up some other spiritual practice. Eastern practices, particularly Buddhist meditation, have become so popular that the term *Jew-Bu* has been coined. Jews are incorporating Quaker practices as well as frequenting Unitarian churches. These religions tend not to have a strong theological system and distinctive doctrines of God and lend themselves to borrowing by Jewish and other believers.

It is doubtful, however, whether an attempt to combine Jewish and other religious forms into a new synthesized faith can meet with much success. For one thing, any combining of religions and spirituality can be plain confounding to most of the rank and file in congregations who may be unschooled in Jewish basics, not to mention Buddhist or Hindu teachings. A brief examination of different denominations can lead one to conclude that there have not been many successful attempts—in terms both of stability and growth—to mix and match two different faith systems into hybrid forms.

All this talk of consumerism and a spiritual free market assumes that Reform Judaism and any other religions and spiritualities will be accessible to outsiders and interested in bringing them into the fold. It is this matter of seeking converts that continues to roil Reform and other branches of Judaism. On one hand, Reform has already been receiving more converts than the other branches through intermarriage. On the other hand, it is often suggested that Jews may not be prepared for the sharp separations between Jewish ethnic and religious identity that may take place as more converts outside of intermarriages join the ranks. However, synagogues may experience a change of mind. Newcomers bring excitement and innovation, as well as new challenges, to congregational life. As the importance of spirituality and belief overshadows ethnic identity in American Judaism, and as a growing number of Jewish leaders call for the acceptance of non-Jewish converts, which seems to be taking place, a greater acceptance of recruiting converts may follow naturally.

Of course, welcoming and integrating new members into congregational life is difficult even for the most evangelistic of faiths. Many churches are discovering the importance of providing nontraditional points of access to help the newcomer move into congregational life. For instance, the large, multipurpose Protestant megachurches run a whole gamut of small groups—Bible studies, self-help groups, groups for singles and divorced people—and many newcomers participate in these activities before attending the main Sunday services. In a similar way, Jewish community centers, once largely based around secular endeavors such as adult education and recreation, are adding religious programs to their menus. Like Christian megachurches, they provide nonthreatening entry points for disaffiliated Jews to move into Jewish life. Reform synagogues may have to form similar programs. The popular classes in deciphering "Bible codes" held in many synagogues, however questionable their premises, are one example of out-reach to the disaffiliated community.

Commitment and Consumerism

Reform's compatibility with the workings of the spiritual marketplace goes only so far. Even if traditional elements are mixed into the melange of American spir-ituality, this may not satisfy or generate the commitment that can keep a syna-gogue vibrant. Those faiths that have relatively strict standards and demand a high level of commitment, such as attendance, giving, and adherence to teaching, tend to prosper. Religious groups that have lax standards, permitting a greater number of free riders (those who may have weddings, bar mitzvahs, or baptisms in congregations without contributing to them) tend to decline. In other words, groups that demand a lot from members tend to generate commitment and loy-alty. In a Jewish context this dynamic is evident in a Conservative Jewish syna-gogue in Washington, D.C., which has attracted young urban professionals by emphasizing lay leadership. But the synagogue also follows the traditional approach to observing Jewish law. The rabbi said of the congregants, "The fact that our service is more demanding does not scare them away; on the contrary, that is what they want. Their attitude is, 'If I am going to do this, I might as well really do it.'"[2]

If this theory, known as rational choice, holds true, than Reform may have trouble attracting and, more important, keeping new members. While there is a move toward more observance and acceptance of traditional practices, the denomination allows a large degree of pluralism that rules out enforcing uniform standards and practices. Those synagogues that use the new pluralism in the denomination to select more demanding and traditional practice and also restrict lax practice may experience the most growth. It may also be the case that those returning and converting to Judaism may come into the faith through Reform, but as they become more conservative or traditional, they may move on to Conservative or Orthodox expressions (a trend that is already occurring among a small number of observant Jews).

In any event there may also be growing conflict between the traditional and observant members and those taking a more nonritual and pluralistic approach to the faith. This conflict is already evident among those older members who find the introduction of traditional rituals and observances something foreign and in conflict with their own conceptions of Reform worship and life, one that stressed social concern and universal brotherhood. However, neither party will likely claim unqualified victory in these "worship wars." Reform rabbis and congre-gants will most likely want to hold on to a distinctive identity, which now includes some form of traditional observances and rituals, while also finding new ways to reach out to the disaffiliated and potential converts.

A Role for Laity and Women in Reform

Other aspects of Reform life seem to flow strongly in the direction of current trends in religion and spirituality. As we have seen, when seekers become believers and committed members of a congregation, they don't necessarily stop being consumers. Yet active members of a religious community are contributors of time and talents as well as consumers of services. Reform and other branches of American Judaism have traditionally allowed laypeople a greater variety of roles and influence within synagogues than have been found in many Christian bodies. Today within a wide range of denominations and congregations there is a shift of power away from the clergy as the primary bearers of the faith and teachers to the laity, who are taking up these new roles.

Computers and information technology utilize networks and relationships in preference to autocratic leadership. Rising education levels in postwar generations are creating a demand for greater participation and shared decision making. A model of "servant leadership," where the clergy seeks to enable and empower the laity to use their talents and gifts in the congregation, is emerging in many congregations. Another factor in this trend is the growth of small groups. Centralized authority in the rabbinical and pastoral office tends to become dispersed as these groups require the delegation of authority from clergy to congregation members who are leading these activities.

The expanding role of the laity has also been aided by one of the major trends in the last three decades—the leadership of women in religious institutions. Reform and mainline Protestant bodies have been the main carriers of this development, but women's leadership has also been felt in places as disparate as Orthodox prayer groups and conservative megachurches. Most of the mainline and Reform seminaries report rising enrollments of women students and in some women are the majority. Research on women clergy suggest that they are changing the style and in some places the content of their faith. Their preaching and style of leadership stress the sharing of personal information and put less distance between clergy and laity. Women clergy will accelerate the move from strictly hierarchical forms of leadership to team leadership models, according to many observers.

Such innovations as inclusive language and other feminist theological currents have moved from the seminaries to congregations as women take to the pulpits. In Jewish circles feminist attempts at rewriting the liturgy tend to stress the immanence (or nearness) of God rather than His transcendence. For instance, God might be referred to as the "wellspring of life," rather than as "king" or "judge." While these concepts may seem commonplace in the culture of more liberal seminaries, they can be disturbing to the laity, who sense, not incorrectly, that changing the text in some ways changes parameters of the faith. The attempt to introduce feminist revisions, particularly involving changes in worship, may at a certain point ignite another round of "worship wars," pitting more traditional believers against innovators. Critics have also noted that Reform synagogues (and most other religious congregations in the United States) are attended by women far more than by men. It is not difficult to envision many men being put off by a synagogue that has removed masculine references in the liturgy, is attended and led by women, and is presided over by a woman. This seems to be the place where team leadership (consisting of men and women) and small groups catering to men and their relationship to Judaism may play a vital role in Reform Jewish life in the future.

The Future of Reform

Readers may have noticed by now that only a few words in this essay were directed at Reform denominational structures, programs, and statements. That was not an accident, as it appears that Jewish as well as Christian denominational structures are increasingly irrelevant both to individual seekers and believers as well as to congregations. This does not mean that wider traditions and new forms of religious oversight and connections will be unimportant. But the centralized structures that demand loyalty and support from congregants and members are being met more with indifference than with respect. This can be seen in Christian churches in the decline of benevolence giving beyond one's own congregation. In Judaism denominational seminaries are now having to compete against new nondenominational schools, such as the Academy for Jewish Religion, as the old distinctions between Conservative, Reform, and Reconstructionist (if not Orthodox) no longer seem useful to a new generation of students. There is also the phenomenon of synagogues from the different branches in a given area convening to privately ordain rabbis. One of the reasons given for these new arrangements is that mainstream schools are too narrow and authoritarian and that their power needs to be checked by more democratic procedures.[3]

Just as Reform temples have generally grown more similar to Conservative and Reconstructionist synagogues, there is also increasing pluralism within all these branches. Like their Christian counterparts, the divisions today fall within as well as between different denominations. For instance, a Reform temple seeking to recover traditional observances may have more in common with the Conservative synagogue across town than with another Reform congregation nearby. One should not expect the newly returned Jew or the convert to understand or care too much about the historical divisions in Judaism or the denominational apparatus; the action and attraction will be at the congregational level.

The spiritual marketplace will have a decentralizing effect as personal choice takes precedence over obligation, ethnicity, and heritage. The give-and-take of the marketplace will likely remove some of the familiar furniture and old certainties on which Reform was built. Yet the same dynamism can also allow new wind to blow into dusty corners and reinvigorate Jewish tradition and create new forms of community.

Notes

1. Richard Cimino and Don Lattin, *Shopping for Faith: American Religion in the New Millennium* (San Francisco: Jossey-Bass, 1998), 22.
2. Walter Ruby, "Reform versus Conservative: Who's Winning?" *Moment,* April 1996, 37–39.
3. Richard Cimino, "Anti-establishment Mood Fuels Post-Denominational Judaism," *Religion Watch,* October 1998, 4–5.

4

Why People in the Sunbelt Join a Synagogue

Jewish Religious Preference in Palm Beach County

JOEL L. LEVINE

Palm Beach County, Florida, with 221,000 Jews, ranks in population among the top six Jewish communities in the United States. Only New York City, Los Angeles, Broward County (Florida), Chicago, and Boston rank higher. However, in 1995 the noted demographer Ira Sheskin of the University of Miami determined that 18.2 percent of all Jewish households in South Palm Beach County belong to a synagogue. This is one of the lowest percentages of any major Jewish community in the United States. (According to Tobin and Berger's 1993 study, the western United States has the lowest regional rate of affiliation, 29 percent.)[1] This percentage could also reflect the overall decline in synagogue affiliation. In 1955 60 percent of all Jews were affiliated.[2] A 1993 study measured that percentage as under 40 percent.

Despite these statistics, Palm Beach County does not necessarily reflect national averages. Jews continue to move in large numbers to Palm Beach County. The Jewish community of Boynton Beach alone is the fastest-growing community in the entire state. Moreover, by the year 2010 the south Palm Beach County communities of Boca Raton, Delray Beach, and Highland Beach will be home to about 220,000 persons in Jewish households. I have served as a rabbi in Palm Beach County for over two decades, and I continue to see members of the Jewish community affiliating with synagogues due to factors unlike those of Jewish communities elsewhere in the United States.

The purpose of this chapter is to examine the unique factors that determine why 18.2 percent of this rapidly growing Jewish community chose to affiliate with synagogues. I have found that these factors differ from those of Jewish communities of North America with long-established congregations, where affiliation is often based on family history. Jews in cities such as Baltimore, Boston, Chicago, Cleveland, Detroit, and Philadelphia are members because of their parents, grandparents, and great-grandparents. Yet once they move to Palm Beach County, new factors enter the picture. In this chapter I will suggest that these factors have little to do with either denomination or family history. Guided by Sheskin's statistics, studies cited elsewhere in this chapter, and my relatively long tenure as a rabbi in Palm Beach County, I will demonstrate that as a broader Jewish community, we have unique lessons to learn from the affiliated synagogue members of this rapidly growing Jewish population.

Two Kinds of Synagogues

Palm Beach County is home to a large number of Jewish seniors: 76 percent of south Palm Beach County's Jewish population and 67 percent of north Palm Beach County's Jewish population are age sixty or over. This has led to two distinct kinds of synagogues: the condominium congregation and the family congregation. There are approximately fifteen condominium congregations and fifteen family congregations in all of Palm Beach County. A condominium congregation, overwhelmingly populated with seniors, is located either on the grounds of a condominium development or close by. Dues are kept to a minimum and are levied per person instead of per family. Religious services and programming are aimed at the needs of seniors. Rabbis are often retirees and are engaged on a part-time basis. Cantors are also part-time.

In contrast, family congregations provide a full range of religious, cultural, and social activities similar to congregations in other North American cities. With the exception of three, Palm Beach County family congregations are not located in neighborhoods of Jewish households, so one must drive to a family congregation. Dues average $1,000 per family, and the majority of family congregations have building funds. Full-time rabbis are supported, with cantors, soloists, educators, executive directors, program directors, preschool directors, and youth directors employed on a full- or part-time basis. All but two of the county's Reform congregations are family congregations. Twelve Conservative synagogues are condominium congregations, and seven are family congregations.

Reasons for Joining Palm Beach County Congregations

Religious denomination is clearly not a reason for joining a synagogue in Palm Beach County. Since the majority of Jews there emigrated to the area in the last twenty years, family history is also not a reason for affiliation. According to Sheskin's 1996 study, the most important factor in determining affiliation is the quality of the rabbi.[3] This is followed by the need to identify with the Jewish community and the friendliness of the congregation. The quality of the cantor and cost are the least important.

Synagogue or Shul Shopping

For twenty-one years I have observed the phenomenon of "synagogue shopping." Synagogue or shul shopping is most intense in Palm Beach County from mid-August until the day of Kol Nidre. During this period Palm Beach County synagogues are overwhelmed with the flow of newcomers. They visit a different synagogue each Shabbat until they feel comfortable filling out a membership application. Savvy shul shoppers understand that the summer months are vacation months. Every Friday synagogue volunteers tell the same story. Telephone caller after telephone caller wants to know whether the rabbi will be conducting services that night. Many also want to know if the cantor will be chanting. In the weeks and even days prior to Rosh Hashanah and Yom Kippur shul shopping reaches a feverish pitch. I will never forget the time when the husband of our membership chairperson threw his hands up in the air as his telephone continued to ring until the moment his family left the house on Kol Nidre night.

The Palm Beach County phenomenon of shul shopping has compelled synagogues to engage in extensive newspaper and radio advertising. My synagogue takes a unique approach by advertising on our local public radio station in addition to the local press. I have found that a large number of young retirees not only listen to public radio but also frequently contribute their time and money during the year. Many are part of the steady stream of new residents who belonged to synagogues in their former communities. They are more motivated to join a Palm Beach County synagogue but do not know what is available.

On one Friday evening two weeks prior to Rosh Hashanah my synagogue was filled with shul shoppers who fit this profile: young retirees new to Florida who had heard our advertising on public radio. Judging from Sheskin's 1996 demographic study, additional young retirees will continue to move to Palm Beach County. Since they have created a market for synagogue membership, synagogues will need to find new advertising methods to inform them of the choices available.

Quality of the Rabbi

The results of the frenzy of shul shopping are very revealing. Sheskin's 1996 study found that the quality of the rabbi is the most important factor in synagogue affiliation. This varies somewhat with age: 64.9 percent of those under 35 years of age think the quality of the rabbi is very important, compared with 57 percent of those age 35–49, 60.2 percent of those age 50–64, 56.9 percent of those age 65–74, and 52.6 percent for age 75 and over. The figure is 60 percent of all females compared to 50 percent of all males. Further, the quality of the rabbi is more important to 67 percent of conversionary couples (married couples in which one spouse is a convert) and 58 percent of in-married couples (where both spouses are Jewish by birth) than those in intermarriages (45 percent). However, in my own experience in Palm Beach County I have found that intermarried couples place the quality of the rabbi on an equally high level. I have also found a difference in what shul shoppers expect from the rabbi. Retirees evaluate how the rabbi conducts the service, explains the Torah reading, and delivers the sermon. Parents keenly observe how the rabbi teaches and reacts to their children. Nonretired singles expect the rabbi to meet their unique spiritual and social needs.

The Need to Identify with the Jewish Community

The second most important factor in synagogue affiliation is the need to identify with the Jewish community. In Sheskin's 1996 study 46 percent indicated that this factor is very important. This factor does not vary significantly by sex or by geographic area. The need to identify with the Jewish community is much more important to couples where both spouses were born Jewish (49 percent) than those in intermarriages (23 percent).

The responses show a consistent relationship with age: 48 percent of those age 65 and over as compared to 39 percent of those age 35–64 cite the need to identify with the Jewish community as important. In my observation of the condominium synagogues I have found that the need to identify with the Jewish community is a very important consideration. Of the fifteen condominium synagogues only two boast continuing rabbinical leadership; yet all fifteen synagogues maintain consistently high levels of membership.

As for the fifteen family congregations, the need to identify with the Jewish community is less important, as confirmed by Sheskin's 39 percent figure for this group. The quality and tenure of the rabbi remain the primary factors. One family congregation had over 700 family members on its rolls twenty years ago. With the loss of five senior rabbis membership is around 150 families. As one family emphasized to me, it was very important to them to have the same rabbi who officiated at their son's brit milah officiate at the child's bar mitzvah. I have found that families find spiritual comfort and meaning in developing a long-term relationship with the same rabbi, who officiates at all life-cycle events.

Friendliness of a Congregation

The third most important factor in synagogue affiliation is the friendliness of the congregation. Sheskin found that 44 percent indicated this as very important and 26 percent as somewhat important. Friendliness of the congregation is therefore critical to about 70 percent. This factor is more important to younger respondents than to older ones, with 56 percent of those under age 35 rating friendliness as very important. This compares to 48 percent of those age 35–64 and 42 percent of those 65 and over. Figures vary only slightly according to gender. However, in-married couples (44 percent) find friendliness more important than do inter-married couples (34 percent). Having been intimately involved in my own congregation's membership campaign for over eighteen years, I find that friendliness is a high-priority, determining factor that cuts across all the ages. Conversionary, in-married, and intermarried couples also look for friendliness as a critical factor when they shul-shop.

It is significant that one congregation in Palm Beach County marketed itself as the friendliest congregation in Florida. In a workshop with my own temple board the mastermind of that campaign, now a past president, told us that he framed the entire membership drive around this slogan of friendliness. At a recent convention of my professional association, the Central Conference of American Rabbis, we rabbis were urged to personally greet people as they enter the synagogue rather than participating only in the traditional receiving line following services. During my own synagogue's membership campaign, we have receiving lines before and after services. The president of the congregation and I have found that this makes people feel more comfortable about being in the synagogue. In Palm Beach County this is extremely important because not only are so many residents newcomers to our community, but many have not been to a regular Shabbat service for a number of years.

Quality of Cantor and Cost

Sheskin called quality of cantor and cost the least important factors; 37 percent indicated quality of cantor and 32 percent indicated cost.

With 37 percent, the quality of the cantor ranks number four in the list of reasons people affiliate with a given congregation. The two major groups who rated the quality of the cantor as very important are those under 35 and those 75 and over. The figures for other groups that rated this factor very important are 27.7 percent of those age 35–49, 34 percent of those age 50–64, and 35.2 percent of those age 65–74. Thirty-nine percent of females rated this factor as very important, as compared to 32 percent of males. Sheskin found that the quality of the cantor is more important to in-married couples (37 percent) than to intermarried couples (20 percent).

Of all thirty congregations in Palm Beach County only two have engaged cantors who are either invested by Hebrew Union College–Jewish Institute of Religion or the Jewish Theological Seminary. The remaining congregations have engaged cantors who either have been recognized by their professional associations for life experience or are cantorial soloists. This compares to twenty-eight congregations out of thirty who have engaged ordained rabbis.

Unlike most communities, where many claim that cost is the main reason why people do not affiliate, in Sheskin's 1996 study cost is the least important factor in affiliation. Only 32 percent indicated cost as very important, and there is no significant difference in statistics by geographic area, Jewish identification, type of marriage, or age. The only variation is by gender. Thirty-five percent of females feel that cost is more important; 26 percent of males feel the same way. In my observations family congregations are very similar in cost, averaging $1,000 per family. On the other hand, condominium congregations charge per person, often under $200. Family congregations usually include High Holy Day tickets in the membership fee but charge extra for religious school and Hebrew school. Condominium congregations often charge extra for High Holy Day tickets.

In my observations I have found that cost does factor into the picture when retirees shul-shop. They carefully compare the dues and expenses of condominium congregations with family congregations, and the high cost of affiliation with family congregations means that many retirees on fixed incomes choose to affiliate with condominium congregations. Several years ago my congregation created a special dues category for seniors 70 and over, a category that is competitive with the cost of joining a condominium congregation. Once this dues category entered the picture, our membership increased significantly in this age group. Within this competitive dues category, retirees 70 and over confirmed Sheskin's primary affiliation factors: quality of the rabbi, the need to identify with the Jewish community, and friendliness.

The Power of a Relevant Message

I now want to take another look at the quality of the rabbi as the most important factor in synagogue affiliation. In this analysis I want to draw upon the work of the late Rabbi Marshall T. Meyer as discussed in Sales and Tobin.[4] In the fall of 1985 Rabbi Meyer was engaged as rabbi of the historic New York congregation B'nai Jeshurun. At that time only eight paying members remained on the rolls of this once-prestigious congregation. B'nai Jeshurun now has over 3,200 congregants and an annual budget of over $1 million. Rabbi Meyer wrote that this phenomenal growth was achieved by one key factor, which he called "the power of a relevant message."

At B'nai Jeshurun Rabbi Meyer not only created a relevant message, but made this message the foundation of every service and program of the congregation. Rabbi Meyer's relevant message embraced inclusion, from opening the synagogue doors to the public on the High Holy Days to welcoming gays and lesbians; egalitarianism with a gender-sensitive liturgy; intimacy, with a chairless pulpit and everyone at the synagogue—including clergy—addressed on a first-name basis; passion in prayer, spontaneity in song, dance, and interactive discussions instead of formal sermons; and a continuing, relevant social action program translating the words of the prophets into compelling programs, such as establishing a homeless shelter and what Rabbi Meyer calls "eco-kashrut."

The Power of a Relevant Message in Palm Beach County

In Palm Beach County the relevant message is set by the rabbi. This is integral to the role the rabbi plays as the primary factor in determining synagogue affiliation. Once again, religious denomination plays no role in this process. During shul-shopping season it is this relevant message that either attracts or detracts people from affiliation. A relevant message may focus on one or two specific themes, such as spirituality, social action, pastoral care and attention, education, or *chevrusa,* the feeling of community. A relevant message can be encompassing, including all of these areas.

One Palm Beach County rabbi focuses his relevant message on spirituality and education. During every Shabbat morning service this rabbi teaches Torah for approximately one hour. He not only introduces the Torah service with a commentary but teaches Torah prior to each aliyah or section of the weekly portion. Every Wednesday from December through March he plans a university-style adult education program that attracts people from all over Palm Beach County.

In another Palm Beach County synagogue the senior rabbi takes a different approach with a relevant message, a task that is particularly challenging because the congregation has well over 2,200 families on its membership rolls. Here the relevant message is designed to embrace the totality of Jewish life. His staff includes an associate rabbi, an assistant rabbi, a cantor, a cantorial soloist, an educational director, a program director, an executive director, and a preschool director. Yet he is not satisfied with having a large staff to assist him with his work. Instead, he teaches his staff to make every member feel important, needed, and involved with his relevant message. Members are not treated as numbers on a vast computer database; they feel valued on a spiritual, educational, pastoral, and social level.

Whether the relevant message is targeted or encompassing, in Palm Beach County a rabbi's pulpit presence is a major factor in why a person affiliates with a particular synagogue. Pulpit presence involves the methodology with which the rabbi delivers the relevant message. Pulpit presence cuts across varying rabbinic styles, such as the formal sermon, the B'nai Jeshurun model of intimate dialogue, interactive Torah study, and even "ask-the-rabbi" sessions. My own observations confirm pulpit presence as a significant factor in quality of the rabbi. When a rabbi delivers the relevant message in a compelling way, Palm Beach County residents will often drive long distances to affiliate with that rabbi's synagogue.

Emotion

Unlike decisions about which automobile to purchase or what color to paint one's house, decisions about church or synagogue membership touch on an individual's ideology and beliefs. Affiliation thus involves deep feelings and is highly emotional. It is also not uncommon for individuals to leave a congregation out of anger, frustration, or disappointment at unmet expectations.[5] In Palm Beach County the quality of the rabbi and the power of the relevant message play into this highly emotional scenario.

As retirees, members of condominium congregations have ample time on their hands. Thus, the subject of the quality of the rabbi and the power of the relevant message become major talking points in restaurants, by the pool, on the golf course, and even in the steam room and sauna. Religious denomination is not an issue. The issue is how the rabbi develops the relevant message, and this is evaluated by many retirees on a compare-and-contrast basis. Since 79 percent of the residents in South Palm Beach County moved there from other states and other Florida counties, such comparison is inevitable.[6] And Palm Beach County retirees often take the technique of compare and contrast to new levels of minutiae. Merely liking a rabbi is not sufficient; retirees become passionately attached to their rabbi. Disliking a rabbi kicks in equally passionate feelings. Palm Beach County's phenomenon of "synagogue waltzing" involves members who grow to dislike their rabbi and then move on to another rabbi at another synagogue. One synagogue-waltzing couple was serious when they told me that could not join my synagogue because they liked me. In every synagogue they had waltzed to and subsequently joined, the rabbi's contract was not renewed.

In contrast, members of family congregations are still working and have far less time to talk about their rabbis. Their emotional attachments with their rabbis are often centered around life-cycle events, notably bar and bat mitzvah ceremonies. Here the quality of the rabbi and the power of the relevant message are often scrutinized. Synagogues are at times selected many years in advance based on how the rabbi officiates at the bar and bat mitzvah ceremonies. Recently a former temple president in another community, now a seasonal resident, based her decision to become an adult bat mitzvah on the way I officiated at a ceremony she attended. Religious denomination played no role in her decision.

Conclusion

Sales and Tobin have found that despite the complexity of the topic of synagogue affiliation and what they call the "multiform routes to its exploration and implementation," affiliation is a valued act.[7] I have found that affiliated synagogue members in Palm Beach County value the quality of the rabbi as the primary factor, followed by the need to identify with the Jewish community and the friendliness of the congregation. Religious denomination plays almost no role in this process.

In over two decades as serving as a pulpit rabbi in Palm Beach County, I have found that people are not concerned about the specific religious denomination of their rabbi. Rather, they are concerned about quality. Drawing on Rabbi Marshall T. Meyer's analysis, I believe that the power of the relevant message is inexorably linked to the quality of the rabbi. The rabbis who have long tenure in Palm Beach County have successfully developed their relevant message as either targeted or encompassing, and this bonds these rabbis with their congregants. This factor cuts across all demographic lines.

Although the majority of Jewish residents are retirees, they have no problem driving to a synagogue where the rabbi is more appealing. Despite previous perceptions that retirees do not like to drive at night, 78 percent of all respondents and spouses age 65 and over indicated in Sheskin's 1996 south Palm Beach County study that they do drive after dark.[8] Even 53 percent of widowed women drive after dark. This shows that driving at night is certainly not a factor in their choice of affiliation. Factors such as the quality of the rabbi, the need to identify with the Jewish community, and friendliness are important enough that retirees will even drive at night to attain them.

These same factors have motivated Palm Beach County residents to drive to the one Orthodox synagogue that is not located in a Jewish neighborhood. Unlike the four neighborhood Orthodox synagogues, I have observed in-married, conversionary, and even intermarried couples affiliate with this congregation primarily due to the quality of the rabbi, enhanced by the power of his relevant message of inclusion and his pulpit presence. The denomination of this synagogue as Orthodox factors minimally into their decision to affiliate.

Two other factors might be unique to Palm Beach County. As previous noted, Sheskin's 1996 study found that for comparison purposes, the quality of cantor and cost are the least important. This finding dispels many popular conceptions. I have observed one condominium congregation growing into one of the largest in Palm Beach County solely due to the quality of the rabbi; congregants talk constantly about the spiritual quality of the congregation's rabbi as their primary reason for affiliation. Cost is not a factor.

Although Palm Beach County synagogues carry denominational labels, the congregational roles are filled with a diversity of religious affiliations. My adult students tell me that once retirees move to Palm Beach County, they often abandon their previous Jewish religious trappings. They have embarked on the quest to build a new life as retirees, and the spirituality that worked for them in their former neighborhood lifestyles may not necessarily work for them in their new retirement locations. Although family members and single members carry different lifestyle expectations than retirees, the reasons for their synagogue affiliation are the same. Unlike their former (often historical) Jewish communities, virtually every Jewish resident in Palm Beach County is a relative newcomer. This means not only a new home, a new neighborhood, and new professional services, but unique reasons for affiliating with a synagogue.

Notes

1. G. A. Tobin, and G. Berger, *Synagogue Affiliation: Implications for the 1990s*, Research Report 9 (Waltham, Mass.: Brandeis University, Cohen Center for Modern Jewish Studies, 1993).

2. J. Sloan, "Religion," in *American Jewish Yearbook*, vol. 5 (New York: KTAV Publishing, 1995).

3. I. M. Sheskin, *Jewish Federation of South Palm Beach County: Jewish Demographic Study Main Report* (Boca Raton, Fla.: Jewish Federation of South Palm Beach County, 1996). Sheskin did a follow-up study in 1999.

4. A. L. Sales and G. A. Tobin, eds., *Church and Synagogue Affiliation: Theory, Research, and Practices* (Westport, Conn.: Greenwood, 1995).

5. Ibid.

6. Sheskin, *Jewish Federation.*

7. Ibid.

8. Ibid.

Legitimacy and Authenticity

The "Sins" of Yesterday and the Controversies of Today

5

When Reform Judaism Was Judaism

JACOB NEUSNER

When Reform Judaism began, its principal theologians did not offer the Jews *a* Judaism—another choice among equally available and comparable alternatives. Nor did they claim merely to modify an authentic, received Judaism in order to accommodate a less than ideal circumstance. Reform Judaism did not present itself as Brand X, and it did not concede it was a lesser version of a good thing that was authentically realized elsewhere, in Orthodox Judaism, for instance. Reform rabbis did not wear head coverings because they did not believe it was correct to do so, the criterion being established by the Torah. That is to say, Reform Judaism thought of itself as Judaism pure and simple: the Judaism that everyone should practice, all Jews and Gentiles as well. It is said that Isaac Mayer Wise thought that by 1900 everyone in the world would practice Reform Judaism. In other words, Reform Judaism began with such confidence, such vigor, such certainty that it claimed to *be* Judaism, which is to say that Reform proudly asserted, "By the light of the Torah, we are right and you are wrong."

That remarkable certainty, resting on systematic scholarship fully coherent with a well-articulated criterion of truth, persisted from the nineteenth century into the middle of the twentieth. It was embodied, perhaps grotesquely, in the Reform rabbi in whose temple I grew up, who insisted on ordering a ham sandwich as a matter of religious right. But that same conviction inspired the courage of the Reformers to define their "Israel" in opposition to ethnicity and nationality, to re-create the liturgy of the synagogue and to reconfigure the entire music thereof, to redesign the spaces and the times of Judaism's realization in buildings and on sacred occasions—in short, not merely to reform but to create.

Such confidence contrasts strikingly with today's failure of nerve, embodied in Reform's claim to renew tradition, tradition then being conceded to the Orthodox definition. Indeed, considering the repudiation of the forms of Classical Reform Judaism (historically the authentic statement of Reform), we lose sight of the true character of Reform Judaism in its creative age: its vitality, its certainty, the power of its logic, and its systemic rationality. Hence any perspective on today's tendencies requires a reconsideration of some of the intellectual sources of Reform Judaism. What demands attention is the character of the propositions, evidence, and arguments adduced on behalf of Reform and represented as not merely change or reform but as something else: a wholly organic step forward in the evolution of a single, linear, harmonious Jewish history reaching its climax in the formation and definition called "Reform."

Reform: Innovative at the Outset

Reform Judaism innovated at the very outset with its debates and platforms, its rabbinical convocations and their decisions. The very fact that it could conceive of such a process of debate and formulation of a kind of creed tells us that this Judaism found urgent the specification of its systemic structure. This gives testimony to a mature, and self-aware frame of mind. We look in vain for equivalent convocations to set public policy, for example, in the antecedent thousand years of the Judaism of the dual Torah. Statements of worldview, as these would emerge in diverse expressions of the received system, did not take the form of a rabbis' platform, on one side, and did not come about through democratic debate on public issues, on the other.

Rather, that worldview percolated upward and represented a rarely articulated and essentially inchoate consensus about how things really are and should be. The received system came to expression in how things were done, what people found unnecessary to make articulate at all: the piety of a milieu, not the proposition of a theological gathering. That contrast tells us not merely that Reform Judaism represented a new Judaism, but, of greater interest, that the methods and approaches of Reform Judaism enjoyed their own self-evident appropriateness.

To begin with, we take up Reform Judaism in its most mature realization in the nineteenth century, in Pittsburgh, Pennsylvania, among rabbis who could point to three or even four generations of antecedents. These were not founders of the new faith—the Judaism before us was born about a generation before anyone identified it as a new thing—but authorities of an established and enduring one. The end of the nineteenth century found Reform Judaism a major component of the Judaic religious life of the United States as well as of Germany, and it was making inroads elsewhere as well. The American Reform rabbis, meeting in Pittsburgh in 1885, issued a clear and accessible statement of their Judaism.

What was this Judaism's formulation of the issue of Israel as political circumstances defined it. Critical to the Judaism of the dual Torah was its view of Israel as God's people, a supernatural polity, living out its social existence under God's Torah. The way of life, one of sanctification, and the worldview, one of persistent reference to the Torah for both rules of conduct and the explanation of that conduct began in the basic conception of Israel. That doctrine exposed for all to see the foundations of the way of life and the worldview that these rabbis had formed for the Israel they conceived:

> We recognize in the Mosaic legislation a system of training the Jewish people for its mission during its national life in Palestine, and today we accept as binding only its moral laws and maintain only such ceremonies as elevate and sanctify our lives, but reject all such as are not adapted to the views and habits of modern civilization. . . . We hold that all such Mosaic and rabbinical laws as regular diet, priestly purity, and dress originated in ages and under the influence of ideas entirely foreign to our present mental and spiritual state. . . . Their observance in our days is apt rather to obstruct than to further modern spiritual elevation. . . . We recognize in the modern era of universal culture of heart and intellect the approaching of the realization of Israel's great messianic hope for the establishment of the kingdom of truth, justice, and peace among all men. We consider ourselves no longer a nation but a religious community and therefore expect neither a return to Palestine nor a sacrificial worship under the sons of Aaron nor the restoration of any of the laws concerning the Jewish state.

I cannot imagine a more forthright address to the age. The Pittsburgh Platform takes up each component of the system in turn. Who is Israel? What is its way of life? How does it account for its existence as a distinct, and distinctive, group? Israel once was a nation ("during its national life") but today is not a nation. It once had a set of laws that regulate diet, clothing, and the like. These no longer apply, because Israel now is not what it was then. Israel forms an integral part of Western civilization. The reason to persist as a distinctive group was that the group has its work to do, namely, to realize the messianic hope for the establishment of a kingdom of truth, justice, and peace. For that purpose Israel no longer constitutes a nation. It now forms a religious community.

What that means is that individual Jews do live as citizens in other nations. Difference is acceptable at the level of religion, not nationality, a position that accords fully with the definition of citizenship of the Western democracies. The worldview then lays heavy emphasis on an as yet unrealized but coming perfect age. The way of life admits to no important traits that distinguish Jews from others, since morality, in the nature of things, forms a universal category, applicable in the same way to everyone. The theory of Israel then forms the heart of matters, and what we learn is that Israel constitutes a "we," that is, that the Jews continue to form a group that, by its own indicators, holds together and constitutes a cogent social entity.

All this in a simple statement of a handful of rabbis forms a full and encompassing Judaism, one that, to its communicants, presented truth of a self-evident order. But it was also a truth declared, not discovered, and the self-evidence of the truth of the statements competed with the self-awareness characteristic of those who made them. For they could recognize the problem that demanded attention: the reframing of a theory of Israel for the Israel that they themselves constituted, the "we" that required explanation. No more urgent question faced the rabbis, because, after all, they lived in a century of opening horizons, in which people could envision perfection. World War I would change all that, also for Israel. By 1937 the Reform rabbis, meeting in Columbus, Ohio, would reframe the system, expressing a worldview quite different from that of a half century before.

Let us briefly summarize this picture of the program of urgent issues and self-evident responses that constituted the first of the new Judaisms of the nineteenth century. The questions we find answered fall into two categories: first, why "we" do not keep certain customs and ceremonies but do keep others, and second, how "we relate to the nations in which we live." So the system of Reform Judaism explained both why and why not, that is, why this, not that, the mark of a fully framed and cogent Judaism. The affirmative side covered why the Jews would persist as a separate group, and the negative would account for the limits of difference.

These two questions deal with the same urgent problem, namely, working out a mode of Judaic existence compatible with citizenship in, for these rabbis, America. Jews do not propose to eat or dress in distinctive ways. They seek "modern spiritual elevation . . . universal culture of heart and intellect." They impute to that culture the realization of "the messianic hope"—a considerable stake. And, explicit to the whole, the Jews no longer constitute a nation. They therefore belong to some other nation(s). If I had to specify a single self-evident proposition taken fully into account by the Judaism at hand, it is that political change has changed the entirety of "Judaism," but the Judaism at hand has the power to accommodate to that change.

So change in general forms the method for dealing with the problem at hand, which is change in the political and social standing the Jews now enjoy. On the very surface Reform Judaism formed a Judaic system that confronted immense political change and presented a worldview and way of life to an Israel defined in those categories opened up by the change occurring. Two questions demand attention. We want to know how this Judaism came into being and how its intellectuals explained their system. That is the point at which the contrast between contemporary and historical Reform Judaic theologians and historians proves stark: the one apologizes for what the other took pride in.

Saving for Jews the Received Judaism

If I had to specify the single dominant concern of the framers of Reform Judaism, I should turn to the matter of the Jews' position in the public polity of the several Christian European countries in which they lived. From the perspective of the political changes taking place from the American and French Revolutions onward, the received system of the Judaism of the dual Torah answered the wrong questions, for the issue no longer found definition in the claims of regnant Christianity.

A new question, emerging from forces not contained within Christianity, demanded attention from Jews affected by those forces. For those Jews the fact of change derived its self-evidence from shifts in political circumstances. When the historians began to look for evidence of precedents for changing things, it was because their own circumstance had already persuaded them that change matters—change itself effects change, so to speak. What they sought, then, was a picture of a world in which they might find a place, and it went without saying that this picture would include a portrait of a Judaic system: a way of life, a worldview, a definition of the Israel to live the one and believe the other that realizes the way of life and accounts for the worldview. The issue confronting the new Judaism derived not from Christianity, therefore, but from political change brought about by forces of secular nationalism, which conceived of society as the expression not of God's will for the social order under the rule of Christ and his Church or his anointed king (emperor, tsar) but of popular will for the social order under the government of the people and their elected representatives, a considerable shift.

When society does not form the aggregate of distinct groups, each with its place and definition, language and religion, but rather undifferentiated citizens (male, white, wealthy, to be sure), then the Judaism that Jews in such a society have to work out also must account for difference of a different order altogether. That Judaism needs to frame a theory of who is Israel consonant with the social situation of Jews who will themselves to be different, but not so different that they cannot also be citizens.

The original, and enduring, Judaic system of Reform correctly appealed to Moses Mendelssohn for its intellectual foundations, and Mendelssohn presented, in the words of Michael A. Meyer, an appeal "for a pluralistic society that offered full freedom of conscience to all those who accepted the postulates of natural religion: God, Providence, and a future life."[1] The protasis presents the important component: a pluralistic society, which, in the nature of things, constitutes a political category. Issues dominant from Mendelssohn's time forward concerned what was called "emancipation," meaning the provision for Jews of the rights of citizens. Reform theologians took the lead in the struggle for such rights. To them it was self-evident that Jews not only should have civil rights and civic equality but should want them. A Judaism that did not explain why the Jews should want and have full equality as part of a common humanity ignored the issues that preoccupied those who found, in Reform Judaism, a corpus of self-evident truths. To those truths, the method—the appeal to historical facts—formed a contingent and secondary consideration.

To the Reform rabbis in Pittsburgh, Christianity presented no urgent problems. The open society of America did. The self-evident definition of the social entity, Israel, therefore had to shift. We recall how the fourth-century rabbis balanced Israel against Rome; Jacob against Esau; the triumphant political messiah, seen as arrogant, against the Messiah of God, humble and sagacious. So Israel formed a supernatural entity and in due course would enter into that final era in God's division of time, in which Israel would reach its blessing. The supernatural entity, Israel, now formed no social presence. The Christian world, in which Christ ruled through popes and emperors, kings claimed divine right, and the will of the Church bore multiform consequences for society, and in which, by the way, Israel, too, was perceived in a supernatural framework—if a negative one— no longer existed. So the world at large no longer verified that category, Israel as supernatural entity, at all. Then the problems of the definition of what sort of entity Israel did constitute, what sort of way of life should characterize that Israel, and what sort of worldview should explain it produced a new set of urgent and ineluctable questions, and, in the nature of things, also self-evidently true answers, such as we find in Pittsburgh.

This brings us back to the birth of this Judaism. Reform Judaism dates its beginnings to the nineteenth century with changes (called reforms and regarded as the antecedents of Reform), in trivial aspects of public worship in the synagogue.[2] The motive for these changes derived from the simple fact that many Jews rejected the received system. People were defecting from the synagogue. Since it was taken for granted that giving up the faith meant surrendering all ties to the group, the changes aimed at making the synagogue more attractive so that defectors would return and others would not leave. The reform of Judaism in its manifestation in synagogue worship, the cutting edge of the faith, therefore took cognizance of something that had already taken place. This was a loss for the received system—as way of life, as worldview, as addressed to a defined Israel— of its standing as self-evident truth.

That loss manifested itself in two ways. First, people were simply leaving. Second, and more important for the group, the many who were staying looked in a new way on what for so long had scarcely demanded examination at all. But, of course, the real issues involved not the synagogue but society at large. It would take two generations before Reform Judaism would find the strength to address that much larger issue, and a generation beyond that for the power of the ideas ultimately formulated in the Pittsburgh Platform to be felt.

To begin with, the issue involved not politics but merely justification for changing anything at all. But that issue asked the wrong question in the wrong way. The Reformers maintained that change was all right because historical precedent proved that change was all right. But change had long defined the constant in the ongoing life of the Judaism of the dual Torah. Generative causes and modes of effecting change marked the vitality of the system. The Judaism of the dual Torah endured, never intact but always unimpaired, because of its power to absorb and make its own the diverse happenings of culture and society. So long as the structure of politics remained the same, with Israel an autonomous entity, subordinated but recognized as a cogent and legitimate social group in charge of some of its own affairs, the system answered the paramount question. The trivial ones could work their way through and become part of the consensus, to be perceived in the end as "tradition," too. A catalogue of changes that had taken place over fifteen hundred years, from the birth of rabbinic Judaism to modern times, therefore will list many more dramatic and decisive sorts of change than the minor revisions of liturgy (for example, sermons in the vernacular) that attracted attention at the dawn of the age of Reform.

We must wonder, therefore, what made the difference at that time, so that change could be perceived as reform and transformed into Reform Judaism. When people could take a stance external to the received mode and effect change as a matter of decision and policy rather than as a matter of what is restorative and purported to be timelessly appropriate, we know that, for those people, Judaism in its received form had already died. The received system no longer defined matters but now become subject to definition, and that marks the move from self-evidence to self-consciousness.

What had brought about the demise of the received system as definitive and normative beyond all argument is something we do not know. Nothing in the earliest record of reform of liturgy tells us. The constructive efforts of the first generation, only later on recognized not as people who made changes or even as reformers but as founders of Reform Judaism, focused, as I said, upon synagogue worship. The services were too long; the speeches were in a language foreign to participants; the singing was not aesthetically pleasing; the prayers were in a language few understood. But that means some people recited the prayers as a matter of duty, not supplication; did not speak the language of the faith; formed other than received opinions on how to sing in synagogue; saw as alien what earlier had marked the home and hearth. Those people no longer lived in that same social world that had for so long found right and proper precisely the customs now seen as alien.

When the heritage forms an unclaimed, unwanted legacy, people nonetheless accept it out of duty. So the reform that produced Reform Judaism introduced a shortened service, a sermon in the language people spoke, a choir and an organ, and prayers in the vernacular. Clearly a great deal of change had taken place prior to the recognition that something had changed. People no longer knew Hebrew; they no longer found pleasing received modes of saying the prayers. We look in vain to the consequent reforms for answers to the question of why people made these changes, and the reasons adduced by historians settle no interesting questions for us.

The more interesting question concerns the persistence of engagement and concern, for people always had the option, which many exercised, of abandoning the received Judaism of the two Torahs and all other Judaisms, too. Among those for whom these cosmetic changes made a difference, much in the liturgy, and far more beyond, retained powerful appeal. The premise of change dictated that Jews would say the old prayers in essentially the old formulation, and that premise carried much else: the entire burden of the faith, the total commitment to the group, in some form, defined by some indicators, if not the familiar ones then some others. So we know that Reform Judaism, in its earliest manifestation in Germany in the early nineteenth century, constituted an essentially conservative, profoundly constructive effort to save for Jews the received Judaism by reforming it in some (to begin with) rather trivial ways.

Not a Judaism, but Judaism

Yet I claim much more. I allege that, from their perspective, the Reformers defined *Judaism*, not *a Judaism*. They set forth Reform Judaism as the natural, right, authoritative, true Judaism and dismissed all others as wrong, inauthentic, and untrue. That attitude derived not from sociology (arguments about what would keep Jews Jewish) but from theology: a systematic, intellectual program built upon logical lines within a well-crafted rationality. So we turn to the evidence for the claim that Reform Judaism promised not a Judaism but Judaism.

What formed the justification for these changes was the theory of the incremental history of a single, linear Judaism, which played a powerful role in the creative age of Reform Judaism. The ones who made changes (it is too soon to call them Reformers) to begin with rested their case on an appeal to the authoritative texts. Change is legitimate, and these changes in particular are wholly consonant with the law, or the tradition, or the inner dynamics of the faith, or the dictates of history, or whatever out of the past worked that day. The laymen who made the changes tried to demonstrate that the changes fit in with the law of Judaism. They took the trouble because Reform, even at the outset, claimed to restore, to continue, to persist in, the received pattern. The justification of change always invoked precedent. People who made changes had to show that the principle that guided what they did was not new, even though the specific things they did were. So to lay down a bridge between themselves and their past, they laid out beams resting on deep-set piles. The foundation of change was formed of the bedrock of precedent.

And more still: change restores, reverts to an unchanging ideal. So the Reformer claims not to change at all, but only to regain the correct state of affairs, one that others, in the interval, themselves have changed. That forms the fundamental attitude of the people who make changes and call the changes Reform. The appeal to history, a common mode of justification in the politics and theology of the nineteenth century, therefore defined the principal justification for the new Judaism: it was new because it renewed the old and enduring, the golden Judaism of a mythic age of perfection. Arguments on precedent drew the Reformers to the work of critical scholarship, as we shall see, as they settled all questions by appeal to the facts of history.

We cannot find surprising, therefore, the theory that Reform Judaism stood in a direct line with the prior history of Judaism. Judaism is one. Let me state the foundation of Reform Judaic self-confidence in a single sentence: *Judaism has a history, that history is single and unitary, and it was always leading to its present outcome, which is Reform Judaism.* Others later on would challenge these convictions. Orthodox Judaism would deny that Judaism has a history at all. Conservative Judaism, also called Positive Historical Judaism, would discover a different goal for history from that embodied by Reform Judaism. But the mode of argument, appealing to issues of an historical and factual character, and the premises of argument, insisting that history proved, or disproved, matters of theological conviction, characterized all the Judaisms of the nineteenth century.

This presents no surprises, since the Judaisms of the age took shape in the intellectual world of Germany, with its profoundly philosophical and historical mode of thought and argument. So the challenge of political change carried with it its own modes of intellectual response, in the academic, scholarly framework. The challenges of the twentieth century exhibited a different character altogether. They were not intellectual but wholly political, and they concerned not matters of political status but issues of life or death. The Judaic systems of the age then would respond in their own way, through forming instrumentalities of collective action and political power, not theory. But we have moved ahead of our story.

To return to Germany and its Judaisms, we observe that the method of the Judaism aborning as Reform exhibited a certain congruence to the locale. Whether we refer to Luther demanding reversion to the pure and primitive faith of the Gospels or the earliest generation of Reform leaders appealing to the Talmud as justification for rejecting what others thought was the contemporary embodiment of the Talmud's requirements, the principle remains the same. Reform renews; recovers the true condition of the faith; selects, out of a diverse past, that age and that moment at which the faith attained its perfect definition and embodiment. This is not change but restoration and renewal of the true modes, the recovery of the way things were in that perfect, paradigmatic time, that age that formed the model for all time. These deeply mythic modes of appeal formed the justification for change, transforming mere modification of this and that into Reform. However, confronted with dubious allegations as to matters of faith and fact, the leaders of change took on the mantle of Reform, for they revised not only a few lines of a prayer but the entire worldview expressed in the accepted liturgy.

The mythic being of the liturgy entailed the longing, in the imagination of the nation, for a return to Zion, the rebuilding of the Temple, and the reconstitution of the bloody rites of animal sacrifice. These propositions formed a critical plank in the response to the Christian view that Israel's salvation had occurred in times past and ended with Israel's rejection of the Christhood of Jesus. In response, the dual Torah had insisted on future salvation, at the end of time, which, self-evidently, had not yet arrived. For ages from the original exile, in 586 B.C.E., the Jews had appealed to a Scripture that explained why they had lost their land, their city, their temple, and their cult, and told them what they had to do to get them back. That scriptural message thus formed a principal plank in the messianic platform of the Judaism of the dual Torah, as we saw, since the sages alleged that if Israel keeps the Torah as they taught it, the promises of the Torah, Pentateuch, and prophets would come true. The Messiah-sage stood for exactly that promise.

To Jews the condition of Israel in exile formed a self-evident fact of politics and culture alike. Speaking their own language, pursuing occupations distinctive to their group, living essentially apart from other peoples of the same time and place (who themselves formed not a uniform nation but a mosaic of equivalent social entities, that is, religion-nations, each with its language and economy and distinct society), Jews knew who they were. They were a nation in exile. When, therefore, the early changes encompassed rewording the liturgy so as to shade off the motifs of the return to Zion and restoration of the cult, these changes signaled that much else already had undergone revision and still more would have to change as well. Reform ratified change now a generation old, proposed to cope with it, to reframe and revise the received "tradition" so as to mark out new boundaries for self-evident truth.

The original changes, in the first decades of the nineteenth century, produced a new generation of rabbis. Some forty years into the century, these rabbis gave to the process of change the name of Reform and created those institutions of Reform Judaism that would endow the inchoate movement with a politics of its own. In the mid-1840s a number of rabbinical conferences brought together the new generation of rabbis. Trained in universities, the rabbis who came to these gatherings turned backward, justifying the changes in prayer rites long in place and effecting some further, mostly cosmetic changes in the observance of the Sabbath and in the laws covering personal status through marriage and divorce. In 1845 a decision to adopt for some purposes German in place of Hebrew led to the departure of conservative Reformers, typified by Zacharias Frankel. The Reformers, however, appealed for their apologia to the received writings, persisting in their insistence that they formed a natural continuation of the processes of the "tradition." Indeed, that point of insistence—that Judaism formed, in the words of eminent Reform theologian Jakob J. Petuchowski in regard to Geiger, "a constantly evolving organism"—formed the centerpiece of the nascent Judaism at hand.[3]

The Crucial Influence of Abraham Geiger

Abraham Geiger enjoyed the advantage of having the finest argumentative mind in Jewry in the nineteenth century. If we want to understand the new Judaisms of the age, therefore, we turn to the leading intellect to show us how people reached their conclusions, not merely what they said or why they found self-evident the positions that they took. Geiger's life presents facts of less interest than his work, and in his work, his way of asking and answering questions tells us what matters in Reform Judaism. For that is the point at which we gain access to what people found self-evident, on one side, and urgent, on the other. The urgency accounts for the questions, the self-evidence for the mode of discovering the answer. To those two matters, everything else takes second place. The question Geiger found ineluctable takes simple form: How can we explain what has happened to us? The answer is that what has taken place—change become Reform—forms the natural and necessary outcome of history. In his emphasis upon the probative status and value of the facts of history he demonstrated those self-evident principles that lead us deep into the consciousness of the man and the Judaism he embodied. What Geiger took for granted, in our terms held as self-evident, is that history proved propositions of theology. Whatever the particular matter of conviction or custom takes a secondary place. The primary source of verification, therefore, of appropriate and inappropriate traits in Judaism, that is to say, the origin of the reliable definition of Judaism, lies in not revealed records of God's will but human accounts of humanity's works. To that principle, everywhere taken for granted, occasionally enunciated, but never systematically demonstrated, Geiger's mode of argument and inquiry took second place.

Since the earliest changes changed into reforms, and reforms of Judaism into Reform Judaism, to Geiger we address our principal questions: Old or new? And how did people explain themselves? Abraham Geiger presented in clearest form the argument that Reform carried forward the historical processes of Judaism, hence positioned both a single, linear Judaism and a Judaism affected by history, that is, by change. He appealed to the facts of history, beginning with the critical study of the Bible. Petuchowski summarizes his view as follows: "Judaism is a constantly evolving organism. Biblical Judaism was not identical with classical rabbinic Judaism. Similarly, the modern age calls for further evolution in consonance with the changed circumstances. . . . The modern rabbis are entitled to adapt medieval Judaism, as the early rabbis had the right to adapt biblical Judaism. . . . He found traces of evolution within the Bible itself. Yet for Geiger changes in Judaism had always been organic. . . . The modern changes must develop out of the past, and not represent a revolutionary break with it."[4] Geiger therefore recognized change as "traditional," meaning that changing represents the way things always were and so legitimately now goes forward. The Jews change, having moved from constituting a nation to a different classification of social entity. The messiah-idea now addresses the whole of humanity, not only speaking of national restoration. Revelation then turns out to form a progressive, not a static fact. In these diverse ways Geiger, and with him Reform Judaism through its history, appealed to history to verify its allegations and validate its positions. Thus do facts turn into the evidence for faith.

Geiger was born in 1810 and died in 1874.[5] Growing up in Frankfurt, he undertook university studies at Heidelberg, then Bonn, with special interest in philosophy and Semitics. University study formed the exception, not the rule, for Jews. By definition, therefore, the change Geiger had to explain in fact came about through the decision of the former generation. Geiger explained change. His parents made it. But among the intellectual leaders in Geiger's day, not only he but his arch-opponent, Samson Raphael Hirsch, founder of Orthodox Judaism, also acquired a university education. So Orthodox Judaism, too, emerged as the result of the decision of the generation prior to the age of the founders.

To both sets of parents, therefore, the value of an education in the sciences of the West proved self-evident; the ways of harmonizing that education and its values with the education in the Judaic sciences were considerably less clear. Earlier generations had not sent their sons to universities (and their daughters would have to wait until nearly our own day for a similar right). So before Geiger and Hirsch could reach the academy, their parents had to find self-evident the value of such an education. Prior to that generation, most parents found self-evident the value of education in the established institutions of the Judaism of the dual Torah, and there alone. Knowledge of another sort, under other auspices, bore no value. So prior to the advent of the reformer, whether the great intellect of Reform Judaism or the courageous leader of Orthodoxy, change had already characterized modes of self-evident truth.

Geiger served parlously in synagogue pulpits, not always appreciated for the virtues he brought to them, namely, flawless German and his questioning of routine.[6] What he did with most of his time, however, concerned not the local synagogue community but the constituency of Judaic learning. He produced a periodical, the *Scientific Journal for Jewish Theology*, from 1835 onward. Wiener epitomizes the purpose of scientific knowledge in the following statement: "They were convinced that, given the historical facts, it would be possible to draw the correct practical conclusions with regard to the means by which their religion could best be served and elevated to the level of contemporary culture."[7] That is to say, through systematic learning Judaism would undergo reform. Reform Judaism rested on deep foundations of scholarship of a certain sort, specifically of a historical character.

What Geiger had in mind was to analyze the sources of Judaism and the evolution of Judaism. If science (used in its German sense of systematic learning) could uncover the sources of the Jewish "spirit," then, in Wiener's words, "the genius of his people and . . . its vocation" would serve "as a guide to the construction of a living present and future." Geiger's principle of Reform remained fixed. Reform had to emerge from *Wissenschaft* (the scholarly study of Judaism), "a term which he equated with the concept of the understanding of historical evolution."[8] To him "Judaism in its ideal for was religion per se, nothing but an expression of religious consciousness. Its outer shell was subject to change from one generation to another."[9] All things emerge out of time and of change, but when it comes to tracing the history of time and change, contemporary categories assuredly defined the inquiry. Thus Geiger produced, out of ancient times, portraits suspiciously congruent with the issues of his own day.

For example, in his account of the Sadducees and Pharisees, the former enjoying a bad press, the latter, in Judaism, a good one, he identified the former with "the strict guardians of traditional institutions, while the latter spoke out in behalf of progress in both religion and politics."[10] Geiger's principal point is as follows: "What Geiger sought to prove by this demonstration [that the text of Scripture was fluid] is quite obvious. It was not the Bible that created and molded the religious spirit of Judaism; instead, it was the spirit of Judaism that left the stamp of its own form and expression upon the Bible—life, and its needs and strivings, change from age to age.[11] What we learn from Wiener's and Petuchowski's accounts of Geiger concerns what Geiger found to be self-evident, truths beyond all appeal that formed the foundation of his life's work as the first and best historian of Judaism. These premises we identify not in the propositions he proposed to demonstrate, but in the facts concerning change and the constancy of change. He proposed to give "Judaism" a history of reform and to give Reform Judaism a history.

In Geiger's theology Reform Judaism renews, it does not invent. There was, and is, only a single Judaism. In the current age Reform undertakes the discovery of that definition. The answer to the question "On what basis does the claim stand?" is clear. Reform lays its foundations on the basis of history, which is to say, tradition. Propositions of a theological character, for example, concerning the dual Torah revealed at Sinai, the sanctified and therefore supernatural character of Israel, the holy people, and the coming Messiah-sage at the end of times—these take their place in the line of truths to be investigated through historical method, in historical sources. Some may see an incongruity between the propositions at hand and the allegations about the decisive, probative character of historical inquiry in evaluating them. For the facts of history hardly testify, one way or another, concerning the character of revelation at Sinai (though we may know what people recorded in that connection), the status and sanctity of Israel (though the social facts and political issues surely pertained to this-worldly Israel), let alone that event at the end, on the other side, of history altogether, the coming of the Messiah.

We cannot ask whether the claim of Reform Judaism finds justification in "the facts." Unlike his twentieth-century continuators, Geiger was a theologian, not a sociologist. The question proves beside the point. Of course it does: the facts are what people make of them, whether discovered in history or imputed in revealed and holy writings, in a canon of truth. We can scarcely say that the position of Reform Judaism, as outlined by a brief sketch of Geiger's thought, even intersects or connects with what had gone before. The appeal to the old, to history, turns out to come after the fact, the system, had already come to ample formation. Once the Judaism at hand had come into being, people knew what they wanted to find out from history, and that was whether or not things change. Geiger followed a far more sophisticated program, of course, since, knowing that things do change (to whom would the proposition have brought surprise?), he asked exactly how, in Judaism, change takes place, and in what direction. That is what makes especially suggestive his discovering, in a mode of self-evidence, that the Sadducees looked suspiciously like the Orthodox of his day, and the Pharisees the Reformers.

What, then, do we find to be the point of self-evidence? It is Geiger's claim that the categories defined in his own day pertained a long time ago. That is the mark of the new Judaism called Reform Judaism: its powerful capacity without a trace of self-consciousness to impose anachronistic issues and categories. So in modern times to claim a movement from self-evidence to self-consciousness distorts the matter. What changes is the repertoire of self-evident truths.

Reform in the United States: The Worldview Unfolds

Clearly, Reform Judaism, once well under way, would have to situate itself in relationship to the past. Geiger's powerful appeal to precedent left no choice, for not all precedents sustained contemporary choices—the system as it had already emerged—and some of the more recent ones surely called it into question. As learning rolled forward, the question emerged as "Precisely what, in history, serves as a precedent for change become Reform?" The answer came down to the appeal to continuing traits of change, the search for constants about change. To advance our understanding of Reform Judaism, we move once more to the United States, the country in which Reform Judaism has enjoyed massive success in the last half of the twentieth century. There we see in full and articulate formulation the world-view of Reform Judaism as it unfolded in a straight line from Geiger's day to our own. What Geiger claimed in nineteenth-century Germany, Jacob Rader Marcus maintained in twentieth-century America: Reform is not a compromise, not a Judaism. Reform *is* Judaism, and here is how he showed that this is so.

Specifically, in his preface to Abraham Cronbach's *Reform Movements in Judaism,* Jacob Rader Marcus, a principal voice in Reform Judaism in the twentieth century, provides a powerful statement of the Reform view of its place in history. [12] Marcus recognizes that diverse Judaisms have flourished in the history of the Jews. What characterizes them all is that each began as a reform movement but then underwent a process we might characterize as "traditionalization." That is to say, change becomes not merely reform but tradition, and the only constant in the histories of Judaisms is that process of transformation of the new to the conventional, or, in theological language, the traditional. This process Marcus describes as follows: "All [Judaisms] began as rebellions, as great reformations, but after receiving widespread acceptance, developed vested 'priestly' interests, failed their people, and were forced to retreat before the onslaught of new rebellions, new philosophies, new challenges."

Nothing in Marcus's picture can have presented a surprise to Geiger, so the fundamental theological method of Reform Judaism in its initial phase, the appeal to facts of history for the validation of theological propositions, endures. However, the claim that everything always changes yields a challenge, which Marcus forthrightly raises: "Is there then nothing but change? Is change the end of all our history and all our striving? No, there is something else, the desire to be free. . . . In the end [the Jew] has always understood that changelessness is spiritual death. The Jew who would *live* must never completely surrender himself to one truth, but . . . must reach out for the farther and faint horizons of an ever Greater God. . . . This is the meaning of Reform." Marcus thus treats as self-evident—obvious because it is a fact of history—the persistence of change. Denying that this is all there is to Reform, at the end he affirms the simple point that change sets the norm. It comes down to the same thing. The "something else" of Marcus's argument presents its own problems. Appeal to the facts of history fails at the point at which a constructive position demands articulation. "The desire to be free" bears a predicate: free of what? Free to do, to be what? If Marcus fails to accomplish the whole of the theological task, however, he surely conveys the profoundly constructive vision that Reform Judaism afforded to its Israel.

For his part, Cronbach sets forth as the five precedents for the present movement the Deuteronomic Reformation, the Pentateuchal Reformation, the

Pharisaic Reformation, the Karaite Reformation, and the Hasidic Reformation. His coming reformation appeals to social psychology and aims at tolerance: "Felicitous human relationships can be the goal of social welfare and of economic improvement. . . . Our Judaism of maturity would be dedicated to the ideal of freedom. Corollary of that ideal is what we have just observed about courtesy toward the people whose beliefs and practices we do not share. "[13] We now have moved far from the position outlined by Geiger, in which a constant conversation with the received canon of the dual Torah yielded important propositions.

Yet our interest in Reform Judaism hardly requires us to criticize the constructive efforts of its theologians. What we want to know is two things: First, is it old or is it new? Second, if a Judaism turns out to be new, as shown by its essentially distinctive principle of selection, then how does that Judaism establish its claim to form the natural, necessary next step in "Judaism"? We find the answers to both questions near at hand. First, does this Judaism ask the questions that for the Judaism of the dual Torah demanded answer, or does it ask other questions? That is a matter of fact. Second, does this Judaism find self-evidently valid the answers of the Judaism of the dual Torah, or do other propositions prove self-evidently true? That, too, is a matter of fact.

Two Lingering Questions

Two questions await attention. First, in the new Judaism at hand, what place do we find for the Judaism of the dual Torah? Second, what questions prove so urgent as to make self-evident the answers of the Judaism in the process of emerging? The answers to both questions lie right on the surface. Given its intellectual strength, Reform Judaism had no difficulty saying precisely what it wished on classic issues.

As to the Judaism of the dual Torah, its questions proved no more compelling than its answers. The whole turned from the self-evident statement of God's will to a source of precedents, available for selection and rearrangement. How to pick and choose formed the principal issue of method. The distinction between the written and oral Torah provided the answer. Pick the written, drop the oral. So the Reform theologians rejected the claim that the oral part of the Torah came from God. It was the work of men, time-bound, contingent, possessed of a mere advisory authority. Whatever precedents and antecedents Reform historians and theologians sought, they would not look in the rabbinic writings that, all together, fall under the name Talmud because there their enemies found their principal ammunition. The Judaism from which Reform took its leave, found its definition in the dual Torah of Sinai, as written down from the Mishnah onward. So, quite naturally, when the Reformers addressed the issue of continuity, they leaped over the immediate past, represented by the Judaism of the dual Torah, and sought their antecedents in the processes of change instead.

But how did they express their judgment of the particular Judaism they proposed to revise? It was in clear and explicit statements that the Talmud at best preserved the wisdom of ordinary mortals, from which, if they wished, contemporary Jews might choose to learn.

A sequence of statements among nineteenth-century authorities expressed the entire consensus.[14] Joshua Heschel Schorr (1814–1895) wrote: "For as long as the Talmud is considered an inherently perfect, infallible monument of true divine tradition and is being accepted as such, no reform can take place through it. That being the case, why do we not get ready to expose the inner imperfections and the many irrefutably obvious faults from which the work suffers? This would clearly prove that what we possess here is a work created by humans, distorted by many errors, and that the writing of this volume is not imbued with one wholly integrated spirit." The study of history therefore carried a heavy freight of theological apologetics for Reform Judaism, a fact we have now confronted time and again. Here it is the very historical character of the Talmud that made the case. It was the work of men, not of God. Its authority was no more than that of other men.

The Talmud will take its place among the works of mortals and lose its position as half of the one whole Torah of Moses, our rabbi. Michael Creizenach (1789–1842) proposed to distinguish among parts of the Talmud. The Talmud presents "a serviceable means for the interpretation of those ritual commandments which, according to the individual concepts of each man, are binding to this day. . . . We regard those portions of the Talmud which do not elucidate the Mosaic laws as merely humanly instituted decrees. . . . We consider those passages in the Talmud which are not consistent with the principle of the universal love of man, as outbursts of passionate hatred of which unfortunately quite often the best men cannot free themselves when they are oppressed in a disgraceful way and when they see that all considerations to which the dignity of human nature gives them undeniable claims are being violated against themselves." The upshot was that the changes that were to become Reform took a clear and distinct step away from the received Torah. No one, even in the earliest generations, pretended otherwise. A new program of self-evident truths had taken the place of the old. A new set of questions now demanded responses, and an established set of issues no longer mattered very much. So at the end we survey the questions people found they had, as a matter of life or death, to answer as well as those answers that gave, and today still give, life.

Conclusion

Reform Judaism was not formed by incremental steps out of the received Judaism ("the tradition"), and it did not move onward along a path in a straight line from where Jews had been to where they wished to go. The system took shape on its own. Judaic religious systems relate only in a common genealogy.

But they cohere—for all Judaisms do contend with one another and regard one another as (unworthy) opponents within the same arena—because, after all, they address pretty much the same people about the same things. Proving that Reform Judaism forms a distinct and autonomous system poses no problem, since the principal theologians of that Judaism claim no less. What we learn from Reform Jews concerns the condition of humanity. The human achievement of Reform deserves a simple observation of what these people did and what they were. With acuity, perspicacity, and enormous courage, the Reformers, in the nineteenth and twentieth centuries alike, took the measure of the world and made ample use of the materials they had in hand in manufacturing something to fit it. Reform did fit those Jews, and they were, and are, very many to whom the issue of Israel as a supernatural entity remained vivid. For, after all, the centerpiece of Reform Judaism remained its powerful notion that Israel does have a task and a mission, on which account Israel should endure as Israel. Reform Judaism persuaded generations from the beginning to the present of the worth of human life lived in its Judaic system. More than that we cannot ask of any Judaism.

That is why, for myself, I am lucky to have been born and brought up as a Reform Jew, in a Reform temple—that, and also to have gotten a first-class Jewish education, so I could benefit from the freedom with which Reform Judaism, and only Reform Judaism, endows the Jewish people.

Appendix: Abraham Geiger in Postmodernist Garments

Since I here follow the conventional, and I believe correct, reading of Abraham Geiger as a principal architect of Reform Judaism and its most systematic thinker, I take account of a new picture of the man. Here he is represented not as a Reform theologian and historian but as an avatar of the postcolonial figure struggling against imperial hegemony, a Jewish Edward Said. The portrait is by Susannah Heschel, in her *Abraham Geiger and the Jewish Jesus*.[15] As I argue in the shank of my paper, Abraham Geiger stands out as the most interesting and original mind in critical scholarship on Judaism in the nineteenth century and a principal theologian of Reform Judaism. That is how he is represented in Max Wiener's definitive biography, *Abraham Geiger and Liberal Judaism* (1962), from its publication the standard work in English on its subject. Here pretentiously masquerading as culture-philosophy in a garment of dreary, sectarian jargon, Heschel's text asks us to read Geiger not as a Reform theologian but as a postmodernist avatar:

> Geiger's work represents a revolt of the colonized, bringing the tools of historiography to bear against Christianity's intellectual hegemony. . . . Intellectually, that hegemony began to end when the Wissenschaft des Judenthums [scholarship

on Judaism] started writing the history of Christianity as a branch of Jewish history. . . . The Wissenschaft des Judenthums . . . is one of the earliest examples of postcolonialist writing. . . . Postcolonial theory's recognition that minority literature is characterized by counterdiscursive practices helps to illumine Geiger's work, inasmuch as the logic of his historical arguments represented an inversion of accepted European self-understanding. Geiger's counterhistory constituted a transvaluation of Christian arguments against Judaism and functioned as a passionate defense of Judaism. (p. 3)

Geiger represented the Pharisees, whom Christian scholarship portrayed in violently hostile terms, as the Reform Jews of their day: "liberal democratizers of Judaism . . . Modern liberal Protestants who seek the faith of Jesus . . . can find it in Reform Judaism." Here Heschel finds "a form of counterhistory": "Counterhistory is a form of polemic in which the sources of the adversary are exploited" and turned against the oppressor. Geiger sought to defend Judaism by writing a counterhistory of Christian counterhistory: "That is, he did not simply offer a straightforward rendition of the history of Jesus and Judaism but presented Jewish history in the context of his own, original counterhistory of Christianity" (p. 14). Heschel further calls on "gender theory" to clarify "some of the hidden motivations" for Jewish theologians' intense interest in the origins of Christianity: "The position of Jews entering the world of Christian theology is not unlike the position of women novelists entering the nineteenth-century literary world . . . women were required to 'kill the angel in the house,' the aesthetic ideal of the female promoted in male literature, before they could generate their own literature. Similarly, Jewish theologians initiated an effort to destroy the image of Judaism within Christian theology as part of their project of self-definition" (p. 18). Predictably, Heschel ends her postmodernist theory of Geiger with attention to Said's *Orientalism*, where she finds nothing new: "The intimacy between knowledge and power may be better known to Jewish historians than anyone else."

This heavy dose of the regnant academic ideology, taken at the start, finds a match at the end of the book in a regurgitation of the same ideology. For Jews, Geiger was "the ultimate overthrow of Christian hegemony. The extraordinary embrace of Geiger's position by modern Jewish thinkers is indicative of their deep satisfaction with their argument." There follows a survey of twentieth-century response to Geiger's position that Jesus was a Jew and a Pharisee. Here Heschel passes her opinion on a great many issues she has not herself investigated, concluding with what must be simply the weirdest discussion of the historical Jesus of recent times. For the bizarre characterization Heschel fabricates, Jesus as a kind of "cross-dresser," only her own words suffice to convey the full idiocy of her interpretation of Geiger's oeuvre:

The dispute over Jesus' religious identity that was set into motion by Geiger's identification of him as a Pharisee has never been resolved. Jews dress him as a Jew,
Christians dress him as a Christian. . . . . The theological situation lends itself to
useful interpretation by means of poststructuralist critical theory. Read in postmodern categories, as cross-dressed, Jesus is at once both a signifier and that
which signifies the undecidability of signification, pointing toward himself but
also toward the place where he is not. . . . The literary theorists . . . have argued
that "transvestism" is a category which reconfigures the relationship between male
and female and places in question binary gender identities previously viewed as
stable and known. For Judaism and Christianity Jesus functions as a kind of literary theological transvestite. (p. 239)

Here I have copied her exact words and have not manufactured a malicious par-
ody of postmodernism or grossly caricatured Heschel's take on Geiger. She
writes with a permanently straight face.

So much for the beginning and the end. But these are tacked on, fore and aft,
and do not ruin the main part of the book at all. The dissertation part of the book
is written in workmanlike, professional prose and in no way invokes the phony
"interpretative framework" promised at the beginning and invoked at the end.
Mercifully, Heschel, once she tells her story of Geiger, forgets where she started,
and at the end does not even pretend to refer to the nub of her narrative, either.
With rare lapses into postmodernist gibberish, what we find in the middle of the
book is a series of professional, well-researched chapters on the life and work of
Geiger, the raw material of a good, if tedious, dissertation.

Take away the gibberish and what is left is this systematic program of biogra-
phy: the creation of a historical theology (early life and education), Judaism,
Christianity, and Islam: prelude of revisionist configurations; reconception of early
Judaism; D. F. Strauss, the Tübingen School, and Albrecht Ritschl; the Jewish
Jesus and the Protestant flight from the historical Jesus; from Jesus to Christianity;
Geiger on the postapostolic era; the reception of Geiger's work. All this is fairly
standard and unexceptionable, if also unexceptional. The author shows herself
industrious and competent, though whether she has improved on Wiener's prior
biography is a judgment that only specialists in the nineteenth-century intellectual
history of Reform Judaism can make. About Geiger the great Reform theologian
and historian, I anticipate they will not learn a great deal from her.

Notes

1. Michael A. Meyer, *The Origins of the Modern Jew: Jewish Identity and European Culture in
   Germany, 1749–1824* (Detroit: Wayne State University Press, 1967), 48.

2. Jakob J. Petuchowski, "Reform Judaism," in *Encyclopaedia Judaica* (Jerusalem: Keter, 1971), 14:23–28.
3. Petuchowski, "Reform Judaism," col. 25.
4. Ibid., col. 25.
5. Max Wiener, *Abraham Geiger and Liberal Judaism: The Challenge of the Nineteenth Century*, trans. Ernst J. Schlochauer (Philadelphia: Jewish Publication Society of America, 1962).
6. Ibid., 11.
7. Ibid., 13.
8. Ibid., 40.
9. Ibid., 42.
10. Ibid., 50.
11. Ibid., 51.
12. Jacob Rader Marcus, "Preface," in Abraham Cronbach, *Reform Movements in Judaism* (New York: Bookman Associates, 1963). Quotations from pp. 7–9.
13. Cronback, *Reform Movements,* 132.
14. All cited in W. Gunther Plaut, *The Rise of Reform Judaism: A Sourcebook of its European Origins* (New York: World Union for Progressive Judaism, Ltd., 1963), 113–19.
15. Susannah Heschel, *Abraham Geiger and the Jewish Jesus* (Chicago: University of Chicago Press, 1998).

6

Reform's Original Sin

ARNOLD JACOB WOLF

In 1885 a small group of radical Reform rabbis led by David Einhorn and his sons-in-law, Emil G. Hirsch and Kaufmann Kohler, produced a document that was to mold American Judaism for decades to come. Its authors were profoundly opposed to Judaism in its traditional form and messianically confident of the glorious future of its alternative, Reform. They were mostly fine scholars in the noble tradition of Abraham Geiger, but they were very poor theologians. Their naïveté and their incoherence led to generations of Reform Jewish belief in a "pick-and-choose" Judaism as the American religion of choice. The fathers' misconceptions can be epitomized thus:

- A god-idea instead of God
- Absolute personal autonomy instead of heteronomy under God
- Anthropocentrism instead of theocentrism
- Negative mitzvot (do *not* keep kosher) instead of obedience to the Torah
- Judaism as a religion instead of the faith of a people
- Individualism over solidarity
- Prophetic texts instead of rabbinic ones
- The (Reform) temple as a central place instead of the home and school
- Freedom above responsibility
- Haggadah instead of Haggadah *and* halachah as the basis for theology
- Aesthetics over authenticity

- Rabbis, not communities, in power
- Reason as the only criterion of truth
- Faceless humanity instead of concrete communities and persons to be addressed
- *Wissenschaft* over *Lernen*
- Timeless "principles" instead of details of observance and decision
- Self-confidence instead of religious humility
- Innovation instead of persistence, for example, late Friday night services and confirmation
- Premature messianism instead of messianic patience

As Emanuel Levinas, the French philosopher, reminds us, "The originality of Judaism consists in confining itself in the manner of being in the least practical endeavor, a pause between us and nature through the fulfillment of a mitzvah, a commandment. The total interiorization of Judaism is nothing but its abolition."

It was precisely the interiorization, the spiritualization of Jewish faith, that Pittsburgh 1885 attempted. This was Reform's original sin. Those rabbis pretended that they were people-in-general, and they offered their vague theology as "news from nowhere." It is no wonder that after a century nobody reads Kohler or Hirsch any longer, while the work of Rav Kuk and Hayyim of Volozhin, their contemporaries, is still important. Just a decade or two later than Pittsburgh, Martin Buber and Franz Rosenzweig began to create a profound non-Orthodox Judaism in the spirit of Hermann Cohen. But of this Kohler and Hirsch, for all of their immense knowledge, were utterly clueless. Radical and imperious, they wore poorly and did much harm to us, their successors. In the thirties and again in the seventies Reform rabbis struggled to undo their theological mischief, with partial success but without permanent victory. We have still not fully overcome the legacy of Pittsburgh 1885. In Columbus in 1937 it took President Felix Levy to make a new platform even possible, after a tie vote. In 1976 Eugene Borowitz and colleagues at San Francisco produced a finely conceived document that, unfortunately, sank without a trace.

Coming back to Pittsburgh in 1999, a new president of the Central Conference of American Rabbis named Levy (Richard) imagined, drafted, and nursed through six or more versions a new statement of principles for Reform Judaism. With enormous courage and patience, Levy, a rabbi whose congregation had been and still was the Hillels of Los Angeles, was determined to reinvent liberal Judaism. Like most of his allies, including this one, he grew up in Reform Judaism, with no need to find reasons to reject an Orthodoxy he had never known. But donning tallith and tefillin for a cover story in *Reform Judaism* magazine, he provoked a hailstorm of dissent and unfair recrimination. Mildly but firmly Levy steered his program through the shoals of lay panic and rabbinical trepidation, and a much modified version of his proposal was passed in Pittsburgh, overwhelmingly.

But how much modified? Is the powerful emphasis on mitzvah and Talmud Torah still apparent? Is it clear that we have indeed abrogated a century-old platform and turned toward a new kind of liberal Judaism? Or has the air gone out of the tire, leaving us with only the memory of a lost opportunity for transfiguration? Have we finally reformed Reform?

The original sin of Reform Judaism is judging Jewish law and theology by standards extrinsic to them and, in many ways, hostile to them. If modernist notions of autonomy and individual choice trump age-old Jewish preference for community standards and response to revelation, then something precious has been surrendered. Even Eugene Borowitz, the most significant liberal theologian of the latter part of this century, qualifies but does not abandon the central place of autonomy in his system. What Borowitz does is to circumscribe the "autonomous Jewish self" with parameters and limitations based on that very self's being Jewish. The community impinges on the self and limits its freedom to choose by changing its will to choose.

However, Judaism is not a religion of ideas but a people's covenant with God, requiring obedience and persistence. These qualities are hardly typical of liberal Jews in America, the most American of all Americans and the most hung up on their right to be themselves. If the typical American slogan is "Says who?" then the American Jewish motto is "I'll decide for myself." In Jewish faith, however, the whole point is deciding for and with God—no easy task, to be sure, but one that is utterly unavoidable. We may not always know for certain what God wants of us, but we must ask that question, not only the easy question of what we want for ourselves. In many, many cases we *do* know what is expected of us, but we just don't want to do what God commands.

Haggadic doing (as Rosenzweig calls it), a random performance of more and more Jewish "ceremonies," will not suffice. Clearly Reform Jews do much more now than they did fifty or seventy years ago. However, we fast on Yom Kippur or give *tzedakah* or study Torah not for God's sake but because we think performing those tasks might be good for us. Judaism is not self-help, and in fact sometimes it does not help us at all: witness martyrdom and self-sacrifice as clear demands of *kiddush ha-Shem* (hallowing God's name). The rewards of obedience are remote and often invisible, but duty remains in place. Reform Judaism knows little of doing what is commanded for the sake of the commandment. But that is decidedly the point of Jewish law: obedience is preferable to mere good will. Doing what we should is more important than wanting to do it.

If you look at recent legislative proposals of our Religious Action Center or the CCAR you find authentic social action initiatives: Criminal Justice Reform, Universal Health Care, Protection of the Environment, Campaign Finance Reform, etc. But if you look at what our congregations are actually concerned with, you find food pantries, tutoring programs, *tzedakah* for the poor, etc.

This second list is wholly meritorious. It is a model of *Gemilut Hasadim*, doing good for people who need our help. But it is far from the kind of issue that galvanized our hesitant congregations a few decades ago, issues like Viet Nam, the Civil Rights revolution, war and peace in Israel. These issues were profoundly controversial, deeply political, even world-historical. Our newer perspectives are far narrower and all too polite. They will not divide a temple membership, nor cost too much in terms of outrage, diminished giving, or resignations. They come perilously close to being mere moral clichés. They employ neighborhood hands-on tactics, with no strategic interest in global or even national choices. They are too little and, in my judgment, too late.

If we staff a food pantry, must we not ask: why are food pantries needed in a rich America? Are there still food pantries in the new millennium? Doing good should lead us to face hard, political questions. We should not be satisfied with band-aids when radical surgery may be required. But first we must call the evils by their names.

Do we act as Jews, or only as humanitarians and liberal citizens? Do we enrich our spiritual dimension by sacrifice and conflict, or do we remain at the level of nice folks doing nice things? Where is the radical concern of our young people? Are they not also too polite to take arms against poverty and injustice in America?

Nor is this all. We choose soft issues, issues that unite us and will not cause struggle or divisiveness. These issues are not unworthy, but I fear they are too easy to remake souls or to instruct our political imagination. I call "soft" gender issues like reproductive rights and gay and lesbian concerns which, however they arouse some other constituencies, are pretty much settled in Reform Judaism. The same applies to gun control, capital punishment abolition, and separation of church and state. Not many in our midst reject the liberal consensus on these issues.

The truly hard issues we do not often face directly: affordable mixed-income housing, minimum wage, equal funding for all public schools (our own children are in the suburbs or in private schools, by and large), universal child care, free college education for all, universal single-payer health care, the end of the failed war on drugs, and the end of "humanitarian" violence to protect "innocent victims" all over the world.

Some issues that come close to our own private world do not appear on our radar screen: the disappearance of Jewish hospitals, mostly in poor and black neighborhoods; the takeover of Jewish funeral homes by mega-corporations without any Jewish direction; redistribution of incomes; the need for clean air and water; justice for the Palestinians.

As for us rabbis, I believe our serious and self-sacrificing assertion of the *mitzvah* of social action could be demonstrated in a single, though very difficult, decision. We should pool all rabbinic salaries and redistribute them according to need. If we had the courage to show the way, our congregations might move somewhere beyond philanthropy toward socialism. That is indeed a utopian, or, at least, a messianic project. In the end, what are we if not premature messianists? And what good is all our doing good if it only delays the end we claim to seek?

Gemilut Hasadim can be a good start. Let's go back to the future, to when we risked jail or even our lives for what we believed, to when seeking Israeli-Palestinian peace seemed to many like treason, to when social action divided many congregations but taught some of us what courage and persistence could accomplish, back to when rabbis counted.

The age of heroism need not be over. If Reform Judaism has anything to teach American Jewry, it is to think hard and work bravely, for the good of our souls and the welfare of our brothers and sisters across America and across the world.

Living in the sight of God in the late twentieth century is very obscure. But that is what Reform Judaism, like any authentic Judaism, must learn to do. The new statement of principles hints at such a life, at such a profound faith. It beckons us toward authenticity and directs us toward recuperation. Our fathers and we have sinned, but repentance is always possible. Of course, it is not only we who have sinned, but we ourselves must turn our own sins into trust.

We should note the commitment both to pluralism and to commitment itself, the right of personal decision fully within a framework of communal obedience. This statement is news from somewhere, from a Jewish people who have gone home to the land of Israel and have also created rich and learned oases in the diaspora of American materialism. Gender equality, a kind of shibboleth for liberals, is affirmed, but the old virtues of home and family are not ignored, despite an inevitable insistence on gay and lesbian rights. God is a reality, not a mere idea. Torah is work to be done, not platitudes left over from prophetic rhetoric. Judaism is not a hobby or a mere version of universalist character but the center to which we must return if we are to be saved.

Commentary and elucidation can only deepen the power of this proclamation. Ours may be a time when the movement is finally ready for transformation. The old Reform Judaism is dead, and a new post-Reform is struggling to be born.

Many years ago I walked with the late Jakob J. Petuchowski from the Tel Aviv Shalom Tower to Jaffa. He recalled that there have been many movements in Judaism of profound revolutionary bent. Some of them finally split off completely from the mother faith, such as the Essenes, the Christians, and the Sabbatians.

Others finally returned to the inner fold, bringing a new message to the Jewish community of which they were part, such as the Pharisees, the Hasidim, and the Zionist movement. He was not sure which group typified American Reform Judaism. Neither was I. Now I am certain that our future as Reform Jews lies deep in the heart of our people and that we rabbis are true inheritors not only of Reformers, of modernizers, but also of Talmudic sages and medieval philosophers, revolutionary rabbis in their time and for our own.

7

From the Christmas Tree to the Yarmulke

*What Separates Classical Reform
from Mainstream Reform?*

HAROLD S. SILVER

When I was ordained in June 1951, the Reform movement in America was on the threshold of a tremendous physical and religious explosion. Before the beginning of World War II the number of Reform congregations in the United States was as little as 250. Within a decade and a half the movement tripled to about 750 congregations, embracing almost a million members. Most of this new congregational growth took place in the booming suburbs of major metropolitan cities. Upon ordination every one of my classmates from our New York school stepped into these brand-new congregations, located mainly in the greater New York suburbs.

I was the only freshly ordained rabbi in my entire graduating class who chose to begin my rabbinical career as an assistant rabbi in a huge, old-line Classical Reform temple that had been founded in Pittsburgh in 1854. I felt that going to Pittsburgh for several years under the guiding inspiration of the legendary Rabbi Solomon B. Freehof, one of the rabbinical giants of the twentieth century, would make me into a better young rabbi and would prepare me for the time when I would choose to lead my own congregation.

The one "downer" in my beginning my rabbinical career in Pittsburgh came when I discovered that their congregational practice of Reform Judaism was mired deep and rigidly in the old-line, early-twentieth-century German Reform Jewish past, which was about 180 degrees apart from the radically new and exciting postwar Reform Judaism. The new Reform, frankly, was not appreciated by the old-line German Jewish Classical Reformers.

The clash between the old and new Reform Jews, which came right after World War II, resulted from the mass infusion of predominantly second- and third-generation East European Jews whose parents and grandparents had migrated to the United States between 1880 and 1924. These new Reform Jews either were in rebellion against the orthodoxy of their own growing up or were uncomfortable in Conservative synagogues, which they felt were still too traditional for their modern Jewish lives. Alternatively, they felt that the Reform movement better satisfied their modern liberal, social, and personal Jewish religious needs.

In the early 1950s, while the East European newcomers were welcome to swell congregational membership and income, they still had to conform completely to the way Reform was originally instituted and carried on faithfully by German Jewish preferences and practice. This approach held first and foremost that ethics and not ritual essentially defined the major hallmark and glory of historic Judaism generally and Reform Judaism in particular. Ritual and ceremony, of and by themselves, were never deliberately meant to be scorned or dismissed out of hand by the early Reform Jews. Rather, they were to be seen as being of secondary importance to moral and ethical commitment. Classical Reform chiefly declared that a fine-tuned religious balance must be struck in this life between morality and ceremony. Fidelity to ritual alone oftentimes can border upon pure sham.

"Paper-thin Jewishness"

The big problem, however, that confronted German Jews in this Classical period of pre–World War II Reform was that the "Jewishness" of their home and synagogue lives became virtually nonexistent, or paper-thin at best. Modernizing the faith in the heady climate of American religious freedom led the early Classical Reformers to the almost total scrapping of Orthodox Jewish customs and norms. Unfortunately, what replaced them was a Judaism and a Jewish lifestyle that proved to be unrecognizably Jewish.

For example, besides the German Reform image of a bare-headed, tallith-free clergy ministering to gender-mixed pews, there was also a virtually Hebrew-free liturgical worship. There was a radical new prayer book that deliberately switched from the traditional right-to-left opening and was replete with King James–style poetic English translations of the standard Hebrew text. There was also the revolutionary organ-pumping, Protestant-church-sounding hymnology that replaced "En Kelhanu" with "God Is in His Holy Temple." There were nonscriptural Sunday morning Shakespearean and social-action lectures in place of the traditional Shabbat morning cyclical biblical portion. It was Sunday-school curricula worlds away from the traditional heder-for-boys-only Jewish education of the past. It was English horns replacing rams' horns for trumpeting in the Jewish new year. It was Yom Kippur without the breast beating and the fasting. It was eggnog and trimming the Hanukkah bushes. It was laughably abbreviated Passover seders and shameful sandwich munching during Passover week. And it was thirteen-year-old (and later fourteen- and fifteen-year-old) bar-mitzvah-type coming-of-age confirmation pageantry ushering in young Jewish adulthood for both males and females.

It must also be acknowledged, however, that while far too many old-line German Jews grew up almost entirely *Yiddishkeit* free, there were still impressive numbers of God-infused and ethically motived German Reform Jews who were very proud of their historical Jewish connection. The blanket charge leveled against all Reform Jews by traditional Jews of their being basically assimilation-ist at heart or simply goyim was really not justified.

On the other hand, in this pre–World War II phase of Classical Reform, the movement as it was perceived and practiced was a very short and far too com-fortable step toward the Unitarian Church and the Ethical Culture movement, where humanism and not Judaism reigned supreme; where liberalism was dei-fied; where Jesus and the Church were soft-pedaled; and where anything that smacked of Jewish particularism was sneered at.

From Classical to Mainstream

Newcomers to mainstream Reform during the past few decades never realized that by the end of World War II the old-style German Classical Reform was in grave danger of almost disappearing as a major Jewish movement in the United States. In a real sense not only did East European Jews rescue the German Reform movement from pending marginalization, if not oblivion, but it was the East European mass infusion that was directly responsible for moving Reform away from its original Classical period into what may be described as its initial "mainstream" era. This was the very same era when I began my rabbinate in Pittsburgh nearly half a century ago—the era of the post-Holocaust nightmare and the era of the incredible emergence of the state of Israel.

The East European Reform Jews wanted no part of old-world or any other Orthodoxy. Yet they still wanted their new religious ties to Reform to incorporate some of the memorable things from their traditional Jewish family and syna-gogue backgrounds, which still resonated warmly with positive and Jewishly enhancing and endearing memories. For example, they wanted Reform to offer the long-ago-dropped ritual of bar mitzvah for their sons and bat mitzvah for their daughters (the female ritual was taken over from the Conservative Jewish move-ment, which pioneered the bat mitzvah in 1924). The biggest headache, however, for *both* of our movements is that in the last half century both Reform and Conservative Judaism have had to confront together the sickening and shameful American Jewish phenomenon of the mass bar/bat mitzvah dropouts from reli-gious schools on the heels of outrageous entertainment extravaganzas that out-orgy the worst of pagan excess.

Another distressing problem confronting mainstream Reform was that the limited Sunday school Jewish education, combined with no solid home parental Jewish role modeling, produced several generations of American Jewish Reform illiterates whose knowledge of Jewish history, skills with the Hebrew language, and emotional and ceremonial ties to the cycle of Jewish holidays were all basically indifferent at best and Jewishly minimal at worst. Unfortunately, this heady new climate of religious freedom quickly degenerated into a personal and group license to strip the Reform movement clean of *any* semblance of meaningful and viable traditional Jewish ceremony and ritual.

The Classical Reform synagogue service is a dramatic case in point. Its welcome brevity, uplifting new music, decorum, vernacular prayers, and mixed pews were all a refreshingly different and welcome spiritual setting for those uncomfortable or unhappy or far removed from the Orthodox worship of their past. One big problem, however, with all of these radical changes brought about by the historic Reform movement was that in far too many Classical Reform–oriented temples, the service quickly degenerated into a cold and impersonal spectator kind of worship that touched, involved, and moved few—where the typical old-line Reform Jewish worshiper might have felt equally at home in a Unitarian, Ethical Culture, or Quaker type of service.

By the time my postwar generation of Reform rabbis came upon the early 1950s Reform Jewish scene, we realized quickly that unless the old-line style of Classical Reform moved substantially away from its bare-boned Jewishness, American Reform could well die out in less than a generation. This was actually happening in the late 1930s and early 1940s. In 1943, a hundred years after our own congregation here in West Hartford was founded, no more than 250 German Jewish families were involved in the congregation. Had it not been for the postwar East European infusion during the next decade, which brought into our congregation a thousand new families, Beth Israel and the entire Classical Reform movement that was similarly exploding would have remained in the background of American Jewish life. Perhaps it might even have faded away before the twentieth century came to an end.

Mainstream Reform, besides reflecting a radically different ethnic Jewish turnover, also witnessed a growingly powerful desire to inject a more meaningful dimension of Jewish-style ceremonialism into twentieth-century Reform that had heretofore been consciously downplayed, deliberately cast aside, or simply rejected. The new mainstream Reform Jews found it quite easy and comfortable to reject Orthodox Jewish ideas and dogmas dealing with the Messiah, life after death, resurrection, and the binding authority of rabbinical decision making.

However, the new mainstreamers were clearly unhappy and unfulfilled with a congregational calendar and a Reform Jewish home life that was barely Jewish in content, practice, feel, and inreach. In *no* way, however, did the new Reformers want to go back to historical Orthodoxy, whether in the first stage of the new and developing mainstream Reform five decades ago or even today at the start of the twenty-first century.

The first mainstreamers originally wanted their worship to include a more Hebraic component that still resonated warmly in their hearts and on their tongues. They were hungry to hear and to sing a style of synagogue music that rang with more familiar, moving cantillations from the past, and that could be blended with a creative dash of the new. They wanted the cycle of Jewish holy days to reconnect their liberal, modern religious lives with some of the best and richest of their past. The first wave of postwar mainstreamers five decades ago fervently sought a style of Jewishness that dignified and honored their Jewish faith and identity, and they wanted to pass this core spiritual identity down to their children. Today many still seek this.

The Year-in-Israel Experience

Allow me just to touch briefly upon a powerful new influence in our Reform movement that is perhaps significantly responsible for some of the new, and allegedly backward, ceremonial and ritual direction of our mainstream Reform of today. This influence is rarely spoken of or alluded to in Reform congregations today. Beginning in the 1970s all entering Reform rabbinical students were required to spend the first year of their five-year postgraduate course of rabbinical studies in the Jerusalem branch of the Hebrew Union College. This mandatory year-in-Israel program, which shortly thereafter was mandated for Reform cantors and educators, was probably the single greatest factor impelling a brand-new generation of Reform rabbis wanting to distance themselves even more dramatically from the movement's Classical Reform past.

The emotional and spiritual high of living and studying in Israel for an entire year is, of course, a thrilling given for today's young men and women committed to being Reform rabbis in the United States. The downside, however, to this year-in-Israel experience has been and remains the shock that these first-year rabbinical students have to absorb when they realize that Reform Judaism enjoys less than minority status in Israeli society, where Orthodox Judaism totally dominates the life and culture of the country, particularly in Jerusalem.

Upon arrival, the fledgling Reform rabbinical students immediately confront the daily fact that Orthodoxy—and particularly fanatic, right-wing Orthodoxy—has a virtual lock on Jerusalem's religious as well as civic life. The students quickly perceive that vast numbers of non-Orthodox Israeli Jews were and still are unhappy enough and depressed enough to move out of Jerusalem to other parts of the country where the heavy religious hand of ultra-right-wing Orthodoxy exerts little theological and legalistic influence over their daily lives and a completely secular type of Jewishness prevails, as in Tel Aviv and Haifa.

Perhaps the most depressing realization for Reform rabbinical students in their year-in-Israel program comes when they confront the almost total ignorance of the history and practices of American Reform among the overwhelming majority of Israel's secular and non-Orthodox Jewish population, which actually represents as many as 80 percent of the Israelis. It comes as quite a shock to Jewish visitors and students from abroad to face up to the fact that most Israelis want to be primarily defined by their Jewish *national* citizenship rather than being exclusively identified by Jewish *religious* status. In a word, most Israelis want to be first and foremost Israeli and not necessarily Jewish. They want their Judaism to be looked upon as a birthright. They want to be intensely proud of it, to be sure, but not to have their lives and culture mandated for them by what they consider to be a suffocating, ultra-right-wing rabbinical control.

Mainstream Israelis, sadly, are completely in the educational dark about any competing variety of or alternative to Orthodoxy. While a growing but still tiny network of Reform and Conservative congregations now exists in Israel, the fact of the matter is that non-Orthodox American-style synagogue life remains a minuscule blip on the religious radar screen of Israeli life.

As a result of this inferiority complex imposed upon the Reform rabbinical students by the scornful Orthodox and the ignorant non-Orthodox secular Israelis, over the years many of the students have attempted in self-defense to don a traditional Orthodox "image" in the hope that the nonstop wearing of yarmulkes, the wearing of the traditional tallith during worship, the sporting of beards by the men, and the observance of kashrut in their private Jerusalem home lives—might somehow help them gain better acceptance among the Israeli Orthodox community. The long and short of it is that for the foreseeable future, the gulf in Israel between Orthodoxy and non-Orthodoxy remains as wide and as deep as ever.

When the rabbinical students finish their first year-in-Israel program and return to New York, Cincinnati, or Los Angeles to finish out the remaining four years of their seminary studies, they nevertheless bring back with them, consciously or unconsciously, a heightened feeling for many traditional Orthodox practices and regimens, which they take to their student pulpits and later to their postordination pulpits across the country. In this long-term process there is a natural, continuing openness and greater sensitivity about wanting American Reform to be vastly more open to and sympathetic toward many traditional rituals and lifestyles.

This new generation of Reform rabbis does not want the Reform movement to become Orthodox. All they basically want is for the ever-changing Reform movement to be vastly more accepting of a good deal of the historical Jewish past, which they fervently believe can, with creative revision, enrich and deepen modern Reform Jewish lives. Hence there is a new push in this present generation for more Hebrew in the service, vastly more congregational participation, a more Torah-centered focus in the service and at home, the richer inclusion of historically Jewish music and cantillation, and a substantially higher prioritizing of Shabbat observance in the home.

Mind you, I am still all for the year-in-Israel program. I just believe that our Reform rabbinical students would be far better equipped to face the hostile Orthodox Israeli scene, as well as the indifferent and uneducated secular Israeli scene, if they were first better grounded here in the United States with at least two or three solid preparatory years in American-style Reform before plunging directly, as babes in the woods, into second- and third-class religious status and intense defensiveness about being Reform in the Holy Land.

Ironically, many poorly educated lay Reform Jews add to their own sectarian confusion by failing to grasp not only where Reform is markedly different from Orthodoxy, but how their own mainstream Reform is a far, far cry from the old Classical Reform. Too many Reform Jews view the proportionately small numbers of their fellow Reformers choosing, for example, to wear hats in the sanctuary, sporting *tallesim* around their shoulders, toying with dietary laws at home, and being open to many rituals of the past as harbingers of a secretly desired mass return to Orthodoxy.

Such, in my mind, is ridiculous and is definitely not the case. What is really going on today in our modern mainstream Reform movement is the mature and inevitable larger recognition that there is, to be sure, a "return" going on here. But the return is a natural and desirable going back to our collective religious senses, which should motivate us truly liberal Jews to do full justice to the best of our entire past—for after all, the past still has so much with which to inspire the present.

Conclusion

I am totally convinced that in the generations ahead we Reformers must follow the dynamic lead of the great Hebrew prophets of old—from whom we must always take our cue—who faced the same great religious challenge as Reform Jews aspire to today. And that is, simply but meaningfully, to try to create a crucial balance between ritual and ethics, where each remains an indispensable and continuing proud hallmark of the Jewish faith and answers the larger and deeper question as to what it essentially means in every generation to "be Jewish."

8

Full Churches, Empty Synagogues

A Defense of Classical Reform

JAY R. BRICKMAN

On a Sunday morning churches in our community, including the Unitarian, are filled to overflowing. Most have two services and some have three to accommodate the crowds. The length of the service is limited to one hour. Children attend for the first part of the service and listen to a story-sermon that is geared to them but interests the elders as well. The children then file out for a brief Sunday-school session, more activity-centered than academic, that concludes at the same time the church service lets out. The service is conducted in English; the words are comforting and inspiring. Hymns are simple and familiar, with the melodies the same ones the worshipers have heard from early childhood. Congregation singing is lusty. The choir is composed of fellow congregants who enjoy performing. Their contribution is warmly received by the audience of friends and relatives. The sermon in a liberal denomination is usually directed to a personal issue with which congregants have wrestled. It attempts to demonstrate how they can derive help in grappling with this problem with insights from their faith. One who attends the service a single time, even someone of a different religion, will understand and feel comfortable with the proceedings, so much so that he may well decide to return.

The Reform temples of our community hold their main service on Friday nights. They are sparsely attended, attracting two to three percent of the membership. The service is almost entirely in Hebrew. Perhaps half those in attendance can read the letters; only the rabbi and cantor know their meaning. The service is replete with traditional gestures, such as bending the knees and bowing at the Bar'chu or rising on the toes for Kedushah, which the novice finds strange and unsettling. The rabbi wears a *tallith* and a head covering, normally identified with traditional worship. The woman cantor wears the same, which is totally at variance with traditional practice. All singing is in Hebrew and therefore unintelligible. Melodies are varied so often that all but the most determined attendees find them unfamiliar.

The service lasts two hours, which, after a long and exhausting workweek, seems very long indeed. There is a Torah procession in which most congregants either touch the Torah with their hand and kiss their hand, touch the Torah with a prayer book and kiss the prayer book, or just touch the Torah with a prayer book. This procedure seems relevant in an Orthodox setting, where people believe or are supposed to believe that the Torah is literally the word of God and that their lives are dedicated to the fulfillment of Torah regulations, but most attendees at a Reform service are neither familiar with the contents of the Torah nor believe themselves commanded by its rulings.

The sermon is often a call to do battle with some overwhelming social issue. Most individuals find behaving with a modicum of decency in their business, civic, and family lives sufficiently challenging. To be called to grapple with world hunger, school violence, or inner-city decay provokes intellectual assent but modest emotional response. The other sermon areas given frequent pulpit attention are the threat of anti-Semitism here and elsewhere, the well-being of Israel, and the importance of Jewish survival. While there are pockets of violent anti-Semitism on the lunatic fringes of our society, most Jews in upper-middle-class suburbia have little experience of rejection. On the contrary, friends and neighbors demonstrate interest in Judaism. In the frequent cases of intermarriage it is normally the Jewish family that experiences consternation. Middle-class, liberal Protestants seem quite content to be linked by marriage with Jewish families.

As for the plight of Jews in other countries, one is familiar with these problems as consequence of frequent solicitations by Jewish fundraising organizations. When Israel was a new social experiment, it was most exciting for American Jews. Many would make regular pilgrimages, perhaps once every two or three years. As Israel becomes more materialistic, more prosperous, and more corrupt, it begins to resemble our own society, and as such provokes less interest. My grandfather, who did not live to see a Jewish state, dreamed constantly of it. I, who remember our pre-state existence, am still deeply appreciative of what Israel represents as a haven for Jews in flight. For my children, the existence of Israel is something they have always known and take very much for granted.

As for the continued existence of our people, a subject much discussed in Jewish periodicals as well as from the pulpit, it is an issue of small concern to all but the professional Jews. It is not that the average Jew does not want our people to survive. It is assumed that if Judaism continues to have meaning in our lives, we will continue to exist as a people. If it does not, we will not. I am reminded of the story of Abraham protesting to God that if he slays Isaac, there will be no progeny to allow for the future existence of the Jewish people. God replies, "You worry about fulfilling my commandments; let me worry about the future of the Jewish people."[1] Faced with a service that is long, unintelligible, foreign in spirit, and with a message not addressed to his or her personal needs, the casual visitor is not likely to return soon.

Given the appeal of the Protestant worship format, why have we not avidly pursued a like procedure? There was a time when we did, in an earlier generation of Reform Judaism; its form is usually identified as Classical Reform. As one of the rabbis who is still loyal to this earlier vision, I question the appellation. It is said that one recognizes a duck when it looks like a duck, quacks like a duck, and waddles like a duck. The present manifestation of Reform Judaism bears so small a resemblance to the vision of our movement's founders, or the historical forces that brought it into being, that it might be more equitable to leave the title Reform (or Reformed, as it was also called) with us and find a new appellation (such as neo-Orthodox) for the present manifestation.

The 1999 Statement of Principles Meets "Niche Marketing"

The most recent effort to articulate the thought and practice of Reform Judaism is the statement of principles adopted May 26, 1999, at the Pittsburgh convention of the Central Conference of American Rabbis (CCAR). The conference was held in the same city where the principles of Reform were set down in 1885. Was this a coincidence, or was a conscious effort being made to repudiate the original document? It is instructive to examine the two documents side by side. The new principles allow for great latitude in the area of theology: "We may differ in our understanding of the Divine presence . . . our varied understandings of Creation, Revelation and Redemption." The sacredness of the Bible is affirmed in the earlier statement as "record of the consecration of the Jewish people as priest of the one God." In contrast, the new text identifies the Torah (not the Bible) as "the foundation of Jewish life . . . a manifestation of ahavat olam, God's eternal love for the Jewish people and for all humanity."

Further, there is clear distinction in 1885 between moral and ritual commandment: "We accept as binding only the moral laws, and maintain only such ceremonies as elevate and sanctify our lives." The new principles commit us to the "study of the whole array of mitzvot . . . Some of these . . . demand renewed attention as the result of the unique context of our own times." Earlier drafts of this statement had called specifically for the reenactment of such rituals as the donning of *tefillin* and the maintenance of dietary laws. Protests from liberal elements in the lay community compelled some verbal compromise, but the reintroduction of traditional rites was clearly the intention of those who authored the new document. The 1885 statement cautioned that "such observance in our days is apt rather to obstruct than to further modern spiritual elevation." The new statement that "the spirit within us is eternal" is less definitive than the earlier "the soul of man is immortal."

While in matters regarding man's relationship to God the 1999 statement offers much latitude, it becomes far more authoritative in affirming relationship to the Jewish people, a subject totally ignored in the prior statement. "We are committed to . . . love for the Jewish people and to . . . the entirety of the community of Israel. [The distinction between these entities is not made clear.] . . . [W]e embrace . . . Jewish life in Israel and the Diaspora [a word shunned by the early Reformers]. . . .We are committed to . . . the State of Israel and encourage aliyah, immigration to Israel." Other new commitments that appear self-serving are to "Progressive Judaism in Israel . . . Progressive Judaism throughout the world." The new principles stress the importance of Jewish education at all age levels and endorse the establishment of Jewish day schools.

There is in every congregation a group of the faithful who will embrace these principles and find great meaning in them. This is the hard-core adult population that attends services, classes, and committee meetings and maintains great interest in Israel. They are the most active element of the membership, and their participation and enthusiasm is essential to the well-being of the congregation. However, this group represents a tiny portion of the membership. Most Jews attend services on special occasions. They do not read books on Jewish subjects (many do not read books at all). Regardless of promotion, they will never participate in a program of Jewish studies. Home rituals are limited to the Passover seder, and lighting candles during Hanukkah and possibly on Friday nights. As far as loyalty to the Jewish collective is concerned, this will continue to diminish with succeeding generations of the American-born. Membership in secular Jewish organizations is down.

In addition, fewer Jewish tourists visit Israel each year. We are living in an age of postnationalism, of the growing importance of the European Union, of the efforts of the United Nations to diminish national rivalries. We have witnessed the frightful devastation that is the consequence of intense ethnic or national loyalties. People of intelligence and sophistication come more and more to view their principal identification as citizens of the world. Anti-Semitism is sharply diminished, so that Jews are seldom reminded of their identity by outside forces. Young people mingle freely, with little awareness of cultural difference. Ask your child if a certain friend is Jewish, and you may be surprised to learn that he or she has no idea. Despite the disapprobation expressed by establishment representatives, the rate of intermarriage exceeds 50 percent, and intermarriage will continue to be rampant so long as Jews and non-Jews mix and Cupid does his job.

Although there was great debate involved in formulating the new principles, it is my strong suspicion that reaction to its promulgation will be near to complete indifference. We are living in a consumer society where it is no longer feasible for leaders to determine what people should do and successfully convince them to fit the mold. We should take warning from the midrash that relates the destruction of Sodom and Gomorrah to the uniformity of bed size. If a man was too tall, they cut him to fit the bed. If he was too short, he was stretched.[2] The most recent concept in retailing is "niche marketing." One begins with where individuals are and what they want or think they want, and endeavors to meet that need. I believe the circumstance of the American Jewish community at this time in our history is not unlike that which faced our forebears at the beginning of the 19th century. Our ideals and our tastes are shaped primarily by the larger culture. We cherish our personal freedom and are unwilling to delegate personal choice to another individual or group. We have deep spiritual needs that cannot be satisfied by such material bounty as wealth, prestige, and power. If spiritual nurturance is not available in a Jewish form, we will look for it elsewhere.

It is to this group of Jews that Judaism must speak. Our doctrine is a sensible one. It does not take extensive study to understand it. As children of a loving God, we are obligated to thank Him for our blessings and to be caring toward persons of all faiths, races, and nations and toward the "lower" creatures as well. The triumphalism of the first Pittsburgh Platform, which asserted that "Judaism presents the highest conception of the God-idea," sounds oddly chauvinistic today. The assertion was probably born as a polemic against the dominant community's assertions that Christianity was the only truth. We recognize in the current universalistic milieu that because there is a single God, there can only be a single faith. However, if we examine the moral affirmation of the great historical religions, we perceive that Buddha, Jesus, and Moses all speak the same moral imperatives. The reason for this is that sensitive individuals have always recognized that the violation of such basic principles make social life an impossibility.

Yet religion is more than ethical affirmation. To keep consciousness of its principles alive and to stimulate enthusiasm for their fulfillment, there is need for saga and for ritual, and these are born out of the cultural experience of different historical communities. In identifying ourselves with Abraham and his wandering, we relive the emotion that accompanied the original experience. We were present at Sinai and felt the encounter of our community with the living God. As Martin Buber has noted, it was not the words of the Torah that were holy, it was the experience that these words endeavored to capture.[3] Sacred texts do not fall from heaven. They are human reactions to divine encounters. We can revere the words revealed to our community without in any way derogating those words honored by other denominations. Their essence is identical.

Ritual is born out of a need to keep alive in consciousness and give symbolic expression to our loyalties. Empty gestures are an abomination to God. When the prophet Amos says, "I hate, I despise your feasts, and take no delight in your solemn assemblies," he is denouncing not ritual but empty ritual devoid of empathy for such spiritual values as justice and compassion.[4] When we bow before the open ark, it should be accompanied with a sense of trying to sublimate our natural inclination to the divine will. The traditional notion that ritual gestures done in the absence of thought and intention will in time provoke the appropriate spiritual underpinning is, I believe, quite incorrect. A service that involves piling one meaningless gesture upon another is a fruitless endeavor. If ritual of any sort assumes real power in the life of an individual or community, it should not be dealt with lightly. Such power is far more difficult to attain than to dismantle.

The early Reformers might have been more successful had they been less impatient in the making of change. In order to retain the earlier momentum and loyalty, rituals should be changed gradually. If it took three thousand years to accumulate the regimen of traditional practice, it need not have been dismantled overnight. So, too, with changes in contemporary Reform. Granted that the early Reformers went too far too fast, our efforts to change what they accomplished should be ongoing but modest. Adding a few more Hebrew prayers, reintroducing kiddush, Kol Nidre, sounding the shofar, were certainly appropriate. Early editions of the Union Prayer Book demonstrated modest change from one edition to the next. Now, however, the genie is out of the bottle and there seems a mad rush among congregations to see which can unearth the most ancient ritual devices.

We have also become creators of liturgy, taking on the mantle of an Amos or Isaiah. Words of the modern liturgist usually fall flat because they are written not by people who believe but by people who would like to believe, and who believe that believing is good for others. With the advent of the Internet, no sooner has a bold new or old/new prayer initiative been tried than it is broadcast across the country and the wandering worshiper finds it everywhere that he or she turns. As the early Reformers taught, rituals themselves possess no holiness, they are vehicles of holiness. To be effective, they must conform to contemporary aesthetic and intellectual norms. A problem exists regarding the degree of ritual with which people are comfortable. In the Protestant community there is a wide variation of possibility. Those whose devotional life is aided by elaborate ritualism may choose an Episcopal church. For those who prefer little or none, there are the Baptist or Unitarian congregations. Such choice had existed in the Jewish community with the Orthodox offering maximal ritualism, Conservatives occupying the middle ground, and Reform synagogues offering the least. As Reform takes on more and more traditional liturgy, those Jews who prefer the simple reading of prayers, hymns, and sermons within a modest time period and minimal ritual accompaniment have no place to go. I fear that unless some accommodation is made to this element of the Jewish population, they may be lost to us, and their numbers may be far larger than we assume.

The existence of a secularized Jewish population, product of the East European Haskalah, was a totally new manifestation in our history. In time it was accepted, even by as pious a leader as the chief rabbi of Jewish Palestine, Abraham Isaac Kuk, that secular Jews such as Golda Meir and Ben Gurion represented a loyal and significant element of the Jewish population. If acceptance can be extended to those who identify themselves as Jews in ethnic or nationalistic terms, why can't the same welcome be extended to those who identify themselves as Jews by religion but have little interest in Jewish peoplehood or Jewish national aspirations? Isaac Mayer Wise wrote in 1898, "Preserving Judaism is one aim . . . the hunger for holiness through the Divine presence is another aim."[5] It is essential for Jewish well-being in our time that those of Classical Reform ideology be welcomed and their viewpoint acknowledged.

In the early years of American Reform, the Jewish population of the United States was small and culturally and economically homogeneous. There was extensive marriage among families of German Jewish background. The consequence was a Reform population that was of limited size and fairly consistent in taste and ideology. It was, as a consequence, possible to give some definition to Reform practice and belief. Members of Reform congregations today come from every manner of background, including a variety of pre-Jewish religious identifications. Any effort to establish a statement of principles, as the CCAR attempted in 1999, must be ambiguous and of little import. A synagogue or Bet Knesset (house of assembly) that is not Orthodox houses people of many perspectives. Rather than seek a single pattern of worship that will satisfy all factions, a large congregation might well consider a variety of offerings. A traditional type of service could be conducted on Saturday morning, a Classical Reform service on Sunday morning, and something middle-of-the-road on Friday evening. With smaller congregations, where it is difficult to muster attendance for a single service, some legitimate compromise can be fashioned. This should be worked out with all groups within the synagogue, even those least likely to attend. Each group should feel a sense of responsibility to care about and respond to the religious needs of the others. All factions in the Reform movement call upon us to be sensitive to the needs of people of different races and regions. We should be no less considerate of the spiritual sensitivities of fellow congregants. It is not disruptive to the service to have some attendees worship with heads covered and others not, some kiss the Torah and others not, and some include names of the matriarchs in reciting the Amidah and others not.

One of the assumptions that underlay the shaping of the new Pittsburgh platform was that Classical Reform was moribund and an alternative formulation was required to give expression to the religious perspectives of contemporary Reform Jews. The outcome of the endeavor may well be the same as happened to the Coca-Cola Company when they attempted to change their formula. There was sufficient protest to compel the reintroduction of the old formula as "Classic Coke." The end product of an effort to reformulate the principle of Reform may reawaken the enthusiasm of those who remain committed to the principles of the old Pittsburgh Platform and who insist upon an equal voice in determining the Reform Jewish future.

Notes

1. Told by Professor Marvin Fox during a lecture at Congregation Anshe Sfard, Milwaukee, Wisconsin, 1960.
2. B. Sanh 109b.
3. Martin Buber, *Writings*, ed. Will Herberg (New York: Meridian, 1956), 192.
4. Amos 5:21.
5. Abraham Cronbach, *Reform Movements in Judaism* (New York: Bookman Associates, 1963), 127.

9

Orthodoxy Confronts Reform

The Two Hundred Years' War

ARYEH SPERO

Viewing life through the prism of age-old traditions and constructs, Orthodox Jews fixate on the origins and sources of given theologies and outlooks and live the present within the framework of the past. While today's props and characters differ from those of yesteryear, for most Orthodox Jews the script by which life is lived has not changed. That having been said, and notwithstanding recent attempts by Reform Judaism to inculcate traditions and mitzvot that in the past Reform rejected, what comes to mind to the average Orthodox Jew when thinking of Reform Judaism is early-nineteenth-century German Reform Judaism and the Pittsburgh Platform of 1885. They are Reform's sources, points of reference.

What the Orthodox perpetually see, therefore, when pondering Reform is mostly yesterday, not today. That German source included (1) the removal of Hebrew, the holy tongue, from the liturgical service; (2) ideological excision from prayer of any reference to or belief in an eschatological return to Zion, the rebuilding of the Beit Ha'mikdash (Temple), or the coming of Mashiach (Messiah); (3) introduction of the quintessential Christian worship instrument (the organ) into, of all places, the synagogue; (4) rejection of oral law and the Talmud; (5) worse, the negation of God in authorship of the Torah; and (6) a concomitant rejection of ritualistic mitzvot such as kashrut, Shabbat, tefillin, and the prohibition of eating *chometz* (leavened items) on Passover. Save Jesus and the Trinity, it, to the Orthodox Jews, resembled Christianity more than it did traditional *Yiddishkeit*.

Many Orthodox Jews still envisage the original intent of earliest German

Reform, which was to denude Judaism of its religious component, its sacred mystery, indeed to view it not even as a religion at all. Thinking still of those early days, Orthodox Jews recall the clarion maxim "We are Germans of Mosaic persuasion" and point to the tolerance early on of intermarriage with Gentile Germans.[1]

When thinking of early American Reform, Orthodox Jews not only recall the reaffirmation of what were, to them, the religious apostasies first enunciated in Germany, but revisit the horror of an early Hebrew Union College event where some members of a rabbinic body, as an act of defiance, requested shellfish. Many, including myself, remember some congregations with services not on Saturday but on Sunday, confirmation in lieu of bar and bat mitzvah, the singing of prayers by temple choirs staffed with non-Jews, and worship before the *aron kodesh* (holy ark) with uncovered heads—in other words, the mimicking of Gentile ways in synagogue life itself.

But that was Reform of yesteryear, not necessarily today. And as Reform is no longer monolithic, with substantial differences within its denomination, likewise today's Orthodoxy is more variegated than would be suggested by its catholic outlook during Reform's incipient days in Germany.

Though the *haredi* (ultra-Orthodox) world is appalled equally by Reform and Conservative Judaism, the modern Orthodox exhibit a degree of tolerance for Conservative Judaism—since many of its rabbis and the Jewish Theological Seminary, in particular, do recognize the importance of halachah—that they do not grant to Reform as a theological construct. All Orthodox Jews, including the *haredim*, do, however, consider Reform and Conservative Jews 100 percent members of the Jewish community, as evidenced by their halachic willingness to marry the offspring of any nonconverted Jews, regardless of affiliation. The differences, therefore, are theological, not biological.

The sense of family and peoplehood—the platform upon which marriage and nationhood are based—prevails, rendering a secular or Reform Jew as biologically Jewish as an Orthodox one. This sense of *am'ha* (peoplehood) extends to the point that all Orthodox Jews feel a responsibility and kinship to Reform Jews qua Jews, manifest in an unhesitant readiness to violate mitzvot and even the Sabbath if that is necessary to save the life of a Reform or secular Jew, as they would toward an Orthodox Jew.

While the distinction between identity acceptance versus creed acceptance may provide little satisfaction to critics of Orthodoxy, especially the element within Reform that has used Orthodoxy's rejection of nonhalachic conversions as a means to demonize the Orthodox as "those who don't accept Reform Jews as Jews," Orthodox Jews find this distinction paramount. The same Orthodox Jew who would question the validity of nonhalachic conversion would vehemently dismiss as a canard any attempt to inauthenticate, for example, Abba Hillel Silver as having been anything but a full-fledged Jew. The rubric is, "Though a Jew may have strayed from Torah, he nonetheless remains a Jew."[2]

"Worldly Involvement"

Orthodox Jews should concede that many of the sociological objections that pre-Enlightenment Central and East European Orthodoxy had regarding Reform have, upon reflection, lost their objectionability given that today Orthodoxy has fully integrated itself into the Western world via professions, secular education, university attendance, its recognition of many Western philosophical and cultural values, the adoption of regional dress, synagogue sermonizing in local vernacular, and the translation, learning, and transmission of holy texts in the national language. While the religious objections do remain regarding the binding force of Sinai, a revealed oral law, the covenantal obligation to mitzvot, Orthodoxy must acknowledge that its present very "worldly involvement" simply postdates by a century Reform's rush out of the ghetto gates into the arena of general society. In fact, were European Jews of a nineteenth-century Polish ghetto to behold their Orthodox progeny in America today, absent the modern Orthodox Jews' religious commitment, they would consider the Americans' dress, tastes, acculturation, demeanor, and professional and entertainment interests Reform.

To be sure, the value of secular wisdom and classical culture and professional training outside the study of Talmud and aligned texts was already recognized by Rabbi Samson Raphael Hirsch of Frankfurt-am-Main in the mid-1800s. The *haredi* world considers Hirsch's paradigm of neo-Orthodoxy, *Torah im Derech Eretz* (Torah and humanism), simply as Hirsch's necessary concession to the alluring challenge and strength of German culture and Reform overtaking Jewish youth. From the point of view of many East European ghetto rabbis yet unaffected by Haskalah and Reform, Hirsch's neo-Orthodoxy, although tolerable for Germany, was not a religious model for them.

The *haredi* perspective on Hirsch is revisionism, for when reading Hirsch, one detects an unmistakable fascination with German high culture and philosophy and, as was the case with Rambam and many others, a belief that a complete Jewish life necessarily involves the integration of God's Torah with the wisdom and formulas by which God created the world and humankind.[3] That is to say, for Hirsch, as for many Talmudic contributors, the sciences and much of the humanities are humankind's attempt to uncover and know the workings by which God created the world, with its corollary being the implementation of such knowledge toward ameliorating the condition of mankind.[4] In Scriptural terms this is the injunction "And ye shall master the world" so as to serve as "a guardian over the Garden" in order to "love thy neighbor" through improving the living standards and awareness of people.[5] Equally clear in Hirsch's conception of the "whole man" is the embodiment of culture, dignity, civility, and creativity, that is, the human in the "image of God."[6]

Although Hirsch did not change the liturgy, he, too, was careful to avoid a contranationalism by avoiding any emphasis on Zionism as an eschatological return to Zion. He identified Jewishness as Judaism, exclusively a religion—something more palatable to Jews wishing to be German yet Jewish.

That being the case, he reinvigorated for the masses the central ideological motif of daily Jewish religious life, which much of the Jewish populace had unconsciously overlooked, given that for centuries, during pre-Enlightenment times, Jewish life, which was universally observant, had not been doctrinally challenged from within. Except for scholars Jewish life was lived mimetically, by tradition. It was a life pattern passed from generation to generation. Hirsch articulated to an ideologically challenged European Jewry that now, for the first time, there was a nonarbitrary internal system by which Jews should decide all religious issues: halachah.

Halachah is a specific traditional Jewish way to approach all questions of Jewish law, of Judaism. While all disciplines value common sense, halachah, like science and mathematics, mandates that even above common sense and current societal proclivities is a set of principles by which Jewish law is to be decided. These principles are contained in the Talmud, the oral law. When new societal circumstances arise not specifically addressed by the Talmud, overarching Talmudic principles and implied precedents are used. These principles are not broad, fuzzy, feel-good, prophecylike platitudes; they are specific, concise, and highly developed legalisms.

Needless to say, rabbis and scholars involved with such decision making must be thoroughly proficient with the vast Talmudic texts, familiar with their nuances and roadways, comfortable with the highly intellectual mode of thinking unique to them, and inherently respectful of Talmudic authority. With a handful of exceptions it is Orthodoxy that has produced rabbis with the comprehensive Talmudic knowledge, and absolute surrender to it, necessary to decide Jewish law; hence the utter reluctance by the Orthodox to accept the opinions of Reform rabbis on issues of Jewish law.[7]

It also goes without saying that Hirsch stressed the eternal nature of Torah, thereby obligating Jews to observe every mitzvah and prohibition—be it the ethical universal or ritualistic particular—except, of course, those that God has made impossible to realize by virtue of historical circumstances. Thus Bible criticism, wherein the Five Books are viewed merely as a haphazard literary compilation of different authors spanning centuries—imbuing the whole with less coherence than Shakespeare's works—is anathema to the believer in a God-revealed Pentateuch spanning at most the forty years from Sinai until the death of Moses. While science, sociology, history, and philosophy are certainly employed in informing our understanding of Torah, they are not a priori accepted as true so as to negate it. Bible criticism was an early departure used by Reform to invalidate complete sections of Torah, its divine authorship, and many of its mitzvot. Bible criticism became a Gettysburg-like battlefield between Orthodoxy and Reform, and that is what it remains today.

To the Orthodox, avant-garde cultural fads, of whatever age, can never be used as the barometer for determining which mitzvot are currently acceptable and which are not. Such domination of cultural trends over Torah's enduring principles has led some present-day Jewish leaders to the horrible proposition that brit milah, covenantal circumcision, is now outdated, no longer Jewishly necessary.

Hirsch was correct in reestablishing for the masses the primacy of divine revelation and the binding nature of mitzvot and halachah—Judaism as a religion, Jewishness as Judaism—for bereft of its religious character, what remains is just ethnicity. Orthodoxy stresses how history has shown that as a Jewish population enmeshes itself within a given society, ethnic ties and ways diminish and evaporate, especially in those cultures valuing individual autonomy. There are other ethnicities, perhaps more engaging and noble than Jewishness. The staying power, the uniqueness of Judaism, is as a religion built upon the Sinaitic divine revelation. It is much more than a political outlook or an affinity for social justice, both of which can be found among other societal entities or upper-class Unitarianism.

Modernism and Rabbinic Control

Another battle comes to mind, which was the battle over who controlled the Jewish communities scattered across Europe. Prior to the Napoleonic emancipation, most of Europe remained under a feudal system, with Jewish communities living as "states within states" where the matters of civil law, punishment, and taxation were bestowed by noblemen onto rabbinic authorities. At their disposal was the ability for rabbis to place in *herem* (excommunication) any Jew deviating from Jewish norms, leaving the excommunicated a nomad, shunned by the Jewish community yet ineligible to enter general society, which was reserved for Christians only.

The Haskalah and Reform leaders resented such control over their personal lives. Here again, age-old antipathies have been carried forward to this day by Orthodox *haredim* reading of Reform's insurrection against venerated holy scholars in books recapitulating how Haskalah and Reform employed government officials in treacherous schemes against the Orthodox rabbis.[8] But as before, with modernism most Orthodox Jews would have to concede the unbearability of living today under a rabbinic theocracy where one's personal choices are circumscribed not by God but by human authorities with the power of communal expulsion, notwithstanding protests by rabbinic loyalists that rabbinic power was a positive force in maintaining "Jewish norms."

The divergence between the *haredim* and the modern Orthodox in harboring continued ill will over Reform's initiatives in the areas of modernism and rabbinic control can be best illustrated by their differing views of Moses Mendelsohn. Mendelsohn, an Orthodox Jewish intellectual and German renaissance man who predated Reform, wrote against rabbinic powers of excommunication. He posited that one's adherence to mitzvot is an obligation of man to God, not a requirement to the *kehillah,* the local Jewish community. That being the case, religious infractions were to be judged by God and were not to be considered as justification for expulsion from the Jewish community—no doubt a highly appealing thesis.

But the *haredi* Jewish commitment embodies more than observance of Torah. For them, *Frumkeit* is an "every-facet" lifestyle, where one lives not a regular life accompanied by mitzvah observance but a specific, complete, rigidly regulated way of life wary of general culture, dress, and secular knowledge not directly related to earning a livelihood—in other words, a life indifferent to Western values. Outside of technology, medical advances, and business manuals, it sees little value in anything not already extant in the religious texts.

Believing that Jewish life is not democratic, pluralistic, or interested in individual autonomy, they would prefer a theocracy in charge of anything touching Jewish life. In fact, self-made ghettos exist today wherein even civil disputes among Jews are adjudicated by local or national rabbis, with those opting for nonrabbinic, U.S. government courts liable to, yes, excommunication: *seiruv.* For them Mendelsohn's belief that the individual need not live for and through the community is sinful. Ironically, living under all-powerful rabbinic rule is akin to living under the medieval Catholic structure. The Church, via the Church fathers, rules. (Rabbi Moses Sofer, the early-nineteenth-century forefather of *haredi*-ism, believed in the divine right of European kings.)

To point to Felix Mendelsohn, Moses Mendelsohn's non-Jewish composer grandson, as proof that Mendelsohn's Western notion of individuality breeds intermarriage is an unfair *haredi* conclusion given that the first and second generations of emancipated Jews were not yet equipped to assimilate Judaism with Germanism. They also did not have philosophical, sociological, or ideological constructs and behavior patterns yet built to balance and merge the two differing outlooks.

Modern Orthodox Jews, however, have reassessed Moses Mendelsohn, realizing that for over a century and a half they have duplicated his profile by melding both worlds, Jerusalem and Athens, into a unity. More Protestant than Catholic in outlook—that is to say, believing that God's obligation devolves on the individual directly as opposed to the individual through the community—the modern Orthodox view Mendelsohn as a highly empathetic and strategic protagonist in the ongoing development of Jewish life.

Haredim, on the other hand, reject any developmental-evolutionary aspect of Jewish communal life—life is simply repeat performances of what was done by previous generations. The modern Orthodox approach to religious problem solving is post-Newtonian; the *haredi* approach is pre-Newtonian. Modern Orthodoxy's attitude is Western; the *haredi* outlook is, really, Eastern. One is religiously proactive, the other reactive. Yet while *haredim* reject planned religious developments through committee, no matter what the current need, a very slow osmosis takes place, as evidenced by their wholehearted endorsement of formal Jewish schooling for girls, a practice not found among *haredi* generations predating World War I.

One more clarification needs to be made about the attitudinal difference between *haredim* and modern Orthodox. To the *haredim* the purpose of life is the *mesora,* the tradition, with people serving as a means to implement that tradition. Tradition can be broken in those circumstances where it is necessary to save one's life so that one may continue to live in order to carry on the tradition. One is an implement; thus there is no notion of the individual finding his or her unique way. The modern Orthodox imbibe a more Western thesis, namely, that the person is the purpose of life, and the mitzvot were given to enrich and provide direction to one's personal journey as specific circumstances arise in life. The Torah can be breached if needed to save a life, not simply because the person's continued life is necessary as an ongoing implement for further Torah observance but because individual life is paramount even absent the tradition. That being the case, non-Jews are equals and non-Jewish life absolute. To *haredim,* however, non-Jews are, basically, accessories to Jewish destiny and needs.[9]

To *haredim,* God is a feudal king whose subjects are entitled to life and liberty only so long as they perform the tasks demanded by the king. To the modern Orthodox, God's law must be followed, as with any sovereign; however, God desires for people life, liberty, *and* the pursuit of happiness, so long as that pursuit stays within acceptable, broad categories.

Both *haredim* and modern Orthodox believe in divine revelation, an actual one-time event, but differ in their conception of God's disposition, a ghetto God as opposed to a *veltlishe* God. The corollary of each thesis of God is seen in one's approach to life, community, government, and other peoples. Quite often it is one's most personal, gut feeling, one's personal psychological makeup and temperament, that determines which camp one will choose as an adult.

Participation in Mixed Rabbinic Boards

Another difference between the modern Orthodox and the *haredim* as relating to Reform is Orthodox participation in mixed rabbinic boards consisting of the different denominations. To *haredim* such participation, as in the New York Board of Rabbis and the now defunct Synagogue Council of America, is forbidden since "participation implies recognition." This proscription was formally pronounced in the 1950s, though Hirsch himself prohibited joint decision making with Reform rabbis in his town of Frankfurt a century ago. (Hirsch's ostensible inconsistency is a subject for discussion elsewhere.)

The *haredi* proscription devolves on rabbinic organizations only, not federations, for it is the recognition of Reform rabbis qua rabbis that *haredim* disapprove of, not individual Reform lay people working in behalf of Jewish community interests and projects. The modern Orthodox accept mixed rabbinic boards under the Western view that people diametrically opposed politically, philosophically, or even religiously must convene—as do conservatives and liberals in the U.S. Senate—to discuss overarching common needs. Still, such participation does not necessarily imply religious recognition, simply reality. By and large even the most modern Orthodox do not subscribe to religious pluralism, although they do recognize sociological pluralism; and Reform rabbis, though halachically inadequate absent a fuller observance of mitzvot, are nonetheless legitimate representatives chosen by legitimate Jews.

The collapse of mixed rabbinic boards such as the Synagogue Council of America was due not to a greater number of modern Orthodox subscribing to "participation implies recognition" but to the deep chasm, to be discussed later in this chapter, now extant as Reform has embraced a whole host of historically radical, and leftist, positions contrary to any honest reading of the specific and pertinent scriptural passages, as well as the patrilineal descent issue. Any society, club, country, or religion must retain certain historical internal standards, non-negotiable requisites, if it is to retain its identity, its original calling. If a Coca-Cola bottling company uses Pepsi syrup when bottling soda, the product is no longer Coke, notwithstanding the bottle's Coke emblem. New Age spiritualism, avant-garde cultural notions, scriptural interpretations befitting Karaites, and radical leftist ideology, even when cloaked in lofty-sounding prophetic garb, remain what they are—not Torah.

While rejecting religious pluralism as a bona fide expression of Torah, most modern Orthodox recognize the laudable social, communal, and charitable achievements of Reform and the communal cohesion it provides its membership and congregants. *Haredim,* on the other hand, rarely acknowledge Reform accomplishments, because of chauvinism, communal immaturity, and tribalism that militate against acknowledging the good done by one's theological opponents. An analogue to this is often found within the entire Jewish community itself when failing to recognize the important role Christianity has played in civilizing the world and how, especially here in the United States, Pilgrim Protestantism—particularly its belief in a Judeo-Christian ethic—facilitated the structure and growth of the most equitable, open, prosperous country in the history of mankind. Like the attitude of *haredim* toward Reform, Jewish fixation on

Christian sins of past times in faraway places has blinded it to the humane spirit and wonderful accomplishments of its past theological foe.

Some *haredim* dismiss Reform accomplishments through delusions that God would have provided these good things, anyway, but by doing so they overlook the scriptural mandate for active partnership of man with God in improving life. At times the fight on behalf of scripture makes one blind to scripture itself. Most believe, even today, that if not for the Reform and Conservative movements, all Jews would be Orthodox and that those denominations suck Jews from the difficult but authentic Orthodoxy to their much easier, religiously relaxed variants.

An honest appraisal, however, results in the inevitable conclusion that because people have different internal mechanisms, and because in a free society they can fulfill themselves uniquely, a substantial amount of Jewry would simply walk away if Orthodoxy were their only option. To that *haredim* answer, "Better they should remain untempled than to attend incorrect denominations, so that if they do return, they will return to authenticity. Better to remain uneducated Jewishly if such education legitimizes the Jewishly illegitimate." They also believe that the soul of every Jew was congenitally programmed to live an Orthodox life.

The attitude toward Reform is not specific to Reform but is symptomatic of an all-or-nothing attitude that yields the same result when confronting any non-*haredi* Jewish project, for example, the refusal to allow its boys to serve in the Israeli army, since the state of Israel is not a halachic-theocratic state. While there may be some merit to espousing the notion that yeshiva boys and girls between the ages of 18 and 26 be allowed to continue their Torah studies, the position is sometimes disingenuous, since (1) not all yeshiva students that age take their studies seriously, (2) modern Orthodox yeshiva boys do serve, (3) the Torah itself, when delineating army exemptions, does not mention yeshiva exemption,[10] and (4) although the *haredim* refuse to recite the prayer for the state of Israel or even the prayer for the soldiers of Israel, this is done religiously every Shabbat in modern Orthodox synagogues. To *haredim* any participation implies a recognition they are unwilling to grant, be it the social accomplishments of Reform, the state of Israel, Yom Ha'atzmaut, secular culture and secular humanities as ends in themselves, or American holidays such as Thanksgiving or the Fourth of July. If it is not theirs, it has no validity.

Haredi citizenship is beneficial, however, since it creates safe neighborhoods where robbery, mugging, or rape will not be visited on strangers walking through it, and where rules of modesty and civilized behavior are the expected norm. When no competitive ideology is involved and a project is under their control, such as burial in Israel or emergency ambulance work in Brooklyn, called Ha'tzalah, *haredim* give of themselves selflessly, exhibiting a concern and kindness that only mitzvah obligation is capable of generating. Forgotten classical notions such as self-sacrifice for the greater good (albeit *haredi* good) are all prevalent. Those coming to its rabbis and rebetzins seeking guidance and religious instruction will be given endless hours of pro bono dedication and warmth, for they are doing "the Lord's work."

The modern Orthodox reject old-world tribalism that sees good only in the specific tribe. It has shed the mental ghettoization that precludes the broadening of one's outlook and personality provided by an affirmative but responsible engagement with the best the world has to offer. *Haredim* will not take that risk and thus, out of fear that their children may find the world enticing, refuse to acknowledge the salutary accomplishments of Reform in areas of general welfare. Quite often the fear of assimilation drives the philosophy of *haredim* more than the actual halachah itself, resulting in the proscription of a behavior that was untroubling to early Talmudic authors.

The reluctance to see any good in our opponents is reminiscent of how Reform Jews, mostly die-hard liberal Democrats, refuse to acknowledge the good done by political conservatives and Republicans in defeating Communism, reviving the notion of individual responsibility, and making patriotism acceptable once again, instead demonizing them and imputing to them all sorts of indifference, inhumanity, and evil. This, too, is done so as not to give any credence to an ideological opponent. Strident ideology, fanaticism—be it *haredi*-ism or left liberalism—saddles the ideologue with holier-than-thou, tribalistic characteristics.

Four Misconceptions

Before moving on to the current dispute between Orthodox and Reform we should be aware of four things. First, the notion that Reform Jews somehow excel in ethics more than the Orthodox, as many a Reformer is wont to assert, is not true and oftentimes is a ruse used to alleviate one's responsibility to ritual mitzvot.

Second, although some Reform Jews think not, it should be noted that Lubavitch is totally in the *haredi* camp; its attitude is very much *haredi*.[11]

Third, *haredim* are not Amish. They are up to date in technology and medicine, and they are politically aware. Their outlet for livelihood is business, a preoccupation in which they generally excel (except for Lubavitch), since they do not have any nonreligious outside interests to distract them and because their heroes, Abraham, Isaac, and Jacob, are all portrayed in the Bible as astute entrepreneurs, wealthy and actively engaged in business enterprises.[12]

Fourth, contrary to conventional wisdom, not all black-hatters are *haredi*, and not all sporters of jeans are modern Orthodox. Generally so, yes; however, attitude is the decisive criterion. Additionally, the great *haredi* rabbis are not militant, nor are many of their followers. Their zealousness is for the law they feel has been entrusted to them to preserve. They are not Iranian mullahs. Finally, within *haredim* there is a distinction between Lithuanian-grounded scholars and Hasidic rebbes, an interesting phenomenon that is irrelevant to this discussion.

Reform Attacks on Orthodoxy

Reform Judaism's anger at Orthodox pronouncements against it is understandable in light of the barrage it has taken for many years. In recent years, however, beginning with Rabbi Alexander Schindler's past tenure, Reform has unleashed unprecedented, ignominious attacks against Orthodoxy, attacks that, curiously, have never been unleashed against the African-American leaders spouting anti-Jewish venom nor against the black leaders culpable in instigating the Crown Heights, Brooklyn, pogroms of 1991. Conservative Judaism has refrained from belligerent statements and actions against Orthodoxy.

The acrimony began with the Who-is-a-Jew issue in Israel, was spearheaded here in the United States, and accelerated later over the issue of patrilineal descent. Regarding patrilineal descent, Orthodoxy claims (and rightly so) that it is not they who have endangered the biological unit of familial Israel, which allows Jews to marry one another regardless of religious belief. Orthodoxy has stayed the historical course. It is the Reform deviation in this matter that will split the Jewish people as a nation with a biological commonality.

Although Orthodoxy has been perennially disturbed by Reform's rejection of mitzvot, it saw the matter as internal to Reform. Not so with the issue of patrilineal descent, which now affects Orthodoxy by making it halachically impossible for Orthodox children to marry the children of non-Jewish, nonconverted mothers married to Jewish men. In this matter Reform, not Orthodoxy, has moved away from the Jewish people, notwithstanding Reform's larger constituency. In such matters propriety is not determined by who has the greater membership but by what is halachically valid.

The Who-is-a-Jew issue is slightly different. Again, while it is impossible to accept as marriage partners children of non-Jewish mothers who have not undergone a halachic conversion, the question is whether Reform can upgrade its conversion standards so that while not matching the high expectations and requirements of an Orthodox Beit Din, Reform conversions can at least meet the minimal Torah requirements and standards for conversion: (1) brit milah, (2) *mikvah* immersion, (3) commitment to Torah and mitzvot, (4) devotional pledge to God, and (5) partnership in Jewish destiny. Such converts would benefit the Jewish people, given their enthusiasm, freshness, newly gained knowledge (which often surpasses that of congenital Jews), and seriousness regarding Jewish practice, as well as the benefit of an expanded gene pool.

To be honest, *haredim* and most modern Orthodox would still not accept even such conversions if performed by Reform rabbis, given that Reform rabbis can hardly extract from a prospective convert a commitment to mitzvot that they themselves do not observe or believe in. And while in the private recesses of their heart some modern Orthodox would accept a Reform Jew-by-choice displaying postconversion dedication to Judaism, official Orthodoxy, on the organizational

level, would not. Nor would Orthodox Jews, who may privately accept such converts as good Reform Jews, allow their children to marry such a convert's offspring absent a new, Orthodox conversion.

Undoubtedly the most heated battle for Reform arises from its campaign for
its rabbis and movement to receive official recognition in Israel, according it religious legitimacy. The *haredim* will never yield on this issue, while many modern
Orthodox would accept in Israel what they already live with here in America.
Furthermore, many modern Orthodox are frustrated by an intractable, often corrupt religious hegemony in Israel, akin to religious Communism, one party for all.
In many ways the Orthodox establishment has not done an adequate job in reaching Israelis, many of whom see themselves as Israelis but not Jews—modern-day
Canaanites. It may be that Israelis harbor not so much a distaste for religious ritual per se as a dislike for the ghetto-type baggage associated with Israeli Orthodoxy,
an Orthodoxy that is ignorant of the American live-and-let-live viewpoint.

The ultimate question is whether Israelis, living as they do in a country where
the movers and shakers are not religious, are less prone to religiosity—as
opposed to the United States, the most religious country in the world on an individual level, where 87 percent of the American mainstream believes in God. Or
is their religious indifference, often hostility, based on the wide cultural and sociological disparities between them and current Israeli-type Orthodoxy? As of yet,
however, there does not seem to be a clamoring among the Israeli public for religious pluralism. The few leftist intellectuals endorsing such pluralism do so not
as much out of a yearning for a religious life as out of a desire to smack the
Orthodox they abhor. Other Israelis fear that Reform's agenda will include affirmative action for Arabs.

Needless to say, the Orthodox bureaucracy in control of Israeli religious life
has been contaminated by the ills endemic to all bureaucracies: unresponsive-
ness, bias, job patronage. Bureaucracies, especially ideological ones, are bastions
of hubris and mediocrity—be it all-powerful unions, Israeli Orthodox hegemony,
or, as in the United States, a public school bureaucracy that has put its interests
over that of its constituency, sinking American big-city schools to pathetic levels.
Such is the corruptive nature of all unchecked entrenchments.

The interesting point in all this is how the battle has developed today in Israel
between a Reform movement wishing to break the state hold by Orthodox rabbis,
just as it did two hundred years ago in the Jewish communities of Europe, then
under Orthodox rabbinic control. As mentioned in the first paragraph of this chapter, to the Orthodox the props and characters may differ, but the script remains
unchanged. The battle endures, merely to be fought on different battlefields.

Tikkun Olam

The very recent CCAR statement of principles emphasizes the centrality of *tikkun
olam* (repairing the world) to its religious agenda. But Reform's approach to

tikkun olam has incorporated only leftist, socialistlike elements. In truth, it is political, basically a mirror of the most radically leftist components of the Democratic Party platform, causing many to say that Reform Judaism is simply "the Democratic party with Jewish holidays."

Unlike *haredim*, mainstream Orthodox see *tikkun olam* as a divine imperative but seriously question a socialistlike paradigm that socially engineers society, demands a conformity that belies human nature and rugged individuality, and has not successfully worked elsewhere.

As explicated in the Talmud, *tikkun olam* primarily involves the promotion of the Almighty to general society, something Reform, through its spokespeople and surrogates, fights, perhaps more so than any other group in America save the American Civil Liberties Union, which is highly populated by Reform members. Judaism's mission is expressed in the Kaddish prayer, the most repeated single prayer in our liturgy: "May His name be exalted and sanctified throughout the world." And, again, in the A'leinu prayer: "To improve the world [*tikkun olam*] as God's kingdom."

Social *tikkun olam* devolves, according to tradition, on the individual and local-regional communities.[13] *Tikkun olam* is never achieved by nation-mandated, utopian, monolithic strategies directed by a chosen few. Central to Torah are the divinelike attributes of individual responsibility and self-reliance, that is, humanity created in the image of God.

According to Zohar *tikkun olam* is simply the discovery through science, commerce (business), and technology of those things that improve the physical condition of humankind. That which is produced by Procter and Gamble—its cleaning products—is an example, for they bring cleanliness, safety from germs, and improved surroundings to our homes, clothes, and body.

Maturity is achieved by accepting upon oneself the requisites of true adulthood: deferment of immediate gratification, acceptance of responsibility, hard work, and the socializing attributes and habits borne of commitment to work, family, and community. Wallowing in victimization or "I can't do it" attitudes is counterproductive. Treating people as pathetic victims forever in need of suckling from an ever-eager nanny-state, one that penalizes sacrifice and hard-won earnings, is paternalistic and cruel. It is feel-good compassion but not productive compassion.

Magnanimous and charitable acts must be forthcoming from individual to individual, not as an enforced paradigm on a national level. History has shown that socialistlike policies do not result in *tikkun olam*, repairing the world, but in its opposite, societal destruction and disrepair.

Not all of those claiming to be victims are correct in their assertion of victimhood; some simply have not grown up or still have thin skins. Quite often people who ascribe to or proclaim victim status display a sense of entitlement, resulting in a mind-set that sees a right to receive without a corresponding obligation to give—to give to society, to sacrifice for the community and one's family. Torah, which countenances good citizenship, cannot therefore be happy with *tikkun olam* policies that engender such sad consequences.

On the road one hears how liberal Jews arrogate to themselves the notion that they know what is best for all of us, constantly rebuking society from atop its modern-day-prophet pedestal. Could it be that the movement that rejected religious chosenness has made itself the politically and culturally "chosen"? Can it be that the denomination that frowns on Orthodox/*haredi* application of halachah to details of daily life has itself constructed a leftist and political "halachic" system as zealous and demanding as Orthodoxy's is in regard to ritual? Holier-than-thou attitudes abound equally in both groups, simply in different categories.

Reform: The "Religious Left"

While coming closer than ever before to an awareness of the need for particularistic mizvot, Reform still does not see God as commander of those mitzvot, for to do so obligates the commandee, the Jewish people, to choose God's will over societal pressures and personal beliefs. The notion of a commanding God remains, for many, distasteful and unsophisticated. Certainly the Orthodox value of "fear of God" remains untenable to most Reform Jews. The result, however, is a movement that under the banner of civil rights—Reform's cardinal mitzvah—politically champions abortion for whatever reason during any stage of pregnancy and even partial-birth abortion. Though Torah's view of abortion differs from Catholicism's, it is wholly different from that of Planned Parenthood; nor does it take its cue from the National Organization for Women. Reform's position should be stated for what it is: political liberalism. Instead, like the religious right, it extols its political views in religious terminology, as religious imperatives. It is, really, the religious left.

Again, the Torah confers *kiddushin,* the sanctity of marriage, upon the union of man and woman only: "And when a man shall take a woman for a wife."[14] A partnership between same-sex people, whatever it pretends, is not *kiddushin.* Officiation by Reform rabbis at homosexual marriage, and the reference to it by said rabbis as a "sacred" union when Torah calls it an abomination, illustrates once again how disbelief in a commanding God always results in God being vanquished by personal and societal trends. Like adulterers, homosexuals are entitled to routine civil rights, but neither group can claim that its behavior is sacred, neither can assert Torah sanctification, holiness, to their unions.[15]

Throughout history Judaism has produced groups within itself that have wished to remain Jewish while eliminating its two central motifs: a God-commanding entity and the oral law. The Karaites and Sadducees, both believers in a Torah bereft of oral law, had their day but eventually vanished. The early Jewish Christians minimized the importance of actual mitzvah observance in favor of "living the spirit of the law." They eventually became non-Jews. In biblical times there was *a'vodah za'rah*, wherein Jews worshiped other gods while performing the "optional" Jewish practices of kashrut and Shabbat. What they all shared in common was an unwillingness to buck (pagan) cultural trends.

King Ahab and King Menashe are prototypes of those who imbibed both the pagan spiritual culture, which was based on hedonism, and the spirituality of Judaism. Their lives, and those of the majority of Israelites who followed them, show that talk of "spirituality," as opposed to a religious commitment to God's law, devolves into spiritual paganism. Indeed, all of pagan worship revolved around the deep-seated human desire for something transcendent, be it nature, Molech, earth, or the sexual.

Torah saw and warned about the degenerative possibilities in man's quest for the spiritual outside of that which surrenders to the One God and his Mitzvot. A lot of New Age, fashionable spirituality and mysticism being countenanced today in Jewish "religious" circles is simply old-time *a'vodah za'rah*. Endowing animals with "rights," as in ancient Egypt and India, and confusing the protection of the Garden with the Garden's mastery over man himself, are dangerous encroachments of age-old pagan "spiritual" motifs into the body of Judaism.[16]

Some think the purpose of Judaism is to be iconoclastic, to shatter conventional taboos, to disturb the masses. Torah tells us differently. It is to be holy, holiness being the separation from activities the Torah deems unwholesome, soiling.[17]

As with the Hellenists centuries ago, many Reform Jews have expressed a preference for, a greater comfort with, their children marrying an upper-class, socially relevant, liberal Gentile rather than a *haredi* or even a modern Orthodox Jew. To them cultural affinity supercedes common religious ancestry. The degree to which that sentiment prevails is the decisive factor in determining whether Reform has succeeded as a religious movement.

The Reform movement cannot be Orthodox or Conservative. It will choose its way. But to survive as a religious movement it must be God-centered, acknowledging a difference between the sacred and profane, the holy and unholy. It needs *religious* passion, featuring some degree of mystery, faith, a numinous component, a degree of religious surrender.

Absent religiosity among its members, Reform will witness more intermarriage—its sanctuaries will increasingly become a home to non-Jewish spouses, and its rabbis will be ever more frightened to speak about the ills of intermarriage. To maintain its ranks and budget, it will be forced to actively missionize for new members among non-Jews. Such eagerness to find a constituency from without will not upgrade but rather loosen conversion standards.

A liberal social-justice agenda under the guise of religion will not, by itself, retain Reform's young people, since they can do that better by becoming activists in political parties while returning home to future non-Jewish spouses in a home bereft of Jewish ritual and observance. Its membership will still be the largest of all the denominations, but it will be a membership composed of whom? The problem is most acute in the South, Midwest, and mountain states. Only religious passion, a serious religiosity, will link its young people to Judaism as a religion. And such passion and seriousness blossoms when one surrenders one's religious life to a commanding God.

Notes

1. Ben Sasson, *History of the Jewish People* (Cambridge, Mass.: Harvard University Press, 1976).
2. Talmud; *Yoma*; Rambam, Hilchot Teshuva.
3. S. R. Hirsch, *Horeb, Nineteen Letters*, 1800s. Also see such rabbinical scholars as Saadyah (foremost among post-Talmudic Babylonia Gaonim), Ibn Ezra (Spanish commentator on Torah who interprets by virtue of textual meaning as opposed to midrashic coloration), Rambam (Maimonides—original codifier of Jewish law into categories; and foremost traditional Jewish philosopher), Radak (medieval commentator on Prophets), Albo (medieval scholar who constructed an Articles of Faith), Abarbanel (Spanish commentator of Torah during Inquisition period), Hildesheimer (nineteenth-century Berlin rabbi in charge of Orthodox Seminary promoting the need for Torah and secular knowledge), Chajes (Galician rabbi of the nineteenth century who interpreted Talmud and midrash along more rational lines), Reines (nineteenth-century forerunner rabbi of Religious Zionism), Kook (first Chief Rabbi of Israel), Soloveitchik (foremost non*haredi* Talmudist/philosopher of American Orthodoxy, advocate of synthesis between Torah and secular wisdom). Also Talmud Sanhedrin, where it is mentioned that in the study house of the Nasi, Raban Gamliel, philosophy was studied.
4. Hirsch, *Horeb*; Hirsch, *Nineteen Letters*; Talmud, Megillah; J. B. Soloveitchik, *Halachik Man, Lonely Man of Faith* (Philadelphia: Jewish Publication Society, 1983).
5. Genesis 1:28, 2:15; Leviticus 19:18.
6. Genesis 1:27.
7. Lieberman, Feldman, and Roth are among recent erudite Conservative Talmudists. It goes without saying that together with encyclopedic and deep Talmudic knowledge comes a need for perspective and openness when being a *posek*, decisor of Jewish law.
8. The attitude of *haredim* toward Orthodoxy's venerated holy men is a notch less than ancestor worship; they are icons. *Haredim* take personally any attack on such icons, similar to the way some liberals worship the Kennedys and Martin Luther King Jr.. In both cases this iconic status reflects the most personal ideological feelings—the purposeness—of members of each group, a living through them. Thus the personal anger when such icons are attacked. Some Israelis have similarly lionized Yitzhak Rabin.
9. *Haredim* believe that the Jew's *neshama*, soul, is superior to that of the non-Jew's. Converts, then, gain a new soul, or their soul is transmuted or elevated, upon becoming a Jew. Does that happen the moment the convert's head surfaces from the *mikvah* water? To *haredim*, a nonhalachic convert remains with his "non-Jewish soul." Hatam Sofer, father of *haredi*-ism, once posited against a Jew receiving a blood transfusion from a Gentile. The divergence between the *haredi* and modern Orthodox viewpoints can be traced to differing emphasis of

Talmudic sources. Many Western notions are already contained with the Talmud, a fore-runner of much Western thought. Much of *haredi*-ism is the retention today of attitudes and complexes born of the past persecution of the Jewish people.

10. Deuteronomy 20:5–8; 24:4.
11. Lubavitch accepts Reform Jews as Jews with the hope they will become Lubavitchers. They do not, however, accept as valid the Reformness of those Jews. As with all *haredim*, they accept the hoped-for image, the potential, of the Reform Jew, while not accepting him or her, in terms of religion, as an end in himself or herself.
12. Genesis 13:2, 24:1, 26:12–13, 32:6, 33:11.
13. Talmud, *Baba Bathra*, chapter two. Talmud, *Gittin*, chapter four.
14. Deuteronomy 22:13.
15. Leviticus 18:22, 20:13, 18:26, 18:30. In the language of the Talmud: *kiddushin* does not inhere, *aino to'fes ba*.
16. Imbuing animals with "rights," as opposed to them being creatures toward which humans have obligations, as humans do toward all of God's creations, imbues them with "spirit," something unique to humans. Once this is done, a possible next step is the matriculation of them into higher spiritual beings, worthy of worship. Quite often mankind imputes to entities filled with mystery—for example, animals, inaccessible mountains, stars—a sacred veneration exceeding that of immediate humans, with our knowable frailties. Much of ancient Canaanite *a'vodah za'rah* was spurred by the mystery, the anima, within sex. See Genesis 1:28.
17. Leviticus 19:2; Ramban, Commentary on Chumash, Leviticus 21:26.

Personal Status

10

Not by Birth Alone

The Case for a Missionary Judaism

ALEXANDER M. SCHINDLER

The Reform movement recently marked the twentieth anniversary of Outreach, a programmatic thrust well rooted in our tradition, which affirms that Judaism is not an exclusive club for born Jews, that we do not cloak ourselves in an exclusive chosenness, but declare ourselves open to all who would choose us.

The Beginnings of Outreach

Launched in the late 1970s by the North American Reform movement, Outreach was inaugurated at my behest and, initially at least, as a response to the demographic crisis besetting American Jewry. Statistics at that time revealed that the hostile attitude of the Jewish community toward interfaith marriages was not discouraging their rising incidence and was alienating those Jews who were being forced to choose between their religious heritage and their heartsong of love and partnership. Why not render the crisis into an opportunity, I argued, by offering programs that would help ease the burden of intermarried families while cultivating the Jewish identities of their children and, where appropriate, attaining the conversion of the non-Jewish partners?

Worsening figures over the past decades confirmed the need for such an approach. The rate of intermarriage continued to soar. Even the most intensive Jewish upbringing failed to check its rise. For example, Jewish day school graduates are currently intermarrying at a 25 percent rate. These realities cry for an all-out Outreach effort by the Jewish community—the effort to retain the intermarried Jews for Judaism and to infuse new blood into the Jewish body through conversion and Jewish education. A clenched fist and excommunication, I earnestly believe, will not alter the statistics of intermarriage, but a beckoning hand and increased communication may attenuate the phenomenon's impact.

In truth, however, it was not only the statistics that moved me to action in this matter. It was also the painful stories I heard over and over in my travels: from the would-be converts who felt deeply hurt by the rejection of those who were born Jews; from the grandparents who yearned to put an end to the bitterness wrought by their negative response to a son's or daughter's interfaith marriage in order to establish a relationship with their grandchildren; from the adult children of interfaith families who felt Jewish in all but their "accreditation" yet were being denied their rightful place on the *bimah;* from the interfaith couples who had raised their children parve—neither fish nor fowl, neither Jewish nor Christian—only to lose them to the totalism of a religious cult.

While I might be credited for suggesting so radical a shift in the Jewish communal mindscape (that we go from mourning to missionary work in response to the reality of intermarriage), over the past twenty years that suggestion has been elaborated into a plethora of creative programs mainly by others, countless rabbis and lay leaders throughout the continent: Introduction to Judaism courses, Times and Seasons, the development of curricula for the offspring of interfaith couples, the Outreach Fellows program, Stepping Stones, a Taste of Judaism, and on and on. These are but a few of the precious jewels in the tiara that crowns the programmatic efforts of our religious community in the realm of Outreach. They were devised to draw the intermarried back into the synagogue and to break the sense of isolation and alienation that is spurred by the absence of a more genuine communal support. Healing has been brought to many hearts bruised by the misbelief that insofar as intermarriage is concerned the love of family and the love of people are mutually exclusive.

Although reviled at first, Outreach ultimately received the recognition of wide emulation on the North American Jewish scene. Most segments of this community now recognize the compelling logic of Reform's approach to the thorny problem of intermarriage, and that includes those who most disparaged these efforts initially. Indeed, some years before his death, Ha-Rav Soloveitchik, our generation's most respected voice of mainline Orthodoxy, had this to say: "Regarding the plague of intermarriage, from which the Orthodox have not been spared, it is necessary to do what the Reformers are doing—within, of course, an Orthodox context." Today, then, Conservatives, Reconstructionists, and even liberal Orthodox groups, as well as communal organizations and federations, have undertaken outreach activities, each in its own way, though nonetheless joined in a kind of Jewish patchwork quilt of outreach that has forever altered the landscape and the mindscape of American Jewry.

Much the same can be said concerning the patrilineal descent resolution that was spawned by the Outreach revolution. When this principle was first adopted by the Central Conference of American Rabbis (CCAR) in the early 1980s, it was most savagely traduced, even from many in our own ranks. We were warned then that by the year 2000 there would be not one but two Jewish peoples in the world.

Well, here we are, and we are still one. Repeated scientific studies establish that fully 85 percent of America's laity, cutting across denominational lines, are accepting of our bilineal approach, and further—mirabile dictu—that even 7 to 8 percent of the Orthodox rabbinate give it silent acquiescence, that is to say, they *freign nisht keine kashes,* they ask no questions concerning lineage. They sanctify the marriage of all who were raised as and consider themselves to be Jews.

"Fretful Grievances" with Outreach

Outreach does have its critics, to be sure, although these naysayers are but a fractious if vociferous minority. The thrust of their fretful grievances is essentially three-pronged.

The first common misreading of Outreach involves the conceptual error of seeing these programs as counteractive rather than restitutive. They adjudge Outreach to be a failure because intermarriage shows no sign of abatement, and because the conversion rate to Judaism and the percentage of Jewishly reared children continues to be alarmingly low. This is like calling the Salvation Army a failure because homelessness is on the increase. It is like blaming the prophet Elijah, urging that we spill out his cup and close our open doors come next Passover, because the systemic causes of injustice in our world persist.

The goal of Outreach programming all along has been restorative rather than preventive. Its aim is to draw the intermarried back into Jewish life in the hope that the non-Jewish partners will ultimately opt for Judaism and, above all, that the children of these marriages will be reared as Jews and share the destiny of the Jewish people. Realism about the trends of intermarriage, not an inflated sense of power to deter it, inspires Outreach.

Moreover, such objections are based on the convenient distortion of the data. The statistics they cite apply to all of the intermarried, including the vast majority who have not yet been touched by Outreach programs. Yet any rabbi whose congregation is engaged in such activities can testify that Jewish conversion and child-upbringing rates among affiliated interfaith families are substantially higher than the norm. The preponderant majority of interfaith couples who belong to a synagogue rear their children as Jews and only as Jews. Most of these might never have found a home in the Jewish community were it not for the Outreach revolution.

These critics of Outreach efforts are focusing on the wrong target. Instead of attacking such programs, they would do better to support their expansion. Most intermarried couples are not aware that the Jewish community is ready to embrace them. A recent nationwide study shows that relatively few know about

Outreach programs of any kind, and many remain convinced that our community has rejected them.

No, Outreach has not failed. What has failed is Jewish communal understanding of the pressing need to provide adequate funding and creative effort in getting the word out that there is a place within Judaism for those who have not been part of Jewish life in the past.

A second critique holds Outreach responsible for the further attenuation of Judaism. This critique avers that the presence of too many strangers in our midst will inevitably serve to dilute Judaism, to water it down.

Experience teaches otherwise. Substantive Outreach activities that adhere to high standards serve to strengthen Jewish life. More often than not it is the non-Jewish spouse in an intermarriage who sees our religion through fresh eyes and revives the Jewish partner's interest in his or her Judaism. Moreover, Outreach compels those of us who are born Jews to ask ourselves some very fundamental questions: What are we? What do we really believe? What must we know, feel, and do in order to claim to be Jewish? Once we grapple with such questions, an inner transformation takes place.

Harold Schulweis, the widely acclaimed Conservative rabbi of our generation, endorsed Outreach precisely on these grounds: "Something happens to the student who is called upon to teach," he wrote, "something happens to the Jew who is asked to explain the character of his tradition to one outside the inner circle. . . . [K]nowing how to answer is as important to the Jewish responder as to the non-Jewish questioner."

Here is the quintessence of the outreach-inreach dynamic: a renewal of commitment following the process of rediscovery. Invariably when we succeed in touching the non-Jewish partner of an intermarriage, we bring the Jewish partner of that marriage closer to the core. By engaging in the process, we transform ourselves. We, in consequence, become better Jews.

Which brings me to the third most common argument against Outreach, that of "quality versus quantity." These opponents charge that such programs are a waste of scarce communal resources that would be better spent on advanced educational and other programs for the committed, those already strongly involved in Jewish life. The opponents of Outreach demand that the Jewish community focus all its available means on this saving remnant and not on what they see as "lowest-common-denominator" programs that strip Jewish identity of its particularity.

There is a kind of elitism written all over this quality-versus-quantity critique. It is the patronizing belief that only the few deserve to be counted in because of their perceived superiority in learning and commitment. Likewise, this critique expresses a defeatism, an acute pessimism. It sees the glowing sparks of Jewish identity in America as dying embers rather than as combustible coals. It sees the battle for Jewish souls already lost with but a surviving remnant to be guarded, Ezra-like, from foreign encroachment

The notion that Outreach results in a "lowest-common-denominator" Judaism has been most vigorously disproved by our own collective experience. Twenty years of Outreach have brought into our ranks thousands of morally earnest, religiously compelled, and communally alive Jews along with their partners and their children. During those same twenty years there has also been a flowering of Jewish literacy and spirituality that is unfolding at the grassroots level, a new sense of discipline in the performing of the mitzvot, a renewed appreciation of the Jewish calendar, and a greater interest in Judaism's classical texts.

Enlarging the Site of Our Tents

In projecting Outreach twenty years ago, I envisaged it not merely as a response to the issue of intermarriage. Indeed, an Outreach program that limits its efforts to those who are bound to us by marriage is an affront to them. It casts doubt on their integrity, as if to say, "You really didn't choose Judaism based on its merits; you must have done it to please your spouse." This is manifestly not so. For most Jews-by-choice the Jewish spouse was the catalyst but not the cause of their conversion.

No, I envisaged the Outreach program not as an emergency action to repair the holes in our tent but as a long-term effort to "enlarge the site" of our tents, to "extend the size of our dwellings." My dream was to see our Judaism unleashed as a resource for a world in need, not as the exclusive inheritance of the few, but as a renewable resource for the many; not as a religious stream too small to be seen on the map of the world, but as a deep-flowing river, hidden by the overgrown confusion of modern times, that could nourish humanity's highest aspirations.

This is what Outreach was meant to be from its beginning. It calls for more than a passive acceptance, requiring instead an active pursuit. It means something more than welcoming the strangers who choose to live in our midst. It bids us seek them out and invite them in, like the prototype of the proselytizing Jew, Abraham, whose tent was continually open on all four sides for fear that he would miss a wandering nomad and fail to bid him enter.

Why do we continue to resist the notion of an assertive Judaism? Are we ashamed? Is it that our self-image still mirrors the contempt of our traducers? Or do we perhaps think that Judaism has little if anything to offer to our world?

Well, look about you and see. Look at planet Earth, riven as it is by conflicts of every conceivable kind. Would not Judaism's insistence that every human being is created in God's image provide healing for such a fractured world?

Consider the fear that shuts doors to the hungry and borders to the persecuted.

Might not Judaism's emphasis on loving the stranger—and the Jewish experience of being the stranger—help to wedge open the doors of the world's conscience?

And what of the immorality, the unethical business practices born of greed that have come to mark our age? Might not the Judaic understanding of wealth as a stewardship help to restore the integrity of our own people and restore trust in our larger society?

Consider, finally, the yearning in our lands for a life rhythm deeper than the rat race, a reward richer than the accumulation of wealth, a purpose fuller than just "making it." Might not Judaism's sanctification of time and space and of the daily things of life satisfy that hunger?

Yes, Judaism has an enormous amount of wisdom and experience to offer to our troubled world, and we Jews ought to be proud to proclaim it with fervor and with pride. Albert Einstein epitomized this thesis when he declared, "I am sorry that I was born a Jew, because it kept me from choosing to be a Jew."

Let us therefore be champions of Judaism.

Let us not be among those who in their pain and confusion respond to the fear of self-extinction by declaring casualties before the fact, who respond to the suffering of the past by living in the past, who react to the long-drawn isolation of our people with an isolationism of their own.

Let us rather recall and act on those lofty passages from the Tenach and the Chazal, from the Bible and commentary, that define Jewish chosenness not as exclusive but as exemplary, not as separatist but as representative, not as closed but as open, not as rejecting but as all-embracing and compassionate.

11

Patrilineal Descent Revisited

STEVEN BAYME

A prominent United States government official recently explained to a visiting American Jewish Committee (AJC) delegation that the only reason he was not a practicing Jew today was the refusal of his Conservative rabbi to confer the bar mitzvah rite of passage upon him inasmuch as his father had been Jewish but his mother was Gentile. At virtually the same point in time, Rabbi Yitz Greenberg, a prominent modern Orthodox rabbi well known for advocating religious plural-ism, also addressing an AJC forum, condemned as "a first-class disaster" the Reform movement's decision to accept patrilineal descent as a criterion for defin-ing who is a Jew.

Similarly, in 1998, at the board meetings of the Memorial Foundation for Jewish Culture, Rabbi Aharon Lichtenstein, a leading Orthodox scholar, com-mented that he well understood why the Reform movement had accepted patri-lineality as meeting the needs of its constituency. However, as a Talmudic scholar and as a Jew committed to the binding power of Jewish law, he noted he could never accept such a definition. Rabbi Alexander Schindler, immediate past pres-ident of the Union of American Hebrew Congregations (UAHC), responded that the decision was taken only after ascertaining that sufficient scholarly basis within Jewish tradition warranted it.

Both views exist, yet both cannot be correct. The facts on the ground are self-evident. In 1983 the Reform movement accepted patrilineal descent as evidence for presumption of Jewish status within Reform Judaism. Reconstructionist Judaism had done so as early as 1968, yet, given the small number of Recon-structionist Jews, that decision had caused few ripple effects within the Jewish community. By contrast, the 1983 decision of the Central Conference of American Rabbis (CCAR) underscored major debates taking place within the Reform movement, within the broader Jewish community, and between Israel and the Diaspora.

Background

To be sure, as early as 1909 the CCAR had affirmed patrilineality. More recently, in 1961, it had reaffirmed that decision through its *Rabbi's Manual*.[1] For all intents and purposes virtually every Reform rabbi in the United States had been acknowledging patrilineal descent since the Second World War. What changed in 1983, however, was the public nature of the decision and the surrounding communal debate. Until 1983 matrilineality had been upheld in principle, and patrilineality was at most tolerated. From 1983 onward the matrilineal principle no longer was operative exclusively, leading to the irony that in at least some cases, persons considered as Jewish under Jewish law were *not* entitled to Jewish status under the Reform definition of who was a Jew.

By 1990 the National Jewish Population Study (NJPS) reported approximately 150,000 patrilineally defined Jews. Those numbers have doubtless increased since then, owing to continued high rates of mixed marriage. Moreover, in the intervening decade many mixed couples have been raising children. In short, a critical mass of individuals exist whose status in the Jewish community is disputed—acceptable as Jews in some sectors yet unacceptable in others. These differences cross ideological and geographical divides. Even within the Reform movement no unanimity exists. In England, for example, Reform Judaism rejects patrilineal descent while Liberal Judaism practices it.

Therefore, the issue has grown in importance in recent years and promises to become even more significant in the future. For that reason it is appropriate to revisit the issue to ask precisely what has been accomplished, what have been the ripple effects, and what are the implications for the future.

The Crux of the Debate

The issues and considerations in the debate may be quickly summarized. The decision in effect affirmed long-standing Reform practice to accept as a Jew the child of either a Jewish father or a Jewish mother, provided that the parents expressed commitment to Jewish continuity through engaging in specific acts of Jewish affirmation in the child's upbringing. Many have sought to explain the decision as one of principle that is irrelevant to the intermarriage phenomenon generally. Traditional rabbinic law had defined identity via the mother. In an age of gender equality, should not equal weight be given to a Jewish father?

Moreover, Reform leaders pointed to the anomaly of children of Jewish fathers raised as Jews yet not being recognized as such, whereas children of Jewish mothers who had never identified in any substantive or even symbolic way as Jews were automatically recognized as Jews under Jewish law. Traditionalist Reform rabbis, in fact, pointed to their refusal to officiate at marriages in which one partner was born of a Jewish mother but had never affirmed membership in the Jewish community.

Yet in addition to questions of principle, the patrilineal descent decision must also be considered in the sociological and demographic context of American Reform Judaism. For one thing, the overwhelming majority of Reform rabbis had been practicing patrilineal descent since World War II by their de facto acceptance of children of Jewish fathers and non-Jewish mothers as Jewish. Moreover, Reform rabbis who opposed patrilineality in the name of communal unity had to face the harsh reality that the Orthodox rabbinate was unlikely to accept Reform conversions in any case. Finally, and most important, as the number of interfaith marriages increased, the numbers of children of Jewish fathers and non-Jewish mothers within Reform temples naturally increased as well.

However, objections to the patrilineal descent decision are considerable. First, its effects on Jewish unity weigh heavily. For the last two thousand years the Jewish community has acted upon a single principle of matrilineal identity. Any child of a Jewish mother, no matter how involved or uninvolved in Jewish activity, claimed equal status as a Jew under Jewish law. Orthodox and Conservative Jews agree on the continuing validity of this principle. Thus, individuals who are told by Reform rabbis that they are Jews would find their Jewishness rejected, in the absence of formal conversion, by Orthodox and Conservative Judaism alike.

To be sure, Orthodox rabbis generally rejected Reform conversions in any case. Yet the decision for patrilineality, rather than for insistence upon the conversion of children of Jewish fathers, drove a wedge between Conservative and Reform Judaism, the two largest religious movements within contemporary American Judaism. Finally, as Reform rabbi David Polish noted, the insistence that the Jewishness of children of either Jewish mothers or Jewish fathers depends upon certain Jewish "affirmations" itself threatens to divide the Reform movement over differing criteria of what such affirmations might be.[2]

Equally serious are the implications for Israel-Diaspora relations. Reform leaders, like their Conservative and even many Orthodox colleagues, oppose proposed changes in the Law of Return that would have the effect of denying Jewish status to those who convert to Judaism under non-Orthodox auspices. They argue that the state of Israel, through legislative action, ought not drive wedges between Israeli and Diaspora Jews by declaring that converts to Judaism in the Diaspora are less than full Jews. This argument, however, collapses in the face of the patrilineal descent decision.

The Reform movement itself has driven such a wedge by declaring offspring of Jewish fathers as Jewish. Should Israel now be compelled to amend the Law of Return in a more liberal direction, extending the definition of who is a Jew to children of Jewish fathers, recognized as Jews by the Reform and Reconstructionist movements in America, yet whose Jewishness is denied by more traditionalist sectors of Jewry? Significantly, the Reform movement in Israel itself recognized the implications of the decision for its claims to recognition within Israel and vociferously, yet vainly, opposed the patrilineal descent resolution.

Finally, we must weigh the consequences of the patrilineal descent decision on conversion to Judaism in the United States. In theory patrilineality may obstruct rather than encourage conversion. Intermarried couples are now offered the message that even absent the conversion of the Gentile mother the offspring of such marriages are still Jews. They may well be entitled to ask why the non-Jewish partner should convert at all. Why submit to a rigorous program of Jewish study if the children are already Jews?

Historically one motivation to conversion has been to enable children to be raised within the Jewish faith, a motivation undermined by the patrilineal descent decision. Estimates today are that there are between three thousand and four thousand converts annually—a pathetically small number in the vast sea of mixed marriage. Reform leaders once hailed conversion as a historical response to mixed marriage. Yet no sooner did Reform accept patrilineality publicly than the numbers of converts to Judaism began to decrease remarkably.

In the final analysis the patrilineal descent decision, motivated by legitimate concerns for expanding Jewish numbers and by the principle of gender equality, may not be taken out of the context of the Outreach movement and the intermarriage phenomenon. Patrilineal descent affirms the growing reality of intermarriage and says to intermarried couples that any of their children who identify with Judaism are still presumed to be Jewish, even without conversion. As laudable as such a statement may appear, not only does it undermine Jewish unity, but it also goes beyond a pragmatic accommodation of intermarriage and toward ideological legitimization.

Implications

One implication clearly has been the communal dissensus and divisiveness concerning the issue. A 1997 AJC survey discovered that American Jews agreed by 50 percent to 37 percent, that the decision had divided "the Jewish people worldwide, especially between Israel and the Diaspora."[3] Perhaps even more significantly, a 1991 survey of Reform rabbis indicated that one-third opposed the patrilineal descent decision, an additional 7 percent were unsure, and over half agreed that the decision "is one of the most divisive acts in contemporary Jewish life."[4]

A second implication relates to the degree of confusion and misunderstanding concerning the decision. First, the boundary line between Jew and Gentile in America is quite fluid—a significant challenge to a minority group's efforts to maintain its distinctiveness. Patrilineality blurs that boundary even more, because in the public eye it has been interpreted nearly universally as meaning that one is a Jew if one simply has one Jewish parent of either gender. In fact, as noted, the patrilineal decision is more restrictive—in some cases even more restrictive than the definition provided under Jewish law.

Moreover, the NJPS reports that approximately one-third of the children of mixed marriages are being raised at least partially outside the Jewish faith. Patrilineality as a criterion excludes these individuals as Gentiles rather than Jews, for the patrilineal descent decision required the exclusive raising of these children as Jews in order to qualify as Jewish. However, in the public perception, the category of patrilineal Jew encompasses anyone whose father is Jewish and whose mother is not, even if the person was raised partly in another faith.

Reform efforts to draw boundaries on this issue—for example, the decision to deny Jewish education to anyone raised partly in another faith—have not become mandatory for Reform congregations, in turn further blurring the lines and definitions of who is a Jew. For example, even Jewish communal leaders have been known to use the phrase "half Jew," a category unknown to all of Jewish heritage and to all the contemporary Jewish religious movements as well as being at odds with the terms of the patrilineal descent decision. Given this fluidity, one social scientist goes so far as to counsel simple acceptance of all models of Jewish identification irrespective of historical or communal norms.[5] Another sociologist calmly predicts that in the twenty-first century "the mixture of people who comprise synagogue-affiliated families will include ever-greater numbers of intermarried, non-Jews, half-Jews, and patrilineal Jews"—the specter of which should frighten all Jewish leaders, including the most ardent advocates of patrilineality.[6]

The Blurring of the Boundary

In theory, patrilineality has both broadened and narrowed the definition of who is a Jew. Thus, its defenders frequently note how patrilineality may be more stringent in its definition than Orthodox definitions.[7] One advocate, Rabbi Bernard Zlotowitz, even invokes, out of context, the mantle of Rabbi Joseph B. Soloveitchik, dean of American Orthodoxy, as validation for Reform practice.[8]

In reality, however, the trend toward broadening the definition and blurring the boundaries has prevailed in the implementation of the patrilineal descent decision. At a minimum the decision itself has not been understood by the Jewish public and the media, where it is generally interpreted as accepting anyone as a Jew who has one Jewish parent, rather than the far more limited notion of Jewish status resulting from both parents committing themselves to the exclusive raising of the child as a Jew. The latter criterion would in all probability sharply reduce the actual number of individuals claiming Jewish status under patrilineality. In turn, the Reform movement would then find itself in the most difficult position of explaining to large numbers of people why they cannot be accepted as Jews despite the best of intentions.

Other questions flow from the blurring of the boundaries. Should, for example, community day schools, theoretically open to all Jews, accept patrilineal Jews as students even though their status as Jews is not accepted by either the Orthodox or Conservative movements? Claims for inclusion de facto contradict the principle of educating children in an environment presumed to consist of only Jewish students. Moreover, the definitional problem of who is a Jew is compounded by contrasting standards of conversion between the religious movements as well as the presence of a critical mass (50,000 to 55,000) of self-declared converts—individuals born as Gentiles who now claim to be Jewish but without having undergone any type of conversion process.

Finally, it should be noted that the blurring of the boundaries between Jew and Gentile is far more critical for American Jewry today than at any other moment in Jewish history. Shaye Cohen offers impressive evidence that biblical Judaism acknowledged patrilineal descent and that both Josephus and Philo were unacquainted with the principle of matrilineality. Only the Mishnah introduced matrilineality as the exclusive operating principle.[9]

Nevertheless, Cohen underscores how rabbinic law strengthened the boundaries between Jew and Gentile and concludes that boundaries are even more necessary today because the contrast of Jew and Gentile ("us and them") has virtually disappeared as existential reality for American Jewry.[10] Matrilineality in effect ensured common kinship of Jewishness. At a time when common faith has virtually disappeared among Jews, surrendering common kinship marked a break with eighteen hundred years of Jewish history and severed one of the few remaining ties universal to all Jews.[11]

Nor has this split in common peoplehood been limited to Orthodoxy versus Reform, a conclusion frequently drawn in media coverage. For example, liberal and secular Israelis have often seized this issue as illustrative of the harmful effects of an Orthodox monopoly in matters of personal status. However, the actual split by patrilineality has also divided Conservative and Reform Jewry and has driven a wedge between Israeli and Diaspora criteria for Jewishness. Significantly, advocates of patrilineality predicted that Conservative Jewry would soon follow the lead of Reform.[12] To be sure, over two-thirds of Conservative synagogue members express personal acceptance of patrilineality in the case of their own families.[13] Conservative leadership, however, has rejected by increasingly larger margins any departure from the matrilineal principle as constituting rejection of halachah, departure from historical Judaism, and a splitting of the Jewish people. In effect, Conservative Judaism has opted for upholding the criteria of Judaism as law, history, and peoplehood over the potential benefits of patrilineality to individual Jews and their families. In fact, Rabbi Robert Gordis, a leading figure within Conservative Judaism, challenged Reform to abandon patrilineality on account of its divisiveness within the Jewish people.[14] The Conservative position upholds the need for boundaries. Its solution for children of Jewish fathers and non-Jewish mothers lies in the conversion of such children, a solution in fact far more acceptable to the concerns of halachists.[15]

Surprisingly, a considerable proportion of Reform rabbis agree. For example, 25 percent of Reform rabbis reported that they themselves would oppose the marriage of their sons to a patrilineally Jewish woman.[16] Jacob Petuchowski, long considered an intellectual dean of the Reform movement, opposed the decision as surrendering a universal standard of Jewish status. Whatever our theological disagreements, Petuchowski noted, Jewish distinctiveness lay in our capacity to recognize one another as Jews. A 1997 joint Simchat Torah celebration of Orthodox, Conservative, and Reform synagogues in New York City illustrated Petuchowski's fears. One of the Jewish communal leaders present praised the event as a statement that we all stood together at Sinai regardless of our differences theologically. Within the assembled crowd others commented that this statement, no matter how well intentioned, simply did not ring true once Reform had accepted patrilineal descent, creating a category of Jews whom some sectors felt did stand at Sinai and others felt simply did not.

Reform leaders acknowledge these costs but do not believe they warrant retreat from the patrilineal principle. UAHC president Rabbi Eric Yoffie, for example, respects the right of Orthodox Jews to reject patrilineal descent but opposes their invoking the coercive power of the Jewish state to endorse that definition.[17] By that logic Israel should reject *any* definition of Jewish status as disenfranchising some who claim to be Jews (for example, Jews for Jesus, Black Hebrews, and so on). Any definition will prove exclusionary to some, and codifying a definition under Israeli law essentially does mean utilizing the coercive power of the state to mandate it. It should be noted that no sentiment exists within any sector of Israeli society (including Israeli Reform Jews) for the patrilineal principle. In this respect the patrilineal descent decision has created yet another wedge between Israel and the Diaspora.

Perhaps the most damaging of the effects of patrilineality has been its impact on the image of Reform Judaism within the Jewish people. Significantly, the Denver Colorado Joint Conversion Institute collapsed in the immediate aftermath of the patrilineal descent decision. Although Reform leaders at the time blamed the collapse of the Denver plan on ultra-Orthodox intransigence, few were willing to question how the decision had in effect undermined those in the modern Orthodox rabbinate counseling greater cooperation with Reform, especially on issues of personal status. Even as liberal a thinker as Rabbi David Hartmann, who embraces Reform as part of the struggle to preserve the Jewish people and praises it for its emphasis on social ethics, condemned patrilineality as breaking the ties of Reform Judaism to Jewish peoplehood and community.[18]

The larger issue of Reform's self-image and communal perception relates also to the question of the limits of freedom and the need for discipline.[19] Is Reform Judaism so elastic as to permit in the name of inclusivity virtually anything that Jews are doing? By accepting patrilineal descent, is Reform in essence sanctioning mixed marriage even as its leaders claim continued opposition to mixed marriage as a phenomenon?

Conclusion

These questions have no easy answers. But the facts on the ground do speak eloquently. Patrilineal descent benefits individuals at the expense of issues of peoplehood and unity. In accepting patrilineal descent, Reform leadership argued for gender equality, inclusivity, and the fact that Orthodoxy would never accept them no matter what they did. The decision clearly resonated with overwhelming numbers of Reform Jews and even large numbers of Conservative Jews.

Aspects of it need to be articulated more clearly and studied more carefully for their impact and effects: the sustaining power of the patrilineal definition (for example, whether patrilineal Jews identify as Jews as adults), the impact on conversion, and so on. Even absent formal study, it may be hypothesized that, given patrilineality, those who are converting to Judaism under Reform auspices are in fact quite sincere in their conversion. In other words, patrilineality permits those who do not desire conversion to retain Gentile status while raising children as Jews. In that sense a side effect of patrilineality may well be to underscore the sincerity of those who actually do convert to Judaism. Moreover, it should be noted that the Orthodox rabbinate may rightly be challenged for its failure to provide even a modicum of support for the Conservative movement's rejection of patrilineality, let alone for Reform rabbis who similarly oppose the decision.

Clearly, however, the decision does signal placing the personal interests of individuals over the collective welfare of the Jewish people. That individuals pursue their own self-interest is understandable. For Jewish leadership to pursue personal rather than collective agendas and aspirations will result in short-term gains and satisfactions but long-term failures.

Notes

1. Charles Silberman, *A Certain People* (New York: Summit Books, 1985), 322; Meryl Hyman, *Who Is a Jew? Conversations, Not Conclusions* (Woodstock: Jewish Lights, 1998), 226.

2. David Polish, "A Dissent on Patrilineal Descent," in *Toward the Twenty-first Century: Judaism and the Jewish People in Israel and America*, ed. Ronald Konish (New York: KTAV, 1989), 230–32.

3. *1997 Annual Survey of American Jewish Opinion* (New York: American Jewish Committee, 1997), 45.

4. Samuel Heilman, *Jewish Unity and Diversity: A Survey of American Rabbis and Rabbinical Students* (New York: American Jewish Committee, 1991), 50.

5. Martha Ackelsberg, "Jewish Family Ethics in a Post-Halakhic Age," in *Imagining the Jewish Future*, ed. David Teutsch (Albany: State University of New York Press, 1992), 152–53.

6. Egon Mayer, "The Coming Refirmation in American Jewish Identity," in Teutsch, ed., *Imagining*, 181.

7. Bernard Zlotowitz, "Patrilineal Descent," in *The Jewish Condition*, ed. Aron Hirt-Manheimer (New York: UAHC Press, 1995), 259, 265.

8. Ibid., 266.

9. Shaye Cohen, *The Beginnings of Jewishness* (Berkeley: University of California Press, 1999), 266–83.

10. *Ibid.*, 343–47.

11. Hyman, *Who Is a Jew?* 73–78.

12. Silberman, *A Certain People*, 323.

13. Egon Mayer, "From an External to an Internal Agenda," in *The Americanization of the Jews*, eds. Robert Selzer and Norman Cohen (New York: New York University Press, 1995), 424; see also Jack Wertheimer, *Conservative Synagogues and Their Members* (New York: Jewish Theological Seminary, 1996), 10.

14. Jack Wertheimer, *A People Divided: Judaism and Contemporary America* (New York: Basic Books, 1993), 158.

15. Hyman, *Who Is a Jew?* 101–3. See also Jack Simcha Cohen, "Pluralism: Halakhic Obstacles and Solutions," in *Conflict or Cooperation: Papers on Jewish Unity* (New York: American Jewish Committee and CLAL, 1989), 66–67.

16. Heilman, *Jewish Unity*, 51.

17. Hyman, *Who Is a Jew?* 178.

18. Ibid., 63–64.

19. Polish, "A Dissent," 233.

12

The Importance of Outreach in Maintaining Reform's Autonomy, Diversity, and Pluralism

ERIC H. YOFFIE

In early 1949, shortly after the creation of the state of Israel, Prime Minister David Ben-Gurion received an urgent telegram from Ehud Avriel, his country's representative in Prague. Mr. Avriel complained bitterly about the hostile attitude of the Orthodox rabbinate in Czechoslovakia toward young couples in which one of the partners was not Jewish according to halachah. In light of the efforts of European Jewry to rehabilitate itself after the Holocaust, Mr. Avriel was incensed that young people wishing to identify as Jews should confront additional obstacles imposed by an unrelenting rabbinate. The rabbis, he wrote, were engaged in "clerical blackmail." This telegram gave rise to a heated debate in the Israeli cabinet, during which Mr. Ben-Gurion summarized his own views as follows: "I do not believe in a doctrine of race. If the children of these couples will grow up in a Jewish home, they will be Jews."

A Jewish revolutionary himself, Ben-Gurion had a sure grasp of those issues that required revolutionary thinking from the Jewish people. In the tumultuous postwar period, when the conditions of Jewish living were changing dramatically, this 1949 Israeli cabinet debate was the first shot fired in what would eventually become a pitched battle over definitions of Jewish identity. But Ben-Gurion had other priorities in those days, and this was not the battle that he was prepared to fight. His reaction, in fact, became a pattern; as frequently as these questions would arise over the next thirty years, one Jewish leader after another would find reason to dismiss them, arguing that the time was not yet right for a small and vulnerable people to confront matters so sensitive and potentially divisive.

Then finally, on December 2, 1978, Rabbi Alexander M. Schindler stood before the national board of the Union of American Hebrew Congregations (UAHC) in Houston, Texas, and gave an extraordinary speech that shook North American Jewry to its very core. Rabbi Schindler believed that the time for timidity had long since passed, that radically new conditions had come into being among the masses of the Jewish people, and that the Reform movement was obligated to rise to the challenge imposed upon us by this new reality.

We all know the circumstances that constituted the background of that speech. The intermarriage rate was spiraling out of control, and although every segment of North American Jewry was affected, we had no idea how to respond. In our synagogues converts to Judaism were at best grudgingly accepted; to be a convert in those days meant to carry a stigma, forged from the history and the prejudices of a once-beleaguered people. More often than not the convert confronted a disapproving family and a none-too-tolerant Jewish community. And remember that this was the reality in Reform synagogues no less than in Conservative and Orthodox ones. We are not talking here about the ancient past but of a condition that prevailed a mere quarter of a century ago.

Intermarried couples were hardly mentioned at all in those days. They, too, joined our synagogues, but exceedingly rare was the temple that both acknowledged their presence and openly confronted the issues that their membership entailed.

In the face of this reality, Rabbi Schindler articulated a clear and unequivocal message that has been the watchword of our Outreach program for two decades.

He said that we would not merely accept or tolerate the convert, we would fully and enthusiastically embrace her or him.

He said that we would not sit shivah for our children who intermarried. This did not mean that we endorsed intermarriage, but it did mean that we refused to reject the intermarried. In our community we would welcome the intermarried into our synagogues and families and homes, draw them near to us, and include them in our celebrations and observances. We would do this with the hope that the non-Jewish partners would ultimately convert to Judaism, and if not, that they would commit themselves to raising their children as Jews.

He also said that in an era of full equality of men and women, the time had come to reconsider the principle that Jewish lineage is determined solely by the maternal line, and he referred the matter to the Central Conference of American Rabbis (CCAR) for its consideration.

These points were important not because they were necessarily new. Their significance lay in the fact that they were presented as a program of action and were proclaimed in a loud voice, for all to hear and understand. Alex understood that a movement that professed to have principles but refused to state them plainly in fact had no principles at all; that caution at a certain point becomes cowardice; and that while we must never surrender to the realities of the world, we must adapt to those realities in a way that is consistent with our most deeply held values. In other words, we could no longer confine our principles to policy statements hidden away in a file or a manual. What was required of us was to delineate them clearly and publicly and then bring our actions into line with our convictions.

And so the Houston speech was followed by the establishment of the Commission on Reform Jewish Outreach, a joint effort of the UAHC and the CCAR, which worked to make real in congregational life those convictions that Alex had so passionately articulated. Permit me to say, on their behalf, that that work has been carried out by an absolutely outstanding staff and by the best lay and rabbinical leadership that our movement has to offer.

And so, after twenty years, have we been successful? We have not accomplished all that we should have, and shortly I will give you my analysis of what is yet to be done. But there is no question that the Outreach work of this movement must be seen as nothing less than a triumph. The easiest way to measure the extent of our impact is to ask what would have happened if that speech in Houston had not been given.

We all know the answer. In the absence of Outreach tens of thousands of intermarried couples who are now members of our congregations would have been forever lost to the Jewish people. In the absence of Outreach innumerable Jews who marry non-Jews would be denied any but the slimmest hope of a Jewish future. Resentment and the sting of rejection would, much too often, be the lot of those who now find a secure place in our community. There would be far fewer Jews-by-choice, and they would still be battling the ambivalent and even hostile attitudes to which they have so long been subjected. Ultimately, ours would be a weaker and more divided movement, denied the surge of energy, religious renewal, and adult learning that is a direct outgrowth of our Outreach efforts.

Of course, if Outreach had not been initiated in 1978, it would have come into being on its own. Individual rabbis and lay leaders would have insisted that doors be opened, attitudes changed, and prejudices rejected; indeed, some were already doing so in 1978. But the fact that Alex Schindler's speech gave rise to an organized, movementwide campaign, supported by both UAHC and CCAR, meant that what would have happened piecemeal over four score years happened instead in a mere two decades. It meant that we are able to acknowledge one of the most remarkable and thoroughgoing revolutions in the history of Reform Judaism and, indeed, in the history of the Jewish people.

Claims against Outreach: Tired Desperation

Outreach, as we know, has not been greeted with enthusiasm everywhere. The 1978 speech by Rabbi Schindler elicited much disagreement, both then and now. Some who attack Outreach focus on the patrilineal descent decision of the CCAR, which is presented as the primary source of disunity in the Jewish world. Others profess to affirm the principles of Outreach but claim that the limited resources of the Jewish community would be better spent elsewhere.

In my own experience, no matter the form these attacks may take, when one probes beneath the surface, they can usually be reduced to a single argument: that intermarriage is the scourge of the Jewish world; that Reform Judaism has not done enough to combat this plague; that Outreach, whatever its original intent, has had the effect of encouraging and justifying intermarriage; and that if only we would retreat from the principles of Outreach, then the Jewish people might yet be saved from destruction.

There is a certain tired desperation to these claims. That they are still invoked today elicits from us not so much anger as sadness and regret. Intermarriage, of course, is a product of modernity and not of any religious stream; the only way to stamp it out would be to return the Jews to the medieval ghetto. Furthermore, no religious grouping has found an answer to intermarriage or has escaped its reach. In the United States, where 90 percent of the Jews identify with Reform or Conservative Judaism, the intermarriage rate exceeds 50 percent; in England and France, where 90 percent of the Jews identify with Orthodox Judaism, the inter-marriage rate is higher still.

This, then, is the sobering reality: when Reform Judaism is there, intermar-riage occurs, and when Reform is not there, intermarriage still occurs, at even higher rates. It is, as Alex Schindler so frequently told us, the sting that comes with the honey of our freedom. And in the real world, Outreach is not a cause of intermarriage but a response to it—one that is necessarily partial but exceedingly effective. And we Reform Jews rightly see it as one of our proudest and most sig-nificant achievements.

Nonetheless, as self-evident as this may be, I respond to our critics with great reluctance. And that is because I believe that the fact of twenty-plus years of Outreach should be an occasion more for celebration than for interdenomina-tional debate, and also because I am convinced that the battle for Outreach is a battle that has already been won. Leaders may carp and complain, but I believe that the grassroots of North American Jewry—Reform and non-Reform—are firmly in our camp. In fact, I am convinced that on no issue is there a greater gap between leadership and membership than on the Outreach question. North American Jews of all stripes want energetic Outreach to intermarried Jews and Jews-by-choice in order to save them for the Jewish people. They want their Jewish community to undertake vigorously and without apology what we have already been doing for twenty years.

Therefore, let me say one final time to all those who ask us to change our direc-tion that there will be no retreat in the Reform movement from the principles or the practice of Outreach. Such a retreat would be unthinkable, contrary to the will of our movement and the desire of our community, and contrary as well to our most deeply held convictions.

Finally, I must note that the Conservative movement has recently taken steps to bar intermarried Jews from positions of lay and professional leadership in their congregations. The leaders of Conservative Judaism are my friends and colleagues, with whom I work closely in many areas. I understand why they have adopted their new policy. But I question its wisdom and suspect that it will be counterproductive. I fear that those who should be drawn near will instead be driven away. Under the circumstances, it is especially important that we hold firm to our convictions and that we continue to offer to North American Jews a thoughtful philosophy of outreach, firmly rooted in clear standards and serious commitment.

Theological Principles Underlying Outreach

Now that Outreach has been with us for two decades, we are understandably inclined to spend more time discussing its practical dimensions than its theoretical foundations. But it is important for us to review from time to time those theological principles upon which our Outreach efforts are based.

We begin with the premise that Judaism is a rejection of tribalism. Yes, there is a biological dimension to Judaism, but it is only one dimension of many; yes, Judaism speaks the language of fate, but it speaks as well the language of choice. A tribalistic view of Judaism would be one that exalts the prestige of blood and that roots Judaism solely in race. Such a view is utterly contrary to our tradition's most basic teachings.

But it would certainly be wrong to conclude that Outreach rests on some vague, love-the-stranger universalism. Judaism is not a universalistic religion. The opening chapters of Genesis specifically reject universal solutions to the human situation. The Tower of Babel, the eternal symbol of a world of "one people with one language," is portrayed as an act of hubris, destined to remain unfinished, no matter how much violence may be committed in its name.

Instead, the starting point for Jewish Outreach and all Jewish theology is our unique destiny as a religious people, tied to God in a covenant that we trace back to Abraham and Sarah. For thirty-five hundred years we have been taught to follow Abraham's example and to "keep the way of the Eternal, doing what is right and just." Developing the nuances of meaning and obligation that flow from this covenant is the ongoing task of the Jews: it guides us in a world that is redeemable but not yet redeemed. We have paid a heavy price for our religious destiny, but we have also been eternally blessed by our conviction that this is the reason for our survival. We know that God has established this covenant with us and has sustained us so that we may offer a taste of goodness and compassion to a despairing humanity.

In short, Outreach begins not with an act of inclusion per se but rather with an act of self-definition. We begin with an affirmation of our particularism, of our apartness, of our unique destiny. This may seem anomalous, but of course it is not. The first step of Outreach—and the single most important step—is to have a clear sense of who we are and of the boundary that exists between us as Reform Jews and the society around us.

If we have learned anything at all after twenty years, it is this: you do not draw people in by erasing boundaries and eliminating distinctions. If there are no clearly defined distinctions between our Jewish values and the values of the world around us, then what reason would serious people—Jews or non-Jews—have to cast their fate with ours?

Intermarried couples are not attracted to us by minimalism or watered-down Judaism. They are attracted by compelling ethical teachings, by ritual experiences rich in meaning, by the mystery of Shabbat, and by the possibility of religious commandment.

The Jews most successful at the work of Outreach are those who know who they are, who communicate the power and beauty of their heritage, and who model proud and assertive religious behavior. Jews who are confused about who they are and what their movement stands for are utterly incapable of opening for others the door to our Jewish world.

The Obligations of an Am Segulah

Once we recognize that we are an *am segulah,* a nation of special destiny that lives in God's presence, the nature of our obligations begins to take form. We know that ever since Sinai, all Jews carry within themselves a fragment of the Shechinah and are linked in a bond of shared responsibility to the Jewish people. It is therefore absolutely unthinkable that we would ever turn our backs on the alienated, the unaffiliated, or the intermarried, or anyone else who has drifted to the margins of our community.

And so for the last twenty years we have been busy building pathways to their hearts. Our successes have been considerable. At the same time, I surely would not suggest that we can in any way be satisfied. To those who still say that there is too much Outreach, I would respond that that there is not nearly enough.

The problem is not so much what we do within the four walls of our synagogues; here we have every reason for pride in our accomplishments. The problem is what we do *not* do *outside* the walls of the synagogue.

An example: in most major Jewish communities, a call is made each year to every Jewish family, even if it is not affiliated with any Jewish institution, to solicit a contribution to United Jewish Appeal. Many of us have participated in Super Sunday phone-a-thons, as we should. But tell me: shouldn't a call also be made every year to discuss with that family Jewish education for their children? Shouldn't a call be made every year to extend an invitation for Shabbat dinner or a holiday celebration? And how many members of our synagogues have hosted even a single unaffiliated or uninvolved individual or family—intermarried or otherwise—for a Shabbat meal during the past year? If we can knock on doors asking for money, we can knock on doors asking for Jewish commitment. If we can show concern for their charitable dollars, we can show concern for their Jewish souls. If it is our intention to rally the spirits of Jews everywhere and to draw the intermarried and the disaffected to our banner, then we must—through our own religious fervor and abiding faith—demonstrate to them that we truly care.

And again, let's be utterly frank: too often, those least able to carry Judaism's compelling message are those who are the most visible on the front lines of this battle.

In 1999, full-page ads placed by a Habad organization appeared in the *New York Times* and in other secular and Jewish publications. These ads contained a picture of the late Lubavitcher rebbe and implied that he was the Mashiach—the Messiah—and is still alive. It is a dangerous and superstition-filled message, an affront to our most sacred principles, and a true *hillul ha-Shem*—desecration of the divine name. How does a movement built on this extraordinary theological presumption maintain such prominence in the Jewish world?

You know the answer, as do I: Habad compensates for its theological primitivism by an outreach campaign that, in some respects, puts the rest of the Jewish world to shame. It is Habad that finds Jews on campus and in out-of-the-way places; that instructs them in the lighting of Shabbat candles and in all manner of Jewish rituals; that reaches out to them with classes, audiotapes, and satellite television. Habad, it seems, is everywhere. Many, many Jews will tell you that a Habad rabbi was the first one to care, to really care, about their spiritual lives.

The irony, of course, is that ours is a philosophy of Judaism that is uniquely well suited to current realities. It bridges the gap between modernity and tradition, and it requires no surrender of critical faculties or ethical sensibilities. Our Judaism, I firmly believe—a doing, dreaming, and choosing Judaism—is the Judaism most likely and best able to draw Jews in.

Yet the passion and deep commitment to spread our message, experienced in full measure by the members of our Outreach commissions, are not yet the possession of our movement at large. Yes, there is broad sympathy for our cause. But the activism that we have generated in our own spiritual homes we have yet to replicate on a grand scale in the community at large.

And so I turn to the Reform leadership and ask for guidance and advice. How can we kindle among the rabbinate as a whole a sense of *shelichut*—mission—to the Outreach cause? How can we promote among our laity a sense of *mesirut nefesh*—self-sacrifice and devotion—to the challenges that lie ahead?

It is our intention to take our case to the public square and to argue for every Jewish soul, persuade every Jewish mind, entice every Jewish heart. And for that we must widen the ranks of those who share our concern for the transformation and spiritual awakening of each and every Jew.

The Place of the Intermarried Couple in the Reform Synagogue

I would like now to touch on the place of the intermarried couple in the Reform synagogue. I return to this topic because I see our work with the intermarried as our most distinctive achievement. We have been especially aggressive in our efforts to make the intermarried feel at home in our congregations, and we alone in the Jewish world have developed a strategy to envelop them in a network of Jewish learning and support. At the same time we have not been afraid to acknowledge that some issues remain unresolved.

When a Jew marries a non-Jew and with our encouragement joins a synagogue, how is the non-Jewish partner to be seen?

In the best of circumstances the non-Jewish partner will see himself or herself and will be seen by temple members as having the status of a *ger toshav*. In the Bible, the *ger toshav* is the stranger who lives among Jews. This individual has not adopted the Jewish faith but has acquired Jewish customs, values, and friends. He or she adjusts to the Jewish surroundings and in some measure even assimilates into them. Portrayed in the most positive manner imaginable by the biblical text, he or she is granted exceptional privileges and protection by biblical law. In fact, the *ger toshav* is someone so special, so deserving of compassion and love, that at a later time the term *ger* comes to mean a convert to Judaism. This, however, was not its original meaning. The biblical *ger toshav* is a stranger but at the same time as close as one could come to being an Israelite without a formal change of status.

Not every non-Jewish spouse fits this category, of course, but our movement operates on the assumption that this is the situation that either does exist or potentially might exist. We do not assume hostility or resentment or indifference on the part of the non-Jewish partner; on the contrary, we assume that the non-Jew who has married a Jew and then joined a synagogue is positively inclined toward identification with our people and tradition. More often than not this is the case, and by conveying our unequivocal acceptance and our enthusiastic welcome, more often than not the non-Jewish spouse comes to see himself or herself as a *ger toshav*, sharing the values of Judaism and participating in the rituals and the customs of our community.

But the first question that arises is whether we should urge the non-Jewish spouse to convert to Judaism. And if so, how and when?

In this instance, too, Alex Schindler gave us vitally important guidance and direction. Alex told us that we need to ask. We must not forget to ask.

And he was right, because the synagogue is not a neutral institution. It is unequivocally value-laden. It admits, without apology, its commitment to building a vibrant religious life for the Jewish people. It wants families to function as Jewish families, and while intermarried families can do so in some measure, it welcomes the decision of an intermarried family to become a fully Jewish family, with two adult Jewish partners. To be sure, Judaism does not denigrate those who find religious truth elsewhere; the existence of our covenant does not deny the existence of other covenants or other truths. Still, our synagogues emphasize the beauty and grandeur of the ancient and awe-inspiring faith known as Judaism, and we joyfully extend membership in our covenantal community to all who are prepared to accept the responsibilities that it entails. And by the way, most non-Jews who are part of synagogue life *expect* that we will ask them to convert. They come from a background where asking for this kind of commitment is natural and normal, and they are more than a little perplexed when we fail to do so.

Special sensitivities are certainly required. We can ask but should not pressure. We can encourage but should not insist. If someone expresses unwillingness, we must respect that; if someone says, "I'm not ready," we must listen. If we pursue conversion with a heavy hand, the result could be to generate anger and resentment.

But none of this is a reason for inaction. And the fact is that we usually do not ask. My conversations with both rabbis and lay leaders lead me to believe that in most instances we do not encourage conversion by non-Jewish spouses in our synagogues. Perhaps this bespeaks a natural reluctance to do what we fear will give rise to an awkward or uncomfortable situation. Or perhaps we have been so successful in making non-Jews feel comfortable in our congregations that we have inadvertently sent the message that we neither want nor expect conversion. But whatever the reason, alongside our lengthy list of Outreach successes, this must be counted at least a partial failure.

I would note as an aside that Rabbi Schindler in his Houston speech proposed that we establish an Outreach program specifically aimed at the unchurched—at seekers after truth who were born into other religious traditions and who are not contemplating marriage with a Jew. His call for an openly proselytizing Judaism was enormously courageous, and I felt, then and now, that in principle he was absolutely right. But two decades later it seems to me that this still remains a program for the future, because the logical place to focus our efforts today is on the tens of thousands of non-Jews who are already members of our synagogues. They are the population most likely to share our aspirations and consider formal conversion.

In this respect I propose some questions about how we as a movement might help them along. What must rabbis do? What must lay leaders do? Are our synagogues sending the right message? Are we offering significant public recognition to non-Jewish spouses who become Jews, as a means of encouraging them and others? Twenty years into the Outreach era, this is one area of our work that cries out for new ways of thinking.

Limitations on the Participation of Non-Jewish Spouses

The second major issue that arises from the presence of intermarried couples in our synagogues is the extent to which we must impose limitations on the participation of the non-Jewish spouse in the governance and ritual life of our congregations. Of course, our primary goal is to include and embrace, but we all understand that if the individual concerned has not converted, there are certain rituals that he cannot participate in and certain decisions that she cannot make. How do we determine where these lines are to be drawn?

It is my belief that by and large we have dealt with this matter in a forthright and responsible way, despite the inevitable differences of opinion that one would expect in our large and diverse movement.

I would suggest that the approach of Reform Jewish Outreach to the question of standards has been guided by four major principles.

1. The first is that there must be standards and boundaries, and they must be defined with reasonable clarity and precision. Healthy individuals define standards for themselves and, as I have already indicated, so do healthy religious traditions. It is by knowing who you are and how you define yourself that you avoid a slide into confusion, minimalism, or syncretism. One of Outreach's most significant accomplishments—one that we must not underestimate—is that it has encouraged us to do what we should be doing anyway: drawing the lines that define our identity as Reform Jews.

2. The second principle is that in most instances we have wisely left the drawing of lines to the local synagogue. Given Reform Judaism's tradition of autonomy, diversity, and pluralism, we have recognized that ongoing attempts by the Outreach commission or the national movement to dictate standards would be unwise. To be sure, we have encouraged our synagogues to develop standards and we have suggested a process for them to follow, but we understand that most decisions about which committee a non-Jew can sit on or what part he or she can take in a religious service are best made on the community level.

At the same time we have also recognized that in some instances a national role is appropriate, particularly in those cases where congregational leadership has asked for direction. When temple educators called for a national policy on the issue of children in religious school who were being educated simultaneously in church schools, the Outreach commission drafted a resolution strongly discouraging that practice. The resolution was then brought to our national biennial, where it was discussed and adopted. Such a resolution can only be advisory, of course, but it was nonetheless influential, precisely because it carried the authority of the biennial assembly. And it demonstrated that when it is important that a line be drawn, the Outreach commission and the biennial assembly are prepared to draw it.

3. The third principle is that setting standards means that someone will eventually rub up against those standards, and that no matter how careful and sensitive we are in drawing them, there is no escaping a certain measure of unhappiness on the part of those who will be hurt and offended. This is self-evident, I know, but it is important to state, because some Reform Jews still find it difficult to acknowledge that any limitation is consistent with Reform belief. I travel to congregations throughout North America, and the Outreach questions that I am most frequently asked relate to some standard set by a congregation or a rabbi that the questioner finds hurtful or offensive. Mistaking me for a higher ecclesiastical authority, the person involved usually pleads with me to set aside the newly established boundary.

   The best answer, as you know, is that setting standards is the surest way to avoid the confusion and misunderstanding that can alienate and offend. Still, there will always be those who will take exception and who will claim, without precisely saying so, that our absolute priority must always be maintaining family harmony and avoiding hurt and rejection. But we have always dismissed such claims because we know that some religious actions and beliefs are simply not consistent with the Judaism that we practice. And a lowest-common-denominator or no-one-must-ever-be-hurt Judaism is not and has never been what Outreach is about.

4. The fourth principle, and the most important, is that as essential as boundaries are, the power of our Outreach work derives from our refusal to be obsessed with them. What distinguishes us from others and accounts for our success is that we have put forth a new paradigm: we emphatically affirm the necessity of standards but do not spend inordinate amounts of time and energy trying to define them with microscopic precision. We believe in boundaries, but we have faith that the average Jew in the average congregation will do a pretty good job of figuring out where they are. We know that

lines must be drawn, but we know, too, that our primary task is to infuse Jewish life with the kind of vibrant Jewish experiences that will create lifelong Jewish commitment.

If the need for boundaries is our primary message and if confronting others with endless demands is the thrust of our program, then we are lost and Judaism is doomed. Instead, we have chosen another path: to expose those on the fringes to synagogues that are genuine centers of learning and holiness, to Jewish homes that are filled with love and joy, to Jewish life rooted in social justice and individual righteousness—in short, to a community that is so nurturing and appealing that no one will stay away.

Boundaries? Absolutely. But a boundary by definition is a barrier, and as Leonard Fein, director of social action at the UAHC, has reminded us, while barriers have their place, bridges are always more important.

Practical Tasks That Lie Ahead

I would like to conclude with a few thoughts on the practical tasks that lie ahead of us.

The Commission on Reform Jewish Outreach and the Commission on Synagogue Affiliation engage in a multiplicity of important programs. Most are familiar with them, and I will not review them now. Each one is valuable and deserves our support.

If we confront questions about our practical work, we do so as a direct result of our successes. Congregational Outreach committees that were created to welcome Jews-by-choice, integrate the intermarried, and set the parameters of non-Jewish participation in the synagogue now often find that there is less urgency to the tasks in which they have long been engaged. And the reason, of course, is that many congregations have already adopted policies and adjusted their cultures in order to respond to the issues that we have raised. More than one rabbi has told me that she or he woke up one day to discover that there was no longer a need for an Outreach committee—not because of lack of interest but because the committee members had become so involved in mainstream congregational activities that they felt less need for and less investment in Outreach work.

It is also true that the line between Outreach programs and other programs has become hopelessly blurred. Taste of Judaism, one of the proudest accomplishments of our Outreach commission, reaches many intermarried couples, but it also reaches non-Jews and unaffiliated Jews in roughly equal proportions. Is it a program designed to reach out or one designed to reach in to those already engaged in synagogue life? Indeed, there is more than a little irony in the fact that those who have decried Outreach because it exists at the expense of inreaching programs have failed to notice that many of the Jewish community's strongest educational programs are administered by our Outreach network and serve born Jews no less than intermarried Jews. Our own Commission on Synagogue Affiliation, which operates under Outreach auspices, runs superb membership-retention programs that defy classification and could easily be claimed under either an Outreach or an inreach umbrella.

What conclusion do we draw from this somewhat confusing picture? Surely we should resist any suggestion that our Outreach efforts are no longer necessary. Despite our accomplishments, we cannot take for granted the acceptance and integration of Jews-by-choice and intermarried couples into our synagogues. The changes that we have witnessed are indeed immensely encouraging, but the Outreach revolution is so radically new that it would be a mistake to become complacent. We have many more years of work to do before we can declare victory for our principles of inclusion. At the same time the fact that Outreach and inreach efforts so frequently converge should serve to strengthen our claim on our community's resources and attention.

But we are also in need of some creative thinking and new initiatives. I have already suggested a campaign to encourage non-Jewish spouses in our congregations to formally embrace Judaism. I feel as well that we should build on our experience with Taste of Judaism to create courses that target those populations most likely to be in search of Jewish meaning and connection. For example, young couples thinking about having children or already expecting children are very often struggling with religious questions in a serious way for the first time. Using the Taste of Judaism model, we should be offering in major cities throughout North America courses on birth, naming, and child rearing in the Jewish tradition. Such courses, if offered at no cost to the participants, would draw large numbers of intermarried and unaffiliated Jews at precisely the time when they are most open to Jewish education and direction.

There are also opportunities currently available to us that we have yet to explore. Several hundred Reform synagogues currently run nursery school programs. Some have strong Jewish content and some do not; some offer special assistance to intermarried couples and some do not; some promote synagogue membership in a sophisticated way and some do not. Our movement, in the meantime, has nothing to offer these schools. We provide no curricular assistance, no teacher training, no forum for the exchange of ideas and problems. Incredibly, we have ignored an institution that in many ways is best positioned to serve the young intermarried and unaffiliated population. I have asked the UAHC's Budget Committee to allocate money for staff so that we can begin to remedy the situation, and I hope that it will agree. If it does, we will need our Commissions on Outreach and Synagogue Affiliation to work with us and our congregations to offer the strongest possible Jewish programs to this generation of young people.

And finally, twenty years is barely a speck in the collective history of the Jewish people, but in our individual lifetimes it is a long time indeed. It is long enough for Outreach to become fully institutionalized and totally respectable, the domain of experts and specialists—in short, the outstanding success that I have described. But special care is required. We must be very careful not to lose the sense of excitement that followed Alex Schindler's speech in 1978 and the sense of personal commitment and involvement that so many of us felt then.

Maimonides says that if you love God, then you will want to share that feeling with others. Our obligation as Reform Jews and as servants of God is to reach out to unaffiliated and disenfranchised Jews, to intermarried couples, and to all those on the margins and to communicate to them the power and the beauty of our Jewish heritage. And even though it is often easier to speak out on behalf of a principle than it is to impact the life of a single individual or family, Outreach is still, more than anything else, something that is done by Reform Jews who care and who do this work one on one: the work of extending our hands, teaching Torah, and sharing with others a joyous holiday celebration. It is lighting a fire ourselves under a Jew or a potential Jew and being energized again and again by the response. As long as we do not lose that passion and personal commitment, Outreach will go from strength to strength.

Facing the Future with Optimism

And so we face the future filled with optimism and determination. Abraham Joshua Heschel, the great Jewish thinker, pointed out in a different context that one of the tragic failures of ancient Judaism was the indifference of our people to the ten tribes of Israel, who were taken away into exile after the Northern Kingdom was destroyed. Uncared for, unattended to, overlooked, and abandoned, those tribes were consigned to oblivion, and in the end they vanished. We are here because of our determination—our absolute determination—that we will not be part of another such failure, another dereliction of duty.

Will we attract enormous numbers of intermarried couples and unaffiliated Jews? We cannot know for certain. But even if we draw in only 20 percent of those on the periphery, we will have added upward of half a million Jews to the ranks of the Jewishly committed.

And in any case, our ultimate motivation runs deeper, relating not to numbers but to faith. We do the work that we do and bring our message to the community—to the affiliated and unaffiliated alike, to the intermarried and the Jew-by-choice—because we are confident that being a Reform Jew deepens one's love of God, promotes the practice of Torah, and strengthens our shared destiny as a holy people.

13

Why I Officiate at Mixed-Marriage Wedding Ceremonies

HILLEL COHN

The position of a rabbi who has chosen to officiate at mixed-marriage ceremonies must be one of explaining why he or she chooses to depart from the traditional position as well as to dissent from the two operative resolutions of our rabbinic conference, the one passed in 1909 and the one adopted in 1973.

While I could simply invoke the argument of personal autonomy, that is, the right of each rabbi to determine his or her own practices while always being aware of and guided by the decisions of the Central Conference of American Rabbis (CCAR) and the actions of the other institutions of our Reform movement (although not necessarily governed by them), there are a number of compelling reasons why I choose to officiate at intermarriage ceremonies. I cannot say that the reasons I give are those given by my colleagues who have similarly decided to officiate at intermarriage ceremonies, nor are they the only reasons. They are the reasons that dictate *my* decision, and so this is a personal statement.

Yet no statement that I as a rabbi make is totally personal, something of individual whim. It is guided primarily by the act that for me took place in 1963 when Dr. Glueck ordained me as a rabbi in Israel. When I look at my *semichah* (rabbinical ordination), I am constantly reminded that my ordination as a rabbi "authorized and licensed" me to "perform all rabbinical functions in the name of God and Israel." My decisions as a rabbi are, for me, guided by that mandate.

All of the years of my rabbinate have been spent serving the same congrega-

---

This essay is based on a talk given to the Board of Trustees of the Union of American Hebrew Congregations, December 1996, in Los Angeles.

tion and community. For the first seven years I did not officiate at mixed marriages. Over those years I began to question the wisdom of my position and ultimately concluded that the reasons I gave for not officiating were outweighed by
the reasons for officiating. And so in 1970 or 1971 I informed my congregation
of my decision to officiate at mixed-marriage ceremonies. Over more than three
decades I have met with hundreds of couples, one of whom was not Jewish. Many
have communicated with me and expressed their appreciation for the insights
they gained from our discussions and from the values that were imparted to them
through the symbols and rites of a Jewish marriage ceremony. The Jewish partners of those mixed marriages have in the great majority of those cases not only
maintained their ties with the Jewish people but have strengthened those bonds,
a strength expressed in the creation of homes where children are being raised as
proud and participating Jews. I wish I had saved all of the notes I have received
over the years. But my memory has kept all of those affectionate and loving
expressions of appreciation, the looks exchanged between Jewish brides or
grooms and their parents or other loved ones that clearly revealed their comfort
and satisfaction in having their marriage ceremony be a Jewish ceremony.

An Unscientific Review

Recently I conducted a very informal and unscientific review of the last one hundred marriages at which I officiated as of December 1996.

In twenty-eight of those one hundred marriages both parties were born and
raised as Jews. In nine of those one hundred marriages one partner was not born
and raised a Jew but converted to Judaism prior to the marriage. In four cases the
one partner not born Jewish converted subsequent to the marriage. Out of those
twenty-eight marriages ten couples would not be having children. Sixty of those
one hundred marriages involved a native Jew and a non-Jew. My review shows
that in the last twenty-eight of these marriages the children were certainly to be
raised as Jews and the non-Jewish partner was essentially not practicing his or
her faith yet was not of a mind to convert. In twenty of those sixty marriages I do
not know for certain how the children are being raised, although I suspect that
the majority are not raising their children in any non-Jewish faith, I do not know
for certain that they are being raised as Jews. In twelve of those sixty marriages
there was no expectation of having children.

Some interesting things have emerged from this review. First, the overriding
concern with how children of a mixed marriage will be raised is not necessarily
as significant an issue as one would think. A number of those couples are beyond
child-rearing age or for some other reason would not be having children.

I know that twenty-eight of those mixed couples certainly will have homes
that express Jewish identity, with children being raised as Jews. The expression
of that identity will obviously take many forms, just as it does in homes where

both husband and wife are Jewish. The non-Jewish partner in these twenty-eight cases is basically a nonpracticing Christian who will not convert to Judaism but who will respect and support the Jewish partner. A few years ago I devised a modified form of a *ketuvah* for just such occasions. It contains a statement that the Jewish partner "reaffirms a strong commitment to the Jewish people" and the non-Jewish partner is "intent on respecting and supporting" the Jewish partner in that commitment.

One such wedding especially sticks out in my memory. The bride was a product of our congregation, a daughter of a past president. She was president of our youth group and a camper at Camp Swig as well as a National Federation of Temple Youth board member. She went on to enroll at Hebrew Union College and received her degrees in education and Jewish communal service. Her first marriage, to a Jew, ended in divorce. I officiated at her second marriage, to a brilliant man who is not converting but is totally committed to supporting a Jewish home. He is not converting because he personally continues to find meaning in his Christian faith, though he does not attend church. That faith and his family heritage are important loyalties. This couple now has a son, and the child is being fully raised as a Jew. They are members of a synagogue. Their Jewish marriage ceremony remains for them a significant moment. It was a moment that brought greater strength to our Jewish people.

In the four weddings where the non-Jewish partner at the time of the marriage ceremony converted later perhaps the most important reason was my own feeling that in some cases it would be best to defer conversion until later so that marriage not be the reason for conversion. At the time of the ceremony these were, by definition, mixed marriages.

In the twenty marriages where I do not know for certain what will be, I am inclined to believe that as a result of our counseling and as a natural outgrowth of the ceremony there will be a continuation of Jewish loyalty and identity by the Jewish partner, and that if there are children, they most likely will be raised as Jews but certainly will not be raised as Christians. Most likely they will be taught about Judaism and Christianity, and the chance for their opting for a full Jewish commitment is certainly good. That the door is opened wide for that development is due, in large part, to my readiness to officiate at a Jewish ceremony. This group, for better or worse, falls into the same category as couples where both partners are Jewish, but their Jewishness is rather marginal.

Departing from Tradition

Now, why depart from the traditional stand? It is not, I hope you understand, an isolated departure. As a Reform Jew, I have consciously departed from a number of Jewish traditions. In all cases I have done so with what I believe are conscientiousness and responsibility. These departures are not made for convenience or for approval. They are made as the result of soul searching. One such example is the ceremony of Pidyon ha-Ben, the Redemption of the Firstborn. It is based on the traditional division of Jews as Priests, Levites, and Israelites, something I feel is antithetical to the democratic impulse in Jewish thought and experience. That reform Judaism abandoned that act long ago made sense. Since we are focusing attention on a life-cycle ceremony, I could add to the list of such departures our abandonment of the requirement for a get and our abandonment of the strictures related to *taharat hamishpacha,* family purity. And I could also add our embracing of the nontraditionally accepted bat mitzvah, which includes an aliyah, and of course the ordination of women as rabbis.

There are instances when I have consciously dissented from a standard set down by the Central Conference of American Rabbis. Those standards represent the majority's will but are not entirely binding on each and every member of the CCAR. An example of this is the work done in the area of responsa over the years by some of the most scholarly members of the rabbinate. I find their decisions to be interesting but not necessarily binding. Autonomy of the rabbinate is indispensable. Responsible and conscientious exercise of that autonomy is equally as indispensable. Still another example is the prevailing use of the prayer books published by the CCAR but which some congregations, my own included, do not use.

The Role of Jewish Law

It seems to me that the first consideration of a rabbi in determining whether or not to officiate at mixed-marriage ceremonies ought to be the role that Jewish law plays in the matter. Clearly Jewish law does not allow for a Jewish marriage ceremony to be conducted unless both parties to the marriage are Jews. Beyond that the law goes on to qualify who can be married. A descendant of the *kohanim* cannot marry a divorced person or one who was descended from an illegal marriage of a *kohen.* Later expansion of that included the proselyte as well. However, the rabbinical conference held in Philadelphia in 1869 determined that those qualifying laws had lost "all significance and are no longer to be respected." I believe that all reform rabbis, with no exception, agree that such laws should not be imposed and therefore the restrictions pose no impediment to a marriage. Similarly, the law requiring that both parties to a marriage be Jewish has, for some of us, lost significance and need no longer be binding.

Jewish law does accept the validity of the marriage of a Jew and a non-Jew even though it obviously discourages such unions. But were one to invoke halachah, Jewish law, in this matter, then one must invoke it in other matters as well. For we who are liberal Jews, halachah is *not* binding. We say that as a statement of neither pride nor guilt. Rather, it is a defining statement of who we are, of our liberality. We turn to Jewish law for guidance but not governance. As

Mordecai Kaplan, founder of the Reconstructionist movement, put it so well, "We look to the past for a vote, but do not empower it to give us a veto." It surprises me, then, to see Reform rabbis invoke halachah to justify their stance with regard to not performing mixed marriages. I cannot in good conscience invoke halachah in one area if I am not prepared to invoke it fully.

I do not, for example, invoke the halachah when determining the order of aliyot in my congregation, with the *kohen* and the Levite receiving the first two aliyot. I do not invoke it in my view of gays and lesbians. I do not invoke it in my determination that men and women may be seated side by side in the synagogue, nor in hundreds of other practices. Though I have a great respect and appreciation for custom and tradition, I am equally comfortable in departing from it, reshaping it, or creating new customs or practices.

The words of the Jewish marriage ceremony need not be taken literally any more so than many other words we use in prayer. We often will sing "*Vezot ha-Torah asher sam Moshe,*" "This is the Torah which Moses placed before the children of Israel," yet we do not take those words literally, as we accept a more scholarly understanding of how the Torah came into being. The words of the blessings we teach every child to chant before the haftarah speak of the words that came from Moses, the servant of God, the people of Israel, God's people, and the prophets of truth and righteousness, yet we find that not each and every word of the prophets continues to ring out in absolute truth for all of us. Certainly the formula of the Kol Nidre is taken less than literally, and the words of the Unetane Tokef, speaking of the decree being written on Rosh Hashanah and sealed on Yom Kippur, is taken somewhat less than literally by most of us. Why have the words of the marriage ceremony become so sacrosanct that they are not also open to nonliteral meaning? *K'dat Moshe v'Yisrael* for us means not the exact laws of Moses and the people of Israel but the spirit of the tradition, which is one of love and devotion between husband and wife.

Guiding Principles

What, then, guides me as a Reform rabbi in determining whether to officiate or not officiate at a mixed marriage?

First is the relationship of the act to the survival of the Jewish people. The matter of concern for Jewish survival is *not* the same as acceptability to the wider Jewish community. Long ago I ceased worrying about whether what I do as a Jew is acceptable to the wider community. Those of the Orthodox and Conservative movements who want to reject our legitimacy as Reform Jews find plenty of grounds on which to do that, much to our chagrin. Will a rabbi's officiating at an intermarriage provide the non-Reformer with grounds on which to condemn us? Yes. But so will lots of other things we do for good reason and based on sound principle, such as our openness to gays and lesbians, our acceptance of patrilineality, our rejection of the obligation for a get to be issued prior to remarriage, our burial of cremated remains in our cemeteries, our encouragement of our people to be organ donors, and others.

I have found that Jewish strength and solidarity might even be *better* served by performing the mixed-marriage ceremony than by refusing to perform it. I would point to many leaders of my synagogue and other synagogues, including some people who sit on national boards of our Reform institutions, who are involved in Jewish life and the synagogue because a rabbi did not turn them away at the time of their marriage but enabled them to be married with the symbols and words of the Jewish marriage ceremony even though one partner in the marriage was not a Jew.

I should also add that my agreeing to officiate at an intermarriage in no way undermines my encouragement that Jews marry Jews. One often hears the objection that we cannot effectively argue for inmarriage while performing intermarriages. That is not so. There are many other settings in which we can and do articulate our hope and desire that Jews marry Jews and give substantial reasons for that being a good thing to do. But I have yet to be convinced that when it comes to falling in love, people ask, "Is this what my rabbi approves of?"

In my counseling sessions prior to a marriage I have opportunities to help a couple explore their religious views on a level that I know is deeper and more comprehensive than they have experienced before. The questions I ask and the manner in which I steer the discussion are important. Often the non-Jew is surprised at what the Jew believes or does not believe and vice versa. Sometimes I suggest that there is too much of significance separating them to hold out the prospects of a good marriage. Those counseling sessions would not be possible if a caller is told, "The rabbi doesn't officiate at such marriages." And they are certainly not possible when we direct them to well-intentioned civic officials, judges, or others whose role is simply to perform the rite and who are not equipped by training or position to provide such counseling.

I know that some of my colleagues insist that while they do not officiate, they always convey to the couple that they are ready to receive them in the synagogue and that they are fully and warmly welcomed. But the rabbi saying, "I'd like to talk to you and the synagogue welcomes you but your marriage is not one at which I would officiate because it is against Jewish law or tradition" is taken as a double message. There are members of my congregation who are members precisely because they felt that a rabbi in another synagogue who does not officiate was giving them the message that their marriage was not accepted. I find that my officiating gives me an opportunity to expose the non-Jew and his or her family to the values, symbols, and words of the Jewish marriage ceremony, which enhances an appreciation of Judaism and thus contributes to the positive survival of the Jewish people.

I have also found, as have many of my colleagues, that when I agree to officiate at an intermarriage, I open the door to further exploration of Judaism by the non-Jew that might ultimately lead to his or her choosing to be Jewish and formalizing that choice in conversion or functioning as a de facto Jew. The conversions that take place *after* marriage rather than as a prerequisite for a Jewish ceremony are often done with greater sincerity than the other. And when the conversion does not take place, the support by the non-Jew of the intent of the Jewish partner to practice Judaism and the determination to raise children as Jews, which is often made, are all things that make for Jewish survival.

A second consideration is one that I believe flows most deeply from the mainstream of Jewish tradition. If it is not the letter of Torah, it is most surely the spirit of Torah as we understand it. Thus I ask how the decision of a rabbi to officiate or not officiate relates to the human situation. It has never been the Jewish way to ignore the human situation, and it is most certainly not the liberal Jewish way. We are universalists, not particularists. The principle operative in the tradition and the law concerning the right to abrogate any and all commandments for the preservation of life is one that exemplifies that position. In the matter of mixed marriage we are dealing first and foremost with human beings, people with genuine feelings. We are not dealing with abstract concepts. These couples and their families have feelings. Not only do they feel love for each other, they feel they want to do right by their families, and this is found to a higher degree among the Jewish partners, who for the most part have been nurtured more passionately on the importance of family.

By the same token I think we need to be sensitive to the non-Jewish bride or groom who may be rather indifferent to Christianity but who out of love and respect for her or his parents just cannot convert to Judaism. It is time we realized that non-Jewish parents experience as much pain and discomfort when their child embraces Judaism as would Jewish parents whose child might choose to be a Christian. I have come to believe that the human situation is better served by my willingness to officiate. I use that as a guideline for my decisions in many other life-cycle matters. Why not in this matter? I think of this as a mitzvah. A mitzvah is not restricted to the 613 commandments. It is a life-affirming and humanly elevating act. I think it was a mitzvah that led me not long ago to participate in a funeral mass at an Episcopal church for a dear friend and community leader. I think it is a mitzvah to be engaged in a variety of interfaith activities. I think it is a mitzvah to hug a kid. Mitzvot come in many shapes and forms.

A third consideration is whether there is a consequence of the act that has a favorable outcome for the Jewish individuals involved. While I certainly have regard for all people, I readily admit to a high degree of Jewish chauvinism. I became a rabbi especially to serve Jews and Judaism. I have found that my decision to officiate at an interfaith marriage enables a Jew and his or her family to gain a new or renewed appreciation of the role of Judaism in their lives and enables them to avoid the pain and discomfort of participating in either a civil or church ceremony at such a significant moment in the life of their family.

These are important factors that I considered when I decided to officiate at intermarriages. Whenever I meet with an interfaith couple, I make clear to them that in the Reform rabbinate there are rabbis who will officiate and rabbis who will not, and both are right. I convey to them the importance of freedom and autonomy in Reform in general and in the Reform rabbinate in particular. I hope that I always convey to them the respect I have for my colleagues who hold a position different from mine. I am not always sure that my colleagues reciprocate with equal respect.

Finally, while it is certainly not a major consideration, I must also mention that I will often agree to officiate so that the couple will be spared from falling into the clutches of those few colleagues who have made a business out of officiating at mixed marriages. I am distressed by their exorbitant and somewhat extortionary fees and the absence of counseling that I hear of.

In summary, some thirty years after I decided to officiate at mixed marriages, I find no reason to change that view. In fact, I feel more convinced than I did then about the correctness of that position for me.

Gender

14

A Worthier Place

Women, Reform Judaism, and the Presidents of Hebrew Union College

KARLA GOLDMAN

Every March the Hebrew Union College–Jewish Institute of Religion (HUC-JIR) observes Founders' Day, celebrating the founding presidents of the two institutes for rabbinical study that eventually merged to form the American Reform movement's present-day College-Institute. On Founders' Day the school's early leaders are remembered, and those rabbis who graduated from the College-Institute twenty-five years earlier are awarded honorary doctoral degrees in recognition of their years of service as rabbis. Until March 12, 1997, every rabbinical honoree at the Founders' Day celebrations held at the various branches of the College-Institute in Cincinnati, New York, and Los Angeles had been a man. But that particular March day was a special one, as it marked the first time at one of these occasions that a woman would be honored for having had the opportunity to serve the Jewish people as a rabbi.

Given the opportunity to speak on that Founders' Day in 1997, and aware that I was the first woman to speak at Cincinnati's annual commemoration, I could not help but reflect that Founders' Day is usually spent talking about men. There were certainly women in Cincinnati and elsewhere among those who supported the creation of the Union of American Hebrew Congregations in 1873 and Hebrew Union College in 1875. Hundreds of women from seventy-nine different localities, from Atchison, Kansas, to Zanesville, Ohio, joined Hebrew Ladies' Educational Aid Societies in 1877 by pledging to donate $1 a year "for the support of the indigent students of the Hebrew Union College."[1] Members of the National Federation of Temple Sisterhoods (now Women of Reform Judaism), founded in 1913, have supported Hebrew Union College since their organization's inception, providing many scholarships and funding the construction of a student dormitory that opened in 1925. As much as women may have contributed to framing the education of America's Reform rabbis, however, the hopes and direction that shaped the first one hundred years of Hebrew Union College belonged to men who first dreamed of and then realized the possibility of training young men to be rabbis for an American Israel. And so I, too, was compelled to turn to the vision of these male dreamers and builders.

Wise, Kohler, and Female Equality

Despite the clear male orientation of the founding and most of the history of Hebrew Union College, the question of women's religious equality and the possibility of female Jewish leadership threads an insistent pattern through the history of the school, raising challenges that still speak to the present moment's assumption of gender equality and apparent acceptance of female religious leadership. As it happens, Isaac Mayer Wise and Kaufmann Kohler, the first two presidents of Hebrew Union College, were among the earliest exponents of female equality within American Judaism. Early on in his American career Wise, who seemed to care about and comment on everything, identified the cause of women's rights as a useful weapon with which to push the cause of reform. In 1855 he argued for mixed choirs, suggesting that any objections to female participation could only "appear ridiculous" in light of contemporary sensibilities. "In our days," he argued, "only men who lacked full command over their intellectual faculties" could countenance the "queer notion of prohibiting ladies to sing in the choir." Further, Wise argued that it was "most desirable and recommendable that our ladies should take an active part in the synagogue." Such involvement could only add "to the devotion of the heart, the solemnity of the ceremonies, and the decorum of the divine place of worship."[2]

As the design of Cincinnati's Plum Street Temple, where he served as rabbi, suggests, Wise believed that a public and impressive Judaism should be expressed in grand sanctuaries that reflected the prosperous respectability of America's Jews. At the same time he expressed his disdain for the petty concerns of what he called "kitchen Judaism," denigrating the domestic religiosity that had so long been the domain of women's religious authority. It becomes more interesting in this context to see that although Wise may have eloquently articulated a call for women's equality within Judaism, he did not always implement his egalitarian suggestions.

Even though Wise was happy to take credit for pioneering the abolition of the women's gallery, family pews were not one of the reforms that he brought to Cincinnati when he arrived from Albany in 1854. It was not until Plum Street Temple opened in 1866, when family pews had already become part of the evolving national synagogue landscape, that mixed seating came to Cincinnati. Wise's inspiring call for a female college as a counterpart to his proposed men's seminary never found institutional expression, although his early college did host a number of girls and women in its courses.[3] In 1876 Wise called upon synagogue leaders to give women "a voice and a vote." Reform would not be "complete," Wise affirmed, until women were welcomed as members of congregations and congregational governing boards both "for the sake of the principle and to rouse in them an interest for congregational affairs."

Yet although he declared himself "ready to appear before any congregation" to plead the cause "of any woman wishing to become a member," his own congregation, over which he had a great deal of influence, never considered such a reform during his lifetime.[4] While Wise articulated a clear position of gender equality, he could not overturn the social, religious, and institutional boundaries that continued to limit opportunities for women within late-nineteenth-century American congregations.

Kaufmann Kohler, who became president of the college in 1903, had early in his career argued that, viewed historically, "only the Jewish religion assigned woman a worthier place" than other faiths by recognizing that her spiritual and "ethical nature" was equal to that of a man.[5] Kohler affirmed that Reform had a role to play in emancipating women from the oriental influences that had suppressed their public voices, and, like Wise, he insisted that "Reform Judaism will never reach its higher goal without having first accorded . . . equal voice to woman with man" in the congregational council and in the entire religious and moral sphere of life.[6]

At the same time, however, he revealed a profound discomfort with the possibility that bringing women's voices into public Jewish life might add to the dimming of "religion's fire" that "has almost burned out on the domestic altar."[7] Although the Reform project that Kohler championed was driven by the force of reason, at the same time he yearned for the "beautiful Sabbath lamp of household piety and devotion," a Judaism that touched the soul and heart.[8] The problem with modern society, Kohler argued, was that "the blood has all rushed up to the brain and the heart emptied of its vital fluid has its chills and fevers." Kohler looked to women for a solution but not to "the intellectual woman," whose circulation also sent "blood rushing to the head and away from the heart." Rather, it would be "the hearty, the whole-souled tender-hearted Rebecca-like woman" who would finally bring "the lost paradise back to man."[9]

Kohler rejected the idea of a woman who might not fit his definition. For him the threat of meaninglessness in a posttraditional world was exemplified in the figure of a woman refusing to play her proper role. Even the possibility of such a creature seemed profoundly disturbing to Kohler: "A woman without tenderness, without gentleness, without the power of self-suppression to an almost infinite degree is a creature so anomalous that she cannot fail to do enormous harm, both to her own sex and the other. . . . She . . . becomes a devil in disguise."[10]

When Kohler looked to women to maintain familiar, if updated, feminine roles, he imposed upon them the responsibility for maintaining the distinctiveness of Judaism. In his question "Is it woman's calling to become a man?" Kohler struggled with the need to place limits upon certain essential markers of identity.[11] Although Reform Judaism sought to meet the modern needs of both men and women, the only vital future Kaufmann Kohler could envision for Judaism was one in which women would continue to embody and sustain the Jewish past.

Pushing the Reform Establishment

For all their engagement in questions of women's religious status, neither Isaac M. Wise nor Kaufmann Kohler had to seriously consider the question of women's religious leadership. This was not the case for their successors. Soon after Kohler's retirement, Martha Neumark's pursuit of studies at Hebrew Union College and her desire to serve a High Holy Days student pulpit pushed the Reform establishment to confront practical questions regarding the proper callings for men and women within Judaism. In an extended discussion by the Central Conference of American Rabbis (CCAR) in 1922 Kohler's successor, Julian Morgenstern, excused himself from "express[ing] any opinion upon this subject," although he did encourage the busy conferees to expend "as much time as may be necessary for a thorough discussion of the question." Morgenstern asked them to look at the question pragmatically: "Namely, is it expedient, and is it worth while?"[12] In the end the 1922 conferees did resolve that given Reform Judaism's other departures from tradition, women could not "justly be denied the privilege of ordination." HUC's board of governors, however, chose to overturn this less than emphatic affirmation, arguing that the question was not one of practical import.[13]

At New York's Jewish Institute of Religion Stephen Wise enthusiastically acceded to the request of Irma Levy Lindheim to enter the course of study at his new institution in 1922. The faculty's response to Lindheim's subsequent petition to change her status from that of special student to that of a regular student was reflected in the school's surprising 1923 charter, which, in describing the institute's mission to "train, in liberal spirit, men and women for the Jewish ministry, research, and community service," perhaps suggested the faculty's view that women students should be training themselves for something other than the rabbinate. In any case Lindheim withdrew from the curriculum before the issue of her ordination could become a reality, and when Helen Levinthal completed the JIR curriculum in 1939, faculty reluctance to certify her as a rabbi resulted in her being granted a master of Hebrew letters degree rather than ordination.[14]

A 1956 report to the CCAR submitted by a committee that included HUC-JIR president Nelson Glueck stated clearly that the conference should "endorse the admission" of women students to the College-Institute. This suggestion was laid aside, however, purportedly until the other side of the issue could be considered.[15]

The Reform movement's hesitation in following through on its stated commitment to the realization of women's equality might have continued indefinitely. But as societal expectations of women's roles shifted in the 1960s, and as Sally Priesand advanced through the Cincinnati campus's undergraduate and rabbinic course, the question was finally resolved without any grand statements from the movement's governing bodies. Nelson Glueck made it clear that he would ordain a female candidate for ordination when the opportunity arose. In 1972, after Glueck's death, Alfred Gottschalk was able to carry through on his predecessor's commitment.

A Generation of Women Rabbis

Now, at the start of a new century, we can literally say that we have had women rabbis or at least a woman rabbi for a generation. Clearly HUC-JIR's step in allowing women to take on the most prominent role of Jewish religious leadership has had profound symbolic and practical implications for the Jewish people, with an impact that resounds far beyond the rabbinate and the Reform movement. The Reform movement's innovation was followed quickly by the Reconstructionist Rabbinical College and, eleven years later, by the Jewish Theological Seminary. The presence of women in Jewish leadership positions has reconfigured expectations of what women should be allowed and encouraged to do in a wide variety of Jewish settings. As women have responded to the range of possibilities so recently opened to them, a worthier place for women has been created in the public realm of Judaism.

In keeping with this achievement and cognizant of remaining challenges, the Statement of Principles for Reform Judaism, adopted by members of the Central Conference of American Rabbis when they met in Pittsburgh in 1999, pledged "to fulfill Reform Judaism's historic commitment to the complete equality of women and men in Jewish life." The spirit of this commitment would have been familiar to Wise, Kohler, Morgenstern, and Glueck. Indeed, although the leaders of today's Reform movement face an order of challenges different from those encountered by their predecessors, they must also struggle to bring reality into conformity with their rhetoric.

We are only beginning to recognize the implications of what happens when, to paraphrase Kohler, a man's calling also becomes a woman's. It is no great secret that despite the fact that the College-Institute has been ordaining women at a rate that for the last fifteen years has approached parity with that of men, we have not put to rest the problem of women's exclusion within our tradition. In fact, at times it seems that all these many women rabbis have done is stir up a lot of new questions.

Once women gained the right of Jewish religious leadership, some among them, almost inevitably, began to question the male orientation of the prayers they were now empowered to lead and the traditions they were now called upon

to interpret. Although the Reform movement placed itself in the forefront of realizing and embracing the challenges of a truly progressive Judaism when it
ordained Sally Priesand, since that day many of the more radical attempts by
women to claim their place within Jewish tradition and practice have arisen outside the Reform movement. More than twenty-five years into this change, some
feminist liturgical pioneers have introduced feminized pronouns and verb forms
to refer to both God and the worshipers in the Hebrew liturgical text; others seem
to have removed God entirely. Feminist scholars have focused a critical eye on a
profoundly patriarchal and hierarchal tradition that, they suggest, will not suddenly become acceptable if we simply omit or modify teachings and practices that
explicitly exclude or denigrate women. Gay activists both within and beyond the
Reform movement have built upon feminist claims and achievements, questioning whether the Jewish marriage sacrament of *kiddushin* should be offered only
to heterosexual couples. They want to know why gays and lesbians should be
made to feel less-than-equal claimants to the richness of Jewish life.

These challenges have found a mainstream response from within the Reform
movement with the creation of gender-sensitive liturgies that insert references to
Sarah, Rebecca, Leah, and Rachel into prayers that refer to the patriarchs and, in
the English text, carefully avoid projecting male identities upon either God or
humanity. Future liturgy projects promise even more compelling engagement
with the challenges raised by feminist liturgical work. Movement policy statements, meanwhile, have accepted gay rabbis (while carefully specifying that only
heterosexual choices should be understood as constituting a Jewish ideal) and
have called for the civil legitimization of lifelong gay marriages or partnerships.
In March 2000 the CCAR further challenged traditional Jewish definitions of
sexuality and family by expressing its affirmation both of the decisions of rabbis
who choose to officiate at "rituals of union for same-gender couples" and the decisions of those who choose not to officiate.

In addition to forcing us to reevaluate our relationship to traditions that have
been created by generations of male authorities, the presence of women religious
leaders has also challenged us to reconsider a professional culture that was built
around the lives and life course of men. Reform leaders at one time may have
wished to believe that all that was necessary to create women rabbis was to allow
women to complete the course of study (at a school that for one hundred years
had been designed to train men), to try to teach everybody fairly, and to hire,
eventually, a few women professors.

All of this has now been achieved, but before we rest satisfied, we must ask a
few difficult questions. Is the model of a successful rabbinate that prevailed when
only men were rabbis still accepted as the appropriate model for success? Do
HUC-JIR rabbinical students have the opportunity to learn from teachers who will
challenge the male orientation of our traditional texts? Are students and congregants within the Reform movement given the opportunity to learn from women's

voices? Do all within the umbrella of the movement's various institutions feel that their voices are heard, that their struggles are recognized, and that they are part of a movement that can respond to their needs? Can we recognize that we may have something to learn from voices that may not sound like our own? Are the questions of those who challenge prevailing patterns heard and treated with respect? Are challenges to our liturgies, our texts, and our theologies—challenges that grow out of a desire to understand how Jewish tradition has belonged to women as well as men—treated seriously as important questions for both men and women? We cannot yet consistently answer these questions affirmatively.[16]

All this questioning, for all of the creative energy that comes along with it, may indeed prove too challenging. When Kaufmann Kohler lost the grounding of the absolute faith of his youth, he cast about for something to hold on to that could continue to tell him who he was. Trying to live in a globalizing economy and amid dizzying technological and social change, even those of us who are committed to a progressive and liberal Judaism may still hope that religious faith can offer simple constructs of meaning and guidance. We, too, would like assurances of where we stand and who we are. In this context feminist challenges to text, tradition, ritual, and theology seem to undermine all that was familiar, everything that told us who we were as Jews. Suddenly we sympathize with Kohler! Can we truly challenge boundaries and hang on to meaning? Can we blur certainties yet remain committed to Judaism? There is nothing simple about this. We can understand why Kohler wanted to hang on to his certainties, why Wise would not push for reforms that might have represented too much of a challenge to the constituencies that he served. When there is already so much work to do, it can seem easier to reject the burden of additional complexity.

When the time came to honor a generation of service from those who became rabbis in 1972, I tried to imagine myself at their ordination service at Plum Street Temple. I wondered what it must have felt like to know that a moment of profound personal and individual import was also a moment that redefined the parameters of Jewish life. Although they sat in his sanctuary, Sally Priesand and her classmates were hardly contemporaries of Isaac Mayer Wise. Yet as they symbolically accepted the burden of changing the world for all of us, they, too, became founders—they helped shape and were part of a moment that redefined the history not only of the American Reform movement, but of Judaism itself.

To the men and women who study for the rabbinate today, Sally Priesand's journey to ordination began a world away in time and experience. What a difference for a girl who grows up wanting to be a rabbi to know that she can be one. But we do a dishonor to the legacy of Sally Priesand and those who supported her if we sit back and assume that these founders did all that needed to be done. If they cannot complete this work, neither are any of those who profess commitment to a progressive Judaism free to desist from it.

Once women's presence was legitimated in the halls of Hebrew Union

College–Jewish Institute of Religion, once women rabbinical students and women rabbis began to redefine notions of Jewish leadership, they found a worthier place for themselves within Jewish tradition than Kaufmann Kohler could ever have imagined. At the beginning of the twenty-first century, with the highly symbolic barrier of women's access to formal spiritual leadership irrevocably breached, today's Reform leaders, students, and congregants must grapple with the evolving challenges that continue to arise from that transformative moment at Plum Street Temple.

If they refuse to believe that the work is done or to accept complacency, if they continue to challenge the assumptions of both traditional and Reform Judaism, if they inherit the struggle pioneered by those rabbis ordained in 1972, then they will do more than merely create a worthier place for those in their own generation. They will follow the course of earlier leaders, and they will emulate the continuing work of Sally Priesand and her classmates. They will struggle to create an American Reform Judaism that can provide a worthier home, a worthier place for those who long for a Judaism that can honor not only our past, but also our future.

Notes

1. Ladies' Educational Aid Societies, "Roles of Honor," Box X-206, American Jewish Archives, Cincinnati, Ohio.
2. Isaac M. Wise, "Does the Canon Law Permit Ladies to Sing in the Synagogue?" *Israelite* 2, 5 (August 10, 1855) and 6 (August 17, 1855): 44–45.
3. Isaac M. Wise, "What Should Be Done?" *Israelite* 1, 4 (August 4, 1854): 29. For a detailed portrayal of the different generations of female students at Hebrew Union College and the Jewish Institute of Religion who preceded Sally Priesand, see Pamela S. Nadell, *Women Who Would Be Rabbis: A History of Women's Ordination, 1889–1985* (Boston: Beacon Press, 1998).
4. Isaac M. Wise, "Woman in the Synagogue," *American Israelite*, September 8, 1878.
5. Kaufmann Kohler, "Das Frauenherz oder das Miriambrünnlein im Lager Israels," *Jewish Times* 2, 5 (February 17, 1871): 812. On Kohler's ambivalent stance on the role of women in modern Judaism, see my article "The Ambivalence of Reform Judaism: Kaufmann Kohler and the Ideal Jewish Woman," *American Jewish History* 79 (Summer, 1990): 477–99.
6. Kaufmann Kohler, conference paper, in "Proceedings of the Pittsburgh Rabbinical Conference, 1885," in *The Changing World of Reform Judaism: The Pittsburgh Platform in Retrospect*, ed. Walter Jacob (Pittsburgh: Rodef Shalom Congregation, 1985), 96.
7. Ibid., 96, 102.
8. Kaufmann Kohler, "Are Sunday Lectures a Treason to Judaism," *Temple Beth-El Sunday Lectures* 16 (January 8, 1888): 7–8.
9. Kaufmann Kohler, "Rocks Ahead," *Reform Advocate* 2, 13 (November 14, 1891): 215; Kaufmann Kohler, "The Jewish Ideal of Womanhood," 1899, Box 6 / Folder 2, Kaufmann Kohler Papers, Coll. 29, American Jewish Archives, Cincinnati, Ohio.
10. Kaufmann Kohler, "Esther or the Jewish Woman," *Temple Beth-El Sunday Lectures* 16 (February 26, 1888): 2.

11. Kaufmann Kohler, "Der Beruf des Weibes," *Jewish Times*, May 21, 1875, 188.

12. Central Conference of American Rabbis (CCAR) *Yearbook* 32 (1922): 167.

13. See Ellen M. Umansky, "Women's Journey toward Rabbinic Ordination," in *Women Rabbis: Exploration and Celebration, Papers Delivered at an Academic Conference Honoring Twenty Years of Women in the Rabbinate, 1972–1992*, ed. Gary P. Zola (Cincinnati: HUC-JIR Rabbinic Alumni Association Press, 1996), 32–33.

14. On Lindheim, see Pamela Nadell, "The Women Who Would be Rabbis," in *Gender and Judaism: The Transformation of Tradition*, ed. T. M. Rudavsky (New York: New York University Press, 1995), 127–31 and Nadell, *Women*, 72–76; on Levinthal, see Nadell, *Women* 80–85, and Umansky, *Women's Journey*, nn. 22, 40.

15. CCAR *Yearbook* 68 (1956): 93.

16. For other reflections on the difficulty of realizing the implications implicit in the creation of women rabbis, see Shulamit S. Magnus, "The New Reality: The Implications of Women in Rabbinical School," *Reconstructionist*, summer 1991, 16–18; Beth Wenger, "The Politics of Women's Ordination: Jewish Law, Institutional Power, and the Debate over Women in the Rabbinate," in *Tradition Renewed: A History of the Jewish Theological Seminary*, ed. Jack Wertheimer (New York: Jewish Theological Seminary, 1997), 2: 483–523. Important observations are also contained in many of the essays included in Zola, ed., *Women Rabbis*.

15

Embracing Lesbians and Gay Men

A Reform Jewish Innovation

DENISE L. EGER

Reform Judaism has been responsible for several revolutions within the ancient traditions. Perhaps the most visible, and one of the main principles upon which it was founded, has been the assertion of the absolute equality of men and women in religious obligations.[1] Out of this conviction came the notion of women as rabbis. Although it took well over one hundred years to actualize, the ordination of women as rabbis and their acceptance as cantors were two of the many factors that have allowed gays and lesbians to be welcomed and returned to the Jewish community through the Reform movement. The notion of the liberation of women, so fervent in the late 1960s and early 1970s, was a part of the larger picture of the so-called sexual revolution of the era. By bringing women into the circles of decision making, as well as smashing our notions of God and gender, the atmosphere was ripe for other innovations as well.

The women's liberation movement also gained strength with the African-American civil rights movement. Thus the notion of equality between blacks and whites also gave strength to the notion of equality between men and women.

A second factor in the return and welcome of gays and lesbians to Jewish life was Reform Judaism's emphasis on the concept of prophetic Judaism. This ideal of championing the cause of the widow, orphan, and stranger gave grounding to the heavy involvement of both Reform rabbis and laity in issues of social justice. For many years social action in Reform Judaism meant involvement in the African-American struggle for civil rights. Many Reform rabbis and the Union of American Hebrew Congregations (UAHC) were deeply involved in supporting the march for justice by our African-American neighbors. So as the gay rights movement grew, Reform Jews could understand the struggle for civil rights and freedom from discrimination that gays and lesbians sought.

A third factor that made Reform Judaism receptive to welcoming gay men and lesbians was the prevalence of both Jewish psychiatrists and psychologists. Many had become familiar with the groundbreaking study of Dr. Evelyn Hooker. Funded by the National Institute for Mental Health and presented in 1956 to the American Psychological Association, Dr. Hooker's revolutionary study was titled "The Adjustment of the Male Overt Homosexual." Her very controversial findings, which were widely publicized, concluded that gay men were as well adjusted as straight men.[2] This rocked the psychiatric world. Since early in the twentieth century homosexuality had been classified as mental illness, psychopathology as well as criminal offense. It took another thirteen years, but in 1973 the American Psychological Association dropped homosexuality from its official list of mental illnesses.

Thus the combination of these three notions—the equality of women, civil rights involvement, and Dr. Hooker's groundbreaking research—helped pave the way for the inclusion of gays and lesbians in Jewish life through the Reform movement.

While the modern gay rights movement often claims the Stonewall riots of the summer of 1969 as its beginning, gay men and lesbians formed their first organizations throughout the 1950s and 1960s.[3] One of those groups, formed in Los Angeles in 1968, was the Metropolitan Community Church (MCC). Founded by the Reverend Troy Perry, a former Pentecostalist minister, MCC was a church by and for gays and lesbians. Perry's organization quickly grew and became a central organizing force for the gay and lesbian community. Many Jews came to the activities of the church and were supporters of the church but were not members. Out of this group of people came the idea for their own place of worship. Thus the Metropolitan Community Temple was born in 1972.

Support from the UAHC and CCAR

They sought assistance from the local Union of American Hebrew Congregations office in helping to form their group and eventually applied for membership status in the UAHC. Rabbi Erwin Herman and Southern California UAHC lay president Norm Eichberg carried the group's banner throughout the UAHC.[4] The group Hebraicized its name to Beth Chayim Chadashim, and after much controversy Beth Chayim Chadashim was finally admitted in 1973 as a full participating congregation in the Reform movement. But this was just a beginning.

Even prior to this start sermons had been given calling for police to stop the harassment of gay people and for the extension of the basic protections of laws as guaranteed in the Bill of Rights.[5] The Central Conference of American Rabbis (CCAR) and the UAHC both had committees that debated the acceptance of a gay congregation into the Union. Following the successful defeat of the Briggs initiative in 1977 in California, Rabbi Allen B. Bennett came out publicly as a gay man. This brave act gave a public face to Jewish gays and certainly to the fact that rabbis were among those who needed the acceptance, love, and support of the Reform Jewish movement.

In 1975 at the UAHC biennial convention a strong resolution calling for full civil rights for homosexuals in the civic arena was passed. This was followed in 1977 by another resolution at the UAHC biennial calling for the same civil rights. By 1977 other gay synagogues had formed, and several had become members of the UAHC including those in San Francisco, Miami, and Philadelphia.

The UAHC continued throughout the 1980s to keep gay rights on its agenda. In 1987 the Union passed yet another resolution, this time to "encourage lesbian and gay Jews to share and participate in the worship, leadership, and general congregational life of all synagogues." This resolution also urged the employment of synagogue personnel "without regard to sexual orientation." However, the specific issue of the ordination of gays and lesbians was referred to the second Ad Hoc Committee on Homosexuality of the CCAR.

Also in the 1980s the UAHC confronted the AIDS crisis in a very strong way. It published outstanding teaching materials, including an AIDS curriculum for the supplemental religious school setting and study guides for some of the early television programs that dealt with AIDS. These materials took Jewish values and placed them in the context of the AIDS crisis, making it possible for Jews to be challenged to care for those with HIV disease. In the early 1980s there was much religious hysteria, especially from Christian fundamentalists about AIDS being God's punishment for homosexuality. Each of the UAHC's publications helped to strongly convince not only the Jewish community but also other religious communities of the fallacy of these fundamentalist ideas.

By 1987 the UAHC biennial even had Surgeon General Everett Koop address the plenum about AIDS and HIV. The Union established a separate AIDS committee that prepared many materials, including a 1987 issue of *Keeping Posted* magazine for youth that was devoted entirely to the issue of AIDS. Rabbi Alexander Schindler, at the time president of the UAHC, spoke eloquently about the plight of people with AIDS at a UAHC-sponsored community service. In the sermon he not only identified with the struggle of gay people but stated, "I declare myself the compassionate ally of every person heterosexual and homosexual, Jew and non-Jew, who is wrestling with the shame, the confusion, the fear, the endless torment involved in the inner struggle for sexual identity. It is, when all is said and done, a struggle for the integrity of selfhood."[6]

The UAHC's AIDS committee also made a quilt piece for the NAMES Project AIDS quilt for all of the many Jews who had died from complications of AIDS. This piece of the quilt traveled to many UAHC congregations before being placed in the larger quilt.

Also in 1989 Rabbi Schindler expanded his comments from the March AIDS service sermon to include in his biennial address to the Sixtieth Assembly of the UAHC an entire section about including gay and lesbian Jews. He expanded on themes from his March address:

> Yes, our resolutions express our resolve to act. There is one realm, however, in which our resolutions have been forthright, but our actions considerably less so. I speak now of the plea of gay and lesbian Jews for fuller acceptance in our midst. . . . To be sure, many of us feel pity for gays and lesbians, and we agree, intellectually that it is a grievous wrong to stigmatize them, to ostracize them, to hold them in moral disdain. But something more than a grasp of the mind is required; there is a need for a grasp of the heart. Something different from pity is called for; we need, as a community to cross those boundaries of Otherness, those fringed boundaries where compassion gives way to identification. . . . We who were marranos in Madrid, who clung to the closet of assimilation and conversion in order to live without molestation, we cannot deny the demand for gay and lesbian visibility![7]

His words did not go unnoticed. Out of his address another resolution was passed at the 1989 UAHC biennial on visibility for gays and lesbians within the movement. These resolutions translated into further concrete action taken by the UAHC Commission on Social Action, which promoted equal employment opportunities in the Reform movement,[8] opposed discrimination against gays in the military,[9] and responded to anti–gay-rights referenda.[10] In 1992 Rabbi Schindler challenged the Boy Scouts of America for its stand against gay men and homosexuality.[11]

The UAHC continued to lead the way on gay and lesbian issues, including resolutions in 1993 for recognizing lesbian and gay partnerships and for supporting the participation of the Commission on Social Action in the 1993 Gay and Lesbian March on Washington. Further, staff from the Religious Action Center of the UAHC testified before Congress and spoke forcefully against the Defense of Marriage Act, which defined marriage as an institution of heterosexual privilege.

The UAHC also created a Task Force on Lesbian and Gay Inclusion that in 1996 published a workbook distributed to all UAHC congregations. This workbook, called *KULANU (All of US)*, is a booklet of programs to help congregations welcome and include gays and lesbians in their midst.

The Central Conference of American Rabbis has also dealt with and passed a number of resolutions strong support for civil rights for homosexuals. In 1977 the CCAR passed a resolution that called "for the decriminalization of homosexual acts between consenting adults and prohibits discrimination against them as persons."[12] In 1981 the Task Force on Jewish Sexual Values of the Central Conference of American Rabbis was formed. During that conference Dr. Sol Gordon presented a workshop on homosexuality, one that widely influenced many who attended. His thesis was based on the idea that one's sexual orientation is determined before the age of five years; therefore it is beyond the ability of the adult individual to change.[13]

HUC–JIR Policies

In 1986 a resolution was introduced to the CCAR by Rabbi Margaret Wenig and Margaret Holub, then a rabbinic student, calling for the ordination of openly gay and lesbian individuals as rabbis as well as revisions of the admission policy of the CCAR and the placement policy of the Rabbinical Placement Commission. The policy of Hebrew Union College–Jewish Institute of Religion, the Reform movement's seminary, had been to deny ordination to anyone who was openly gay. This resolution was referred to committee for study. After four years of deliberation and study the Report of the Ad Hoc Committee on Homosexuality in the Rabbinate was accepted by the plenum of the conference in June 1990 in Seattle, Washington. The report of the committee continued to affirm civil rights for gays and lesbians and the "efforts to eliminate discrimination in housing and employment." Further, the report repudiated hate language and physical abuse toward gays and lesbians.

The document affirmed "monogamous heterosexual marriage as the ideal human relationship for fulfilling the perpetuation of the species and covenantal fulfillment and the preservation of the Jewish people." However, it did note that a minority of the committee affirmed the equal possibility of covenantal fulfillment in homosexual relationships.

During the four years of deliberation of this task force the College-Institute further clarified its admission policy. By the time the report of the committee was issued in 1990 President Alfred Gottschalk of HUC-JIR had set forth written guidelines concerning sexual orientation. The school considers the sexual orientation of an applicant only in the context of a candidate's overall suitability for the rabbinate, his or her qualifications to serve the Jewish community effectively, and his or her capacity to find personal fulfillment within the rabbinate.[14] The acceptance of this report was a hallmark in the spiritual struggle for equality by gays and lesbians. A major mainstream religious tradition had placed no bar on the ordination of gays and lesbians—a major milestone in the struggle for equality.

The CCAR continued to stand for the civil rights of gays and lesbians, including taking a stand against the Boy Scouts of America position excluding gay Scouts and Scout leaders. Also in 1993 the CCAR resolved not to hold regional or national meetings in any state, province, or municipality that had a law after January 1, 1995, denying gays and lesbians legal protection of their civil rights. This resolution was in protest of many of the antigay ballot initiatives that had been forced on voters especially in Colorado and Oregon. In 1996 the CCAR also endorsed civil marriage for gays and lesbians, acknowledging that this "is separate from the question of rabbinic officiation at such marriages."

Following this resolution in 1996 the CCAR formed another committee to look at issues of human sexuality, but once again, at the urging of the CCAR president, the committee's first task was to look at the issues of gay and lesbian wedding ceremonies. While the CCAR had taken a position to endorse civil marriage, the status of a religious ceremony was still left open to debate. In part, the divisive nature of the debate at the CCAR conference that year over the civil marriage resolution led the CCAR leadership to form a committee to examine this issue.

The Ad Hoc Committee on Human Sexuality, after two years of deliberation and study, concluded "that *kedusha* may be present in committed same-gender relationship between two Jews." The report further concluded that gay and lesbian relationships could serve "as the foundation of stable Jewish families, thus adding strength to the Jewish community." Thus, the report states that gay and lesbian relationships are "worthy of affirmation through appropriate Jewish ritual." However, the committee was not prepared to state that this ceremony of affirmation was on a par with *kiddushin,* and further left it up to each rabbi to decide about the issue of officiation according to "his or her own rabbinic conscience." Of course, this leaves the door open for rabbis not to officiate as well.

Concurrent with the work of the Ad Hoc Committee on Homosexuality, the Responsa Committee of the CCAR also entertained the question of whether a Reform rabbi may officiate at a wedding or commitment ceremony and whether or not gay and lesbian unions qualify as *kiddushin.* The majority opinion concluded that a rabbi should not officiate. A vocal minority of this committee indicated that they disagreed, holding that a Reform rabbi may officiate at the wedding or commitment ceremony between two Jews of the same gender.

The Quandary

How can two committees of the same organization deal with an issue and yet come to diametrically opposite opinions? This is a quandary felt by many members of the CCAR and particularly gay and lesbian rabbis. The issue of marriage, which is the final spiritual hurdle of reconciliation of gay men and lesbians, continues to be divisive within the movement in the same way it is divisive within the larger cultural context.

For those in our culture, whether Jewish or not, who believe homosexuality is a sin and aberrant behavior, there is no option for discussion. For those of us who believe that homosexuality is one of the varieties of human expression of love and an innate and unchanging mode of being, then homosexuality, homosexual relationships, and equality flow naturally in the scheme of things. The Responsa Committee's report documents this quite well. It states, "In trying to talk to each other about this question, we discovered as we as a Committee had ceased to share the most elemental kinds of assumptions necessary for a common religious conversation. We were speaking different languages, languages that used similar words and terminology but which defined them in starkly and irreconcilably different ways."[15] The Reform movement that had seemingly championed the rights of gay and lesbian people from a secular and civil rights perspective seems to have gotten hung up in the theological realms. This discussion becomes so explosive when discussed that it has the potential to divide the entire Reform Jewish enterprise.

It was precisely this fear that led to the acceptance of both reports, that of the Ad Hoc Committee on Human Sexuality and that of the Responsa Committee. It was this fear that prevented the Ad Hoc Committee on Human Sexuality from moving forward with a resolution to the floor of the plenum of the CCAR at the June 1998 convention in Anaheim, California. Despite the fact that a third of the membership of the CCAR signed on to a statement that they would officiate or had already officiated at a ceremony of commitment between two Jews of the same gender, the CCAR leadership was petrified of the possible schisms between those who support gays and lesbians in their quest for spiritual fulfillment beneath the *chuppa* and those who oppose this idea.

These two reports were not the final word on this topic. The Central Conference of American Rabbis has appointed a Task Force on Gays and Lesbians in the Rabbinate. This committee task force created workshops and study sessions on the marriage topic for Reform rabbis all across the country, and it will also deal with issues of placement for lesbian and gay rabbis in conjunction with the Joint Placement commission. Further, this task force is charged with finding support mechanisms for gay colleagues within the CCAR.

A resolution on same-sex ceremonies passed overwhelmingly at the March 2000 CCAR conference calling for Reform rabbis to have the option of performing such ceremonies. While each Reform rabbi already has the right to follow his or her own conscience, and many rabbis already officiate at gay and lesbian wedding ceremonies, this resolution will help to give strength to gay and lesbian Jews around the world in their quest for spiritual fulfillment beneath the *chuppah*. The resolution affirmed that "the relationship of a Jewish same gender couple may be worthy of affirmation through appropriate ritual sanctification."[16]

The resolution was introduced by the Women's Rabbinic Network, the organization of Reform women rabbis, once again highlighting the link between the ordination of women as rabbis and gay and lesbian issues. Many members of the WRN were frustrated by the events in the CCAR during the spring of 1998. The opportunity to vote on the Ad Hoc Committee on Human Sexuality was no longer an option. The WRN voted at its March 1999 conference to urge the CCAR to take up the issue of same-gender ceremonies at its Pittsburgh convention. However, the only issue debated at the Pittsburgh convention was the new Pittsburgh Platform. Thus, in the summer of 1999 the WRN introduced an initial resolution to the CCAR for consideration in Greensboro 2000 Conference.

Again, there was a year of discussion at every rabbinic regional conference on the language of the resolution and need for such a resolution.

In the months and weeks leading up to the March 2000 CCAR Convention, the resolution was debated hotly over the Internet in rabbinic email discussions and in person. It was a debate that was not among the movement's shining moments. There were many hurtful and ad hominem attacks made, and the Womens Rabbinic Network was attacked. The misogyny present in these discussions by Reform rabbis was somewhat surprising and somewhat predictable. The WRN was accused of being run by a group of lesbians. It was as if the women rabbis of the CCAR and members of the WRN were out to destroy the safe haven for certain male members of the CCAR. The very existence and need for the WRN was questioned as some kind of rabbinic cabal against the CCAR. The attacks were made as if women rabbis weren't legitimate members of the CCAR.

The leadership of the CCAR had changed at the Pittsburgh convention. Rabbi Charles Kroloff became president of the CCAR, and he was willing and determined to have the issue of officiation at same-gender ceremonies debated under his watch. In addition, Rabbi Paul Menitoff, the executive director of the CCAR gave his full backing and support to the idea of bringing the topic before the plenum of the CCAR.

One area of concern was the Israeli Reform movement. In 1998 when the Ad Hoc Committee on Human Sexuality's report was to be presented, the Israeli Reform movement was adamantly against a resolution of support for officiation at same-gender ceremonies. In fact, MARAM, the Israeli Reform Rabbinic organization, will not permit its members to officiate at same-gender ceremonies. This is in part because of the precarious situation of the Reform rabbinate in Israel.[17] During the spring of 1998 the Reform movement was in delicate negotiations with the Chief Rabbinate in Israel on issues of conversion. One of the many reasons the original resolution of the Ad Hoc Committee on Human Sexuality was pulled from the table was because of concern for the Reform movement in Israel. Thus, for the WRN resolution to be successful, the Israeli Reform movement had to be consulted.

In October 1999 I met with the top leaders of Israeli Reform rabbis, Rabbi Meir Azari and Rabbi Yehoram Mazor, the Av Bet Din of MARAM, during a congregational trip to Israel to discuss the resolution. During the two-hour meeting we spoke about the different situations of North American and Israeli Reform movements as well as the upcoming resolution and how MARAM might find a way to support the resolution. My conversation with them paved the way for further discussion in February when the first WRN trip to Israel—with over fifty women rabbis—met with the leadership of the Israeli Reform Rabbis. Prior to this meeting the strategy that MARAM was going to follow was that they were going to absent themselves from the floor of the convention during the debate and discussion. While many individual Israeli Reform rabbis do support gays and lesbians in their quest for a religious ceremony honoring their relationships, the official policy of MARAM remained firm. By massaging the language of the resolution, given their suggestions, we were able to create language that could weave their reality and ours into the WRN resolution and avoid the scenario of an exodus during the conference.

As the convention drew closer and the Internet debates grew heated, the idea of a possible compromise began to be floated. Some of the opposition to the WRN resolution had submitted an "alternative resolution" that was strong in supporting gay and lesbian civil rights. Yet it omitted any reference to gay and lesbian commitment ceremonies. The alternative resolution merely repeated many of the stands that the CCAR and the UAHC had previously endorsed. Not wanting a pyrrhic victory or a vicious floor fight those of us who authored the resolution agreed to slightly soften some other parts of the language of the resolution. This allowed for the greatest majority to support the document, even those rabbis who are not yet ready to officiate at gay and lesbian weddings or commitment ceremonies. Under the leadership of Rabbi Shira Stern and Rabbi Susan Stone, co-chairs of the WRN, and Rabbi Kroloff, CCAR president, Rabbi Paul Menitoff, Executive Vice President of the CCAR, and Rabbi Elliot Stevens, Executive Secretary of the CCAR, a compromise was fashioned.

By entering into discussion with those who opposed the WRN resolution, the authors of the "alternative resolution" agreed to withdraw their resolution if there were changes made in the text of the officiation resolution. The resolution that was overwhelmingly passed in at the Greensboro 2000 CCAR convention was the product of this compromise.

However, the compromise was a good one. Because the new WRN resolution allowed for the truth to be recognized: that there are rabbis who do officiate at same-gender ceremonies and rabbis who do not. Further, the improved WRN resolution allowed for near-unanimous support and allowed for CCAR as going on record as supporting the dignity of gay and lesbian Jewish same-gender couples.

During the plenum, many questions came up from the floor.

Some supporters of the WRN resolution were very disappointed and felt a stronger resolution could have passed. Many of the amendments from the floor actually made the resolution stronger. In particular, one question from the floor specifically asked, "What can we in good faith call these ceremonies?" It was affirmed from the floor—by the conference president, Rabbi Charles Kroloff, that we could call gay and lesbian commitment ceremonies, weddings, even by the ritual name *kiddushin*. This is the brilliance of the resolution. By affirming Reform Jewish principles of rabbinic autonomy, we speak the truth and yet, begin to institutionalize the reality of Jewish rituals for same gender commitment ceremonies.

While some were disappointed that the language seemed muted, here is what was really achieved. First, the headlines around the world read, "Reform Rabbis Back Blessing of Gay Unions."[18] From San Francisco to Milan, from Tel Aviv to Chicago, a message of support for Jewish gay and lesbian couples and the commitments they wish to make together was visible.

Second, there were five hundred rabbis, all saying yes: saying yes, to gay and lesbian families, gay and lesbian lives. Rabbis with Jewish traditions behind them were saying yes, there is sanctity and holiness about gay and lesbian commitments in the face of the often dehumanizing portraits that are painted about gay people. Those dehumanizing portraits are often made by people who claim moral and religious authority. It was powerful to hear the ayes go up with such unity.

There were only two speakers against the resolution and perhaps less than ten nays. But the room vibrated with spiritual energy. It really felt that we were standing on historic ground. People, gay and straight, were crying tears of relief and joy. People felt good about what had been achieved, even those rabbis who do not yet officiate. The feeling in the large convention hall was electric. There was a tremendous spiritual sense that we were living in a moment of *tikkun olam*. Spontaneously everyone broke out into the Shehkiyanu prayer that says, "Thank you God for giving us life, for sustaining us and for bringing us to the time."

Another important outcome of the vote in favor of the WRN resolution was that the CCAR created a model for coming together even in our differences. This is a strength of our movement.

A third outcome of the vote in favor of the WRN resolution was the hope and comfort that those who still remain closeted will feel in having the largest group of Jewish clergy acknowledge and celebrate gay and lesbian lives. The vote sent a positive message. The institution of marriage is used as a way to legitimize who is family and even who is human. This was certainly true when African slaves were brought to the United States and forbidden from marrying, and it is true today for gay and lesbian people. Thus, the message sent by the CCAR was a victory for all those who believe in the human dignity of all people, including gay men and lesbians.

A fourth outcome—and perhaps the most important—is the institutionalization of gay and lesbian lifecycle events. The WRN resolution called for educational materials and pastoral materials to be developed. This will include gay and lesbian wedding and commitment ceremonies being published in the Reform rabbis' manual. This will include *ketuvot* and commitment documents being developed. It is this part of the resolution that will help transform same-sex Jewish ceremonies from mere exotica to regular ritual, from unique occurrences and rarities to expectations and access. Jewish same-gender couples and their weddings and other ceremonies will become part of the normal, and, yes, regular life-cycle canon of Jewish life. Will it always be called a wedding? Most people will understand what it means, and many Reform rabbis already do use the term *kiddushin*.

In two short years, through study and dialogue, the CCAR was able to come to a consensus on a difficult issue. This was a consensus that affirmed rabbinic choice but upheld the dignity and sanctity of gay Jewish couples beneath the *chuppah.*

The marriage issue is the final ground of acceptance within the reform movement. Reform Judaism in the latter half of the twentieth century became a welcoming haven for gay men and lesbians who wished to be an active part of the Jewish community. Whether in primarily gay and lesbian synagogues or more mainstream synagogues, whether as lay leaders or rabbis or cantors, gays and lesbians have found a home and place at the Jewish communal table. We can say that Reform Judaism has embraced gay men and lesbians. Certainly there will be no going back into the closet.

The Role of the Individual Congregation

The real work of the inclusion of gay men and lesbians must be realized not just on the political and national scale but also within the individual congregation. As it stands now, each congregation determines its own customs regarding gay and lesbian families. While the UAHC has published a guide for inclusion of gays and lesbians in the congregation, this is a resource that needs leadership in order for it to be utilized. The issues of inclusion of gays and lesbians in the life of the congregation is further reinforced by the position of the rabbi on gay and lesbian issues. Thus, if a rabbi is supportive of including gays and lesbians, he or she can be an advocate at the congregational level, helping to make the individual synagogue a welcoming environment. However, if the rabbi is less than supportive, this can send a strong message of exclusion of gays and lesbians. This is perhaps not an issue in larger cities, where there is more than one Reform congregation. But the consequences in smaller communities, where there is only one Reform synagogue or perhaps one congregation, can be devastating. This is particularly true for young people. Since statistics prove that gay and lesbian teens are one-third more likely to commit suicide than teens who are heterosexual, the issue of inclusion or exclusion can have life-and-death consequences.

Further, the present leadership of the UAHC has seemingly steered away from controversial social issues toward issues of religious education. We can only hope and pray that the commitment to the inclusion of Jewish gay men and lesbians within the movement continues to be a priority within the congregational arm of the movement. It seems clear that when the president of the UAHC speaks out on topics, people do listen and the agenda is set. It is my hope that the present leadership of the UAHC will continue to speak out positively on gay and lesbian Jewish issues and will keep the commitment of the UAHC toward inclusion as a vital linchpin in the social justice agenda for the movement.

Each time the UAHC or CCAR speaks out and reaches out to include gays and lesbians in the life of the community, its action hammers away at the often-dehumanizing myths that are still in circulation about gay men and lesbians. The authority of the Jewish voice with which the Reform movement speaks sends a positive message both to Jews and to non-Jews who hunger for spiritual leadership on this issue.

Conclusion

The Talmud teaches that if you save one life, it is as if you have saved the whole world. The positive and inclusive position of the Reform movement has certainly saved more than a few lives. The message of reconcilation of gay men and lesbians to the Jewish community has added a wonderful texture to our congregations and to the Jewish people. One can only hope that this vital message of inclusion continues.

Notes

1. Gunther Plaut, *The Rise of Reform Judaism* (New York: World Union for Progressive Judaism, 1963), 252–55.
2. From "100 Years before Stonewall" exhibit (University of California, Berkeley, June 1994), as quoted in *Out in All Directions*, eds. Lynn Witt, Sherry Thomas, and Eric Marcus (New York: Warner, 1997), 224–25.
3. On June 26, 1969, following a raid by the New York Police Department on a Greenwich Village gay bar, three days of rioting took place to protest police harassment of gay men and lesbians.
4. Both Herman and Eichberg had gay sons, although both have said to me in private conversation that they did not speak to each other about this at the time.
5. Rabbi Steven B. Jacobs, *National Post and Opinion*, May 3, 1968, as quoted in Albert Vorspan, *Jewish Values and Social Crisis* (New York: Union of American Hebrew Congregations, rev. ed., 1971), 230.
6. Rabbi Alexander Schindler, address at the UAHC community service in support of people with AIDS. Leo Baeck Temple, Los Angeles, California, March 12, 1989, 5.
7. Rabbi Alexander Schindler, Presidential Address, Sixtieth General Assembly of the UAHC, November 2–6, 1989, New Orleans, Louisiana, 11–12.
8. Resolution of the Commission on Social Action, 1991.
9. Ibid.
10. Resolutions of the UAHC and the CCAR in 1993.
11. Letter from Rabbi Schindler to the Boy Scouts, 1992, and resolutions of the executive committee of the CCAR, 1992, and National Federation of Temple Youth, 1992.
12. Resolution of the Central Conference of American Rabbis Eighty-eighth Annual Convention, 1977.
13. Report of the Task Force on Jewish Sexual Values, Rabbi Selig Salkowitz, chair, *Central Conference of American Rabbis Yearbook*, vol. 92, 1982.

14. The Report of the Ad Hoc Committee on Homosexuality, *CCAR Yearbook*, vol. 108, July 1997–December 1998, 34.

15. CCAR Responsum on Homosexual Marriage, *CCAR Yearbook*, vol. 108, July 1997–December 1998.

16. Same-sex officiation resolution passed at the 111th annual convention of the Central Conference of American Rabbis, March 2000.

17. The rabbinate in Israel is controlled by the Orthodox. Reform rabbis are forbidden by Israeli law from officiating at civil wedding ceremonies. Reform rabbis also may not conduct funerals officially or convert people. Ongoing negotiations with the Chief Rabbinate in Israel, as well as numerous law suits in Israeli civil courts, have tried to overturn this situation.

18. The *New York Times*, Thursday, March 30, 2000.

16

"Where Kosher Means Organic and Union Label"

Bisexual Women Reembrace Their Jewish Heritage

HINDA SEIF

A central challenge of feminist scholarship since the 1980s has been the exploration of the full breadth of the term *woman* and the interaction of women's multiple identifications, including class, race, ethnicity, and nationality. While there has been a tremendous expansion of writing on gender and Judaism within the past decade, our image of Jewish women raised in the American Reform tradition still too often calls to mind an unproblematic and idealized picture of an Ashkenazi, middle-class, married woman with children.[1] The following is an exploration of an arena of increasing importance to the Reform Jewish movement: the relationship of Jewish sexual minority women to their religion. In specific, it addresses the lives of women who identify as both Jewish and bisexual and are actively participating in American Reform Judaism or have distanced themselves from the denominations in which they were raised by forming Jewish Renewal *havurot* or embracing secular Jewish identities.

This task is accomplished through the analysis of interviews conducted with twenty-seven Jewish bisexual women living in the San Francisco Bay Area, and the transcript from a focus group with six interviewees. An interview methodology is a particularly effective way to look at the complex interactions of individuals and groups with multiple identifications, since people's beliefs and identifications tend to intermingle in their speech. By listening to the words of Jewish bisexual women, we gain a sense of the ways that multiple identifications live and breathe in our daily lives; this complements theoretical discussions of gender, race, ethnicity, religion, and sexual orientation.

A Wall of Denial

When I told people I was joining together Jewishness and bisexuality in a project, they usually laughed. I seemed to have hit a particular wall of denial and chosen a community that people could or would not fathom. There is still a reluctance to acknowledge the interaction of minoritized sexuality and ethnicity or religion, making the term "bisexual Jewish woman" or "Jewish lesbian" stick in some throats or provoking harsh debates in some religious circles.

These terms may be perceived as oxymorons because of an assumption that to "come out" as a nonheterosexual Jew leads to a distancing from Jewish culture, community, and religion. Some may feel there is no room for alternative sexualities within the Jewish religion, thereby forcing bisexually identified Jews to the margins of Jewish life or outside of its boundaries altogether. There is also a fear that we will refuse one of the central, if unevenly fulfilled, mandates of contemporary Jewish culture: that Jewish women must reproduce Jewish children. In his essay "Klal Israel: Lesbians and Gays in the Jewish Community," Jewish Activist Gays and Lesbians (JAGL) member Bob Goldfarb reminds us that most rabbis will not perform commitment ceremonies for gays and lesbians. While the Reform movement has been one of the most willing to address the needs of lesbian and gay Jews, many rabbinical students within this denomination are reluctant to come out because of the unwillingness of many congregations to hire a gay or lesbian leader.[2]

It is especially difficult to envision Jewish bisexuals due to the extreme invisibility of bisexual individuals and cultures. According to bisexual theorist Elizabeth Daumer, "Bisexuality has often been ignored by feminist and lesbian theorists both as a concept and a realm of experiences . . . [d]ue to its problematic political and social position between two opposed cultures."[3] A bisexual identity is not readily available to many people who do not live in major cities; there are few social networks specifically welcoming of bisexuals; and there is little or no sense of bisexual women's history or role modeling, especially since many historical figures who have engaged in both same-sex and other-sex practice have been claimed by lesbian and gay historians and activists.

Yet the Bay Area Jewish bisexuals who participated in this study challenge the aforementioned stereotypes, misconceptions, and silences. Rather than choosing between participation in a heterosexually dominant Jewish cultural and religion or generic sexual minority status, many maintained or reforged their Jewish ties after coming out. Others who had been raised with only tenuous connections to their Jewish heritage and/or religion embraced this identification for the first time in Jewish bisexual religious or social groups: participants' queer identification often moved them closer to their ethnicity and religion rather than farther away. This often occurred after a period of alienation, yet was not a return to traditional forms of Judaism or Jewish community but a movement toward re-created versions. This re-creation is typified by participants' involvement in local queer or queer-friendly synagogues and *havurot* and a support group for Jewish bisexuals, the Jewish Caucus of BiPOL.[4] These gatherings offer a particularly supportive haven for Jews who have been marginalized in multiple ways, not only as nonheterosexuals but often as Jews of mixed heritage, Jews with Christian mothers, Jews from working-class or poor backgrounds, and transgendered or intersexual Jews.[5]

New Forms of Community

The bisexual, Jewish community they create is an example of new forms of Jewish community building that are not based on close kinship groups, the ghettos of the past, or contemporary neighborhoods. It is filled with individuals who have moved away from their geographic communities of origin and are reinventing Jewish community using feminist, ecological, spiritual, queer, and/or anti-racist models. By re-creating idealized versions of traditional Jewish culture, ethnicity, and religion, they attempt to shed assimilationist messages that grow from anti-Semitism and its stepchild, internalized anti-Semitism. These communities are utopian reinterpretations of mostly East European, sometimes Sephardi and Mizrahi Jewish cultures that once seemed to be dying out in twentieth-century United States and in other parts of the world.[6]

The phenomenon of re-created Jewish community has been documented in Riv-Ellen Prell's ethnography of a now defunct southern California *havurah: Prayer and Community: The Havurah in American Judaism.*[7] An anthropologist, Prell demonstrates the ways that the *havurah* movement joined Judaism and countercultural attitudes in "an attempt to synthesize a generational outlook . . . with traditional Judaism" since its inception in the 1970s.[8] She explains that this movement represents a critique of "the suburban and monumental urban synagogue as a viable expression of Jewish life. Its members rejected denominations, impressive buildings, and other imitations of American society and Protestantism."[9] She stresses that "[t]hey did not, however, reject Judaism, only their parents' version of it."[10]

Like the members of the apparently heterosexual *havurah* studied by Prell, many members of the contemporary Jewish bisexual community in the Bay Area share "a desire to create identity and personal meaning within a historical tradition that defines community."[11] Yet this incarnation of Jewish community building also centers around the movements of bisexuality and antiheterosexist struggle. Members of this contemporary Jewish community build a historical foundation for their gender roles and sexualities by connecting them to Judaism and Jewish culture; this is an especially critical rooting because of the contested placement of bisexuality between the more recognized sexual identities of heterosexuality and homosexuality, and the difficulty of maintaining a positive bisexual identification over time.

Writings on Jewish Bisexuality

The recent project of proclaiming Jewish bisexual identity and community in the Bay Area, which started around the early 1980s, is modeled after earlier Jewish lesbian organizing that still flourishes today. Jewish lesbian thought has been documented in writings mostly geared toward a feminist audience that reflects its grassroots origins. The groundbreaking book on Jewish lesbian experience was the anthology *Nice Jewish Girls,* edited by Evelyn Torton Beck.[12] The purpose of this book was "to make ourselves heard and known" as Jewish lesbian feminists. The highlighting of invisibility and visibility in and outside of religious institutions affirms the importance of these issues to Jewish sexual minorities. Since the first publication of this anthology in 1981, there has been an outpouring of writing by Jewish lesbians and their increasing visibility and acceptance in U.S. Jewish culture.[13] This body of work has been reviewed by Naomi Scheman, who observed that "lesbian identity and eroticism can provide a route of return to and affirmation of Jewish identity."[14] Scheman relates her own conflicted experience as a "bisexual woman currently living heterosexually" to the lesbian writings that she celebrates.[15] This points to the presence of Jewish bisexuals at the interstices of both Jewish and lesbian writings and networks.

While there is much work on bisexuality by people of Jewish background, little of it integrates a discussion of Jewishness. Linkages of the themes of bisexuality and Jewishness run through some of the pieces in the anthology *Bisexual Politics: Theories, Queries, and Visions,* edited by two members of the Bay Area Jewish bisexual community.[16] A number of the contributors refer to their Jewish identification in their bios, as "African-American, Jewish, bisexual," "radical Ashkenazi Jewish," and "Queer Jew."[17] The one piece that specifically addresses Jewish bisexuality is, "If Half of You Dodges a Bullet, All of You Ends up Dead," by Orna Izakson.[18] The focus of Izakson's piece is the relative invisibility of Jewish and bisexual oppression, which she sees as key aspects of both identities. The author reflects that "[b]isexuals and Jews occupy a middle ground in the spectrum of oppression. . . . But because bisexuals sometimes have different-sex partners, or because many Jews have white skin, we are not as visible in sharing . . . oppression."[19] According to Izakson, "By looking at both Jewish and bisexual histories, we learn what the oppression of relatively invisible people looks like. We also learn that the most effective way to fight that oppression is by reclaiming a visible identity, not by whitewashing ourselves."[20] Another piece on a similar theme is a personal essay entitled "Passing: Pain or Privilege? What the Bisexual Movement Can Learn from Jewish Experience," by Naomi Tucker, a Jewish bisexual organizer living in the San Francisco Bay Area and editor of the afore-mentioned anthology.[21]

While there is a "new tradition" of personal essays, fiction, and creative writing by and about nonheterosexual Jews, social science methodologies have been less commonly employed to understand nonheterosexual Jewish individuals and communities.[22] A notable exception is Israeli anthropologist Moshe Shokeid's ethnography *A Gay Synagogue in New York,* based on his participant observation at Congregation Beth Simchat Torah (CBST) in New York City.[23]

The author takes what he calls a "secular" approach to his examination of the reasons for and impact of synagogue affiliation on gay and lesbian congregants.[24] He asks the following questions: "Is the choice of sanctuary mainly a strategy to lighten the burden of the stigma of homosexuality? Is this part of the search for a new communitas in the urban metropolitan jungle? Or are these the paradoxical emblems of postmodern men and women?"[25]

Shokeid finds that these scenarios are all true to some extent. He also suggests that joining CBST was a way for gay Jews to "restore their cracked identity" and reconcile their homosexuality with their Jewish background.[26] Additionally, a return to Jewish religion and ethnicity provided a desired "framework for stable lesbian and gay associations" beyond sexually based alliances.[27] This need became especially acute as the AIDS crisis threatened previous gay social practices and networks and brought illness and death as a regular occurrence to the lives of gay men.

Re-visioned Community

Bay Area Jewish bisexuals are collectively engaged in a project of re-visioning Jewishness in order to create progressive Jewish community, lives, and bodies. Although the radical rewriting of some may seem exceptional, they are part of a tradition of constant revision of Jewish ethnicity and religion in the United States. Referring to the work of anthropologist Michael Fisher, Prell discusses the ways that "each generation's ethnic identity is newly made":

> Those who seek to understand their ethnicity, often in search of a unified and coherent life story, individually "invent" and 'reinterpret" their history in every generation. This interpretive process is necessary because second and third generation ethnic Americans inevitably define themselves through 'inter-reference" between the cultural traditions that surround them.[28]

For example, she reminds us that the *havurah* movement was heavily influenced by Black Power struggles and other movements of cultural reclamation by people of color in the United States. Other cultural theorists emphasize the political and definitional struggles that lie behind multiple interpretations of ethnic and religious tradition.[29]

Versions of both Jewish and gay and lesbian history play an important part in the beliefs and practices of participants in this group of Jewish bisexuals. Some espouse a contested rendition of Jewish tradition that challenges Jewish Reform practices and employs Jewish history or biblical passages to demonstrate that new interpretations and directions are culturally embedded and valid. This is often done with a sense of play and an understanding of the selective deployment of history and texts to bolster alternate visions and choices. For example, ritual leader Aliza feels that her unconventional reading of Jewish texts, which emphasizes their woman-centered and "earth-based" (a term used in ecological circles to indicate a centering of nature) aspects, is part of the Jewish tradition of midrash, where passages of religious text receive multiple interpretations: "[I]n terms of the religion, I've basically . . . kind of re-created the religion in a way that's more meaningful to me, and I think also more true to the original roots. . . . And really, everyone, though they won't admit it, takes what they like and leaves the rest."

On a cultural level many community members embrace historical stereotypes of nerdy, effeminate Jewish men and strong, loud, masculinized Jewish woman, using these stories of Jewish gender in the project of creating feminist and woman-loving women as well as antisexist men and woman-man relationships.[30] In this way, butch-identified Jewish women and fag-identified Jewish men find historical roots and justifications for their contemporary gender expressions. While these largely anti-Semitic stereotypes do not accurately represent gender roles in Jewish culture, their reimaginings and recyclings serve a positive and important purpose by offering paradigms for antisexist relationships and masculinities, and by historically and culturally rooting these paradigms and behaviors. I explore this phenomenon of re-created Jewish religion and culture by sharing portions of my visit and interviews.

Jewish Bisexual Women in the Bay Area

When I arrived in Oakland, California, for the purpose of conducting interviews on the day before the San Francisco Pride Parade, I was surprised to learn how many people who identified as Jewish and bisexual wanted their stories to be known. Almost all of the people I interviewed had participated at some point in the Jewish Bisexual Caucus of BiPOL; about half were recruited through the mailing list of this group. Many were members of Jewish religious and spiritual institutions, including the area lesbian and gay Reform synagogue, a queer, bisexually dominated *havurah* and ritual group, and a progressive renewal congregation that welcomes gays and lesbians. Some knew each other from bisexual groups and institutions, including the production team of a national bisexual magazine. Others were part of informal social networks; many had worshiped with, gossiped about, dated, or somehow "schmoozed" with other participants.

I was struck by the heterogeneity of this burgeoning community. The facilitator of the Jewish bisexual support group, Jesse, aptly describes his group as "a most amazing borscht":

> [L]ots of different people come through the group, an incredible variety of people from amazingly diverse backgrounds, and you just would never think . . . You get this incredible cross section of how diverse Jews are. We have lots of Jews from outside the U.S., for example, that participate in the group, people from every point on the religious spectrum and every point on the orientation spectrum. And people who are mixed heritage, and people who are Jews by choice who converted to Judaism, transgendered people—male to female, female to male—I mean, it's really the most amazing borscht.

The community was a place where many Jews who felt marginalized within conventional Jewish institutions could find comfort and acceptance. Yet there were pulls toward conformity that led to varying degrees of alienation for some who were not white, middle-class, able-bodied, urban-raised, or in cross-gender relationship. There was a predominance of women from middle-class backgrounds. While there were women of color in the community, almost all of the women's Jewish backgrounds were of Ashkenazi origin; Sephardi and Mizrahi Jewish women are not represented in my sample. This disparity is reflected in Jesse's imagery of the community as a "borscht," a soup from the Ashkenazi tradition. While there was a range of ages, from twenty-one to sixty-five, most of the women were in their twenties and early thirties. The few community members who had children often had difficulty integrating their parenting into adult-centered community and activities. While there were more women than men in the communities, there were internal struggles around how to welcome bisexual men into a feminist community without elevating them. In the words of one interviewee, "there's a way that men who are really good, really feminist, really cool, really sweet are given more attention than *women* who are really cool, sweet, and feminist. It's something that I'm aware of. And it's tricky." Members struggled with the subtleties of sexism, racism, classism, and other oppressions.

Return to Judaism

In the course of my research I noted that many community members deepened their Jewish identity and commitment or returned to a re-created Judaism through their involvement in Jewish bisexual community. Study participants identified across the religious spectrum, including one Orthodox and ten secular or unaffiliated Jews. Almost all interviewees were engaged in a reclamation of their cultural heritage as Jews. Eleven interviewees were involved in bisexually dominated spiritual groups that engaged in a radical reinterpretation of the

Jewish religion. While this represents a minority of my sample, participants in these groups were leaders of regional Jewish and bisexual thought and organizing, and were engaged in a creative project that is important beyond its numbers. I make no attempt to assess how "true" their perspectives are to the original texts; rather, I share their perceptions of their Jewish beliefs and practices, and what their participation in this project means to them on emotional, spiritual, and political levels.

In the early 1990s, the second incarnation of a *havurah* called Queer Minyan was founded by Aliza, a lesbian-identified bisexual woman, and a "fag-identified" bisexual man. It is a social and prayer group that meets monthly on Friday night to celebrate Shabbat; while most of its members are Jewish bisexuals, it welcomes people who identify as Jewish "queers" and their friends. Leah, a community activist in her early thirties raised with a weak connection to Reform Judaism, explains that Queer Minyan provides a sense of community and offers her a place to explore her Jewish spirituality with others.

In the following statement she refers to a process of becoming "spiritually identified" rather than religiously identified, language that suggests the differences between this reimagined form of Judaism and more traditional Jewish reform practice:

> I never really went through a period of not wanting to be Jewish, not liking being Jewish, not wanting to be part of Jewish community. But what has changed in my life is that I've become more spiritually identified, and that as a child and young adult I always identified as a cultural Jew. . . . I think the reason it's changed is that I finally have found a spiritual community that makes sense to me and that moves me inside, and nothing really moved me spiritually before.

At Queer Minyan, Leah says, she found a form of Judaism that broadly reinterpreted Hebrew texts to fit the ideologies of young, queer-identified members such as herself.

Creating Mishpocheh

According to Aliza, the people in this ritual group became "*mishpocheh*" to each other and helped create space for further Jewish bisexual organizing and community building.[31] Among the people who attend the monthly Queer Minyan gatherings is a smaller group of close friends who form a day-to-day social community together:

> [O]utside of that more formal thing, there's a group of us, about . . . a dozen of us, that tend to hang out a lot and feel like family to each other, and we talk about living together pretty seriously. . . . We pray together, we're sexual together, we do

spiritual stuff together, we help each other on practical levels. It's definitely community, I would say. I feel like living in community is really important and I need that and I want that.

In 1995 Pardes Rimonim ("orchard of pomegranates" in Hebrew), an earth-based, feminist Jewish ritual group also dominated by Jewish bisexuals, conducted its first High Holy Days services. Aliza explains that while some people are members of both Queer Minyan and Pardes Rimonim, Pardes is more focused on "striking a new spiritual path," fusing Judaism with pagan practices in a way that deeply challenges traditional Judaism.

Aliza, who is a ritual leader and the daughter of a Holocaust survivor, describes the ways that her Jewish practice is undergirded by a philosophy of inclusivity: "I'm intuitively searching out the practices and customs and rituals that are meaningful to many people, not only Jews. And especially many people who felt outside of religion of any kind."

This philosophy is demonstrated by the experience of Raquel, a writer, educator, and political organizer. She describes the ways that Pardes Rimonim has offered her a place to link her secular, politically radical Jewish upbringing with her mother's Latina heritage and spirituality. This is captured by her description of Pardes as "a place where . . . kosher means organic and union label."

Raquel outlines her shift over time from a primary focus on her non-Jewish, Latina heritage to reintegrating her Jewish heritage and spirituality:

> I'm feeling very Jewish right now. I spent about fifteen years with the focus of my personal and political work on the Latina side, and over the last . . . five years [I] have really been . . . looking more at the Jewish stuff. I do a lot of workshops on internalized anti-Semitism on college campuses, Jewish radical heritage, and the linkages between racism and anti-Semitism. . . . I recently decided that I want to have a bat mitzvah within Pardes Rimonim, I'm going to be their first . . . and my new partner is Jewish. . . . I want my child to grow up there. I want to do a commitment ceremony with my new partner in that community.

Raquel's status and skills as a feminist and antiracist organizer are seen as relevant to spiritual leadership at Pardes Rimonim. A captivating storyteller, she invokes her family history during group spiritual practice in a way that is personally and socially healing. As Raquel weaves the legend of her "great-great-great-great-grandmother's" life, both her ancestor's struggles and the group's current alternative religious and social practices are validated:

> My great-grandmother's grandmother was the wife of a rabbi in the Ukraine . . . an arbiter of disputes . . . a powerful matriarch in her community. . . . [T]he story

is that she stood up one day in temple and said to everybody there, "Your God is a man," and walked out. . . .

[G]oing to High Holy Days at Pardes Rimonim . . . [I] really fe[lt] . . . for the first time like I had a spiritual community where all of my people were welcome. And not just the Latinos but the anti-religious Jewish ancestors who were always hanging over my head being critical when I was at other celebrations. . . . This was a place where I was seen as not only fully Jewish, but in a way I was getting to be the rabbi that she never got to be. It was a place where I was asked to read a Torah portion and things that were about Latino history, and everyone saw it as relevant to them . . . as Jews . . . [A]nd I think, what would my great-great-great-grandma do? . . . Walk into this room and look around and see all these guys in skirts and these pierced body parts and . . . women kissing each other in the corners. And I'd just take her by the hand and say believe me, this is what you were dreaming of.

Home Rituals

The practice of queer-affirming Judaism is also performed through the home rituals that are a critical part of traditional Jewish religion. Tone, a student in her early thirties, explains that as a person with a Jewish father and a non-Jewish mother, s/he barely identified as Jewish until s/he encountered queer Jewish community three years prior to our interview. S/he is an intersexual activist who is usually assumed to be a butch female by strangers. In the following passage Tone uses her idea of Jewish history to link her multiple identifications and find strength in queer and Jewish survival:

Recently I've been able to equate how Judaism as a tribe has been able to hold together in the face of all this adversity, and equate that to the emerging queer identity. . . . Queers have had the same sort of adversity that Jews have had in a lot of ways, and that people have always hated them, have always wanted to kill them, have carried out pogroms against queers. . . . When I made that connection it totally made me identify even more with my Jewish heritage.

Tone lives in a communally run and owned household with people of different ages and ethnic and religious backgrounds. She considers her home a "hotbed" of transgendered and intersexual political activity. Lighting the Sabbath candles, a ritual that was occasionally observed by her Orthodox-raised father and which she abandoned as a young adult, is now practiced weekly by her entire household in honor of queer and Jewish survival. Using her grandmother's candlesticks gives historical weight to their tribute to both histories and identities. As I heard about the violence that she faced as a youth who did not physically fit into a two-sex system, I understood how Jewish ritual provided an important vehicle for healing and personal empowerment.

Some participants remained alienated from the Jewish religion because of their atheist beliefs or their discomfort with the androcentrism that Judaic studies scholar Judith Baskin considers as "an inherent feature of the classical texts of rabbinic Judaism."[32] Yet almost all of these nonreligious interviewees strongly affirmed their secular Jewish identities through actions such as changing their names from Americanized to Jewish ones and drawing links between their social activism and the East European Jewish political tradition. Orthodox-raised Dona, who rejected Judaism and distanced herself from Jewish culture as a teenager, now honors her Jewish cultural heritage yet will "not touch Torah with a ten-foot pole":

> I'm beginning to feel really happy about embracing my Judaism again . . . in a cultural and traditional way. I still do not touch Torah with a ten-foot pole. It has been a real oppressor and I can't go near it yet. I don't know if I ever will, even with the reinterpretation. . . . I have seen it keep people in a very narrow focus. . . . [I]t has led to a lot of women hating . . . things about being a woman. . . . You really have to twist it other ways to get a more feminist perspective and a more empowering perspective.

Ari is a day care worker in her mid-twenties who grew up in a poor family in a Northeast ghetto area. For Ari, "being Jewish . . . is more a connection to my history and the past and cultural things than it is the religion." She explains that Jewish ideals such as *tikkun olam* have guided her life choices in young adulthood:

> There's definitely certain values that I take from the Jewish tradition that are very important to me. . . . I very strongly feel that in this world we are all responsible for each other, I feel that none of us is free till all of us [are] free. That whole commitment to social justice . . . that's very much part of who I am . . . and I know that part of that comes from being Jewish.

She asserted her queer, butch identity and her Jewish identity a few years ago by changing her name from an Anglicized female name to a Jewish male name. Part of Ari's decision to distance herself from religious Jewish practice comes from her feelings of class alienation from Jewish and bisexual community and religious groups. She tends to express her Jewish culture in an individualized manner, or with a small group of friends who are more sensitive to class issues.

Another participant who considers herself a cultural Jew is Jane, a woman in her late forties who comes from a family that was largely decimated by the Holocaust. While she does not practice the religion, over the past decade she has sensed that her Jewish identity pervades the way she interacts with others.

Jane demonstrated her strong commitment to her Jewish cultural identity by traveling to Auschwitz three years ago. During the week that she spent there so she could "hear the echoes in the middle of the night, the silence in the snow . . . hear the voices," she performed a ritual that united her Jewish and woman-loving identities and symbolically included her circle of Jewish women friends:

> I did make a pilgrimage a few years ago to Auschwitz, and it was very important to me. And one of the things that I did was that I took some things from my women friends . . . and I left them at Auschwitz, right in the doorway of the crematorium in one of the ovens with a note detailing that I am a bisexual, Jewish American woman and that I was leaving stones from the Isle of Lesbos . . . in acknowledgment of the fact that Jews were not the only victims, they were the main victims, but people were killed for other things, too. And being homosexual was one of them. . . . And I put [the stones] in the *yahrzeit*[33] candle that I let burn in the oven.

Embracing Complexity

How do bisexual identities connect with the act of embracing and recreating Jewish culture? During a group discussion, three study participants shared that their religious legacy offers them an ability to "embrace complexity." This facilitates their process of challenging norms of gender and sexual orientation.

> It's not hard . . . to reject a tradition . . . that doesn't allow you to question. But where there's flexibility, you can push against the walls of our tradition, and it can travel from generation to generation.
>
> Our tradition is actually based on . . . iconoclasm . . . going right back to Abraham, who smashed his father's idols. That . . . as Jews and bisexuals . . . there's a certain weight, a traditional weight . . . or authority . . . that . . . comes with . . . challenging, questioning the stereotypes and the mold in which many of us were tempted to be placed.
>
> There is in the tradition a kind of embracing of complexity. And I think that bisexuals are saying, "Yes, let's embrace it all." I see us very aggressively recreating both cultures.

The practices of constructing multiple interpretations of Talmud through creating new midrash, the tradition of Talmudic debate, the story of Abraham smashing false idols, and the long history of resistance to oppression form a religious and traditional buttress for members' questioning not only of compulsory heterosexuality but of the binary opposition of homosexuality versus heterosexuality. These traditions of questioning and debate within Judaism and Jewish culture enable Jewish bisexuals to "push against the walls of our tradition" rather than reject it, "aggressively . . . recreating" both Jewish culture and systems of sex, gender, and sexuality. Not only are the bisexual and queer identities of community members impacted by their Jewish heritage, but bisexuality and queer expression extend the definitions of Jewish culture and community.

Notes

1. For fine examples of this recent outpouring of scholarly work on a diversity of Jewish women, see Lynn Davidman and Shelly Tennenbaum, *Feminist Perspectives on Jewish Studies* (New Haven: Yale University Press, 1994); T. M. Rudavsky, ed., *Gender and Judaism* (New York: New York University Press, 1995); Maurie Sacks, ed., *Active Voices: Women in Jewish Culture* (Urbana: University of Illinois Press, 1995); Marla Brettschneider, ed., *The Narrow Bridge: Jewish Views on Multiculturalism* (New Brunswick, N.J.: Rutgers University Press, 1996); and Miriam Peskowitz and Laura Levitt, eds., *Judaism since Gender* (New York: Routledge, 1997).
2. Bob Goldfarb, "Klal Israel: Lesbians and Gays in the Jewish Community," in Brettschneider, ed., *The Narrow Bridge*, 63.
3. Elizabeth Daumer, "Queer Ethics; or, the Challenge of Bisexuality to Lesbian Ethics," *Hypatia* 7, 4 (1992): 91.
4. According to Naomi Tucker in her introduction to the anthology *Bisexual Politics: Theories, Queries and Visions*, BiPOL is a bisexual political action group that formed in the Bay Area in 1983. Naomi Tucker, ed., *Bisexual Politics: Theories, Queries and Visions* (New York: Harrington Park Press, 1995).
5. "Intersexuality occurs when an individual is born with physical evidence of sexual ambiguity or duality, such as a micropenis, androgen insensitivity (which results in an XY [chromosomally male] child with a vagina who is assigned as a female), enlarged clitoris . . . and/or ovotestes. Intersexed people often receive surgical intervention to assign or reassign their sex while they are still infants; often, this intervention is problematic, physically or psychically, for the treated individual." Dallas Denny and Jamison Green, in *Bisexuality: The Psychology and Politics of an Invisible Minority*, ed. Beth A. Firestein (Thousand Oaks: Sage Publications, 1996), 86.
6. Mizrahi Jews are Jews of Arab or Middle Eastern descent.
7. Riv-Ellen Prell, *Prayer and Community: The Havurah in American Judaism* (Detroit: Wayne State University Press, 1989).
8. Ibid., 15.
9. Ibid., 16.
10. Ibid.
11. Ibid.
12. Evelyn Torton Beck, *Nice Jewish Girls* (Boston: Beacon Press, 1989).
13. For a review of Jewish lesbian writing, see Naomi Scheman, "Jewish Lesbian Writing: A Review Essay," *Hypatia* 7, 4 (1992). For nonfiction on Jewish lesbians, see Rebecca Alpert, *Like Bread on the Seder Plate: Jewish Lesbians and the Transformation of Tradition* (New York: Columbia University Press); Melanie Kaye/Kantrowitz, *The Issue Is Power: Essays on Women, Jews, Violence and Resistance* (San Francisco: Aunt Lute Books, 1992); Irena Klepfisz, *Dreams of an Insomniac: Jewish Feminist Essays, Speeches and Diatribes* (Portland: Eighth Mountain

Press, 1990), in particular the piece "Jewish Lesbians, the Jewish Community, Jewish Survival"; Ellie Bulkin, Minnie Bruce Pratt, and Barbara Smith, *Yours in Struggle: Three Feminist Perspectives on Anti-Semitism and Racism* (New York: Long Haul Press, 1984); *Bridges: A Journal for Jewish Feminists and Our Friends*; and Tracy Moore, *Lesbiot: Israeli Lesbians Talk about Sexuality, Feminism, Judaism, and Their Lives* (London: Cassell, 1995).

14. Scheman, "Jewish Lesbian Writing," 186.
15. Ibid., 187.
16. Tucker, introduction to *Bisexual Politics*.
17. Ibid., xv–xxi.
18. Orna Isakson, "If Half of You Dodges a Bullet, All of You Ends Up Dead," in *Bisexual Politics: Theories, Queries, and Visions* (New York: Harrington Park Press, 1995), 251–56.
19. Ibid., 251.
20. Ibid., 255.
21. Tucker, "Passing: Pain or Privilege? What the Bisexual Community Can Learn from the Jewish Experience," in *Bisexual Horizons: Politics, Histories, Lives*, eds. Sharon Rose, Cris Stevens, et al. (London: Lawrence and Wishart, 1996), 32–37.
22. For fiction and poetry on Jewish lesbian topics, see works by Adrienne Rich, Melanie Kaye/Kantrowitz, Irena Klepfisz, Judith Katz, Leslea Newman, and Sarah Schulman.
23. Moshe Shokeid, *A Gay Synagogue in New York* (New York: Columbia University Press, 1995).
24. Ibid., 238.
25. Ibid.
26. Ibid., 239.
27. Ibid., 241.
28. Prell, *Prayer and Community*, 70.
29. For a discussion of the political implications of reinterpreting community, see Kobena Mercer, *Welcome to the Jungle: New Positions in Black Cultural Studies* (New York: Routledge, 1994), and Ana Maria Alonso, "The Effects of Truth: Re-presentations of the Past and the Imagining of Community," *Journal of Historical Sociology* 1, 1 (March 1988): 51.
30. For an excellent anthology that includes discussion of the progressive reclamation of Jewish gender stereotypes, see Peskowitz and Levitt, eds., *Judaism since Gender*.
31. "Family" in Yiddish. Aliza's use of this word reflects the ways that the group not only re-creates Jewish religion but reinforces Yiddish language and culture. According to Aliza, whose father's Transylvanian Jewish heritage did not include Yiddish, and whose British mother does not speak Yiddish, "I feel even more Jewish than when I was younger now, because I think I'm around more consciously Jewish Jews. For example, when I was younger I didn't speak with Yiddish inflection because my parents' background wasn't Yiddish speaking . . . but then I started hanging around Jews with Yiddish-inflected accents, so I find myself using more Yiddishisms."
32. Judith Baskin, "Rabbinic Judaism and the Creation of Woman," in Peskowitz and Levitt, eds., *Judaism Since Gender*, 126.
33. On the anniversary of someone's death "a memorial candle is lighted in the home, and another in the synagogue, where it burns from sunset to sunset." Leo Rosten, *The Joys of Yiddish* (New York: Pocket Books, 1970).

Visions for the Future

17

Leadership for Profound Change

A Means for Transforming the American Reform Synagogue

SAMUEL K. JOSEPH

Change is *the* key word in synagogue life today. If congregations are to survive, they must respond to the powerful forces pressing on their organizational boundaries. The traditional Jewish family, for example—two parents, married to each other, with children—is by far the minority family structure in American Jewish life. Today a congregation member is much more likely to be divorced, maybe remarried, maybe a single parent with children. A female congregation member is highly likely to be working outside the home. There is a high probability that a congregation member has moved more than once from his or her birth city and is now living quite removed from a support system of family and childhood friends. It is possible that the congregation member may be in a gay or lesbian couple and may have a child with that partner. The congregation member may be a convert or, even more likely, a non-Jew married to a Jew. Clearly the makeup of the congregational membership is vastly different that it was a few decades ago. Yet many synagogues still create programs that assume the traditional family model.

At the same time, planning the congregation's program with different conceptions of the family in mind is, in and of itself, not enough, for the synagogue is a highly textured organization. If creating a Jewish religious synagogue community is the goal, then one has to be able to see the broadest range of possibilities of a complex organization. Does the American Reform synagogue have the structure and the resources to change in order to meet these new realities? In the area of leading the congregation into that future reality, it will require a radical restructuring of both thought and process concerning the nature of congregational life and how congregations work.

Of course, the synagogue does not exist in a vacuum. The surrounding American society, in which the synagogue is embedded, is undergoing great changes. The information age means that communications, data, and news of global events are sent around the world within fractions of a second. Information gathering that once took days or weeks can now be had in a matter of minutes. The traditional great structures of this society—home, school, and religious institutions—are all affected by this age of the Internet and computers. People tell of experiencing more loneliness, alienation, disconnection from society. If nothing else, people lack a "personal touch" from society's institutions. The challenge is building community in this society of individuals, yet community can be created only when its members have a sense of group purpose.

For the synagogue of the future to be successful, it has to be an energized, interdependent community, not just a place where Jews stop off once in a while to attend a bar/bat mitzvah, a High Holy Days service, or a support group for intermarried couples. Gary Tobin writes, "While synagogues are successful in attracting Jews at some point in their life cycle, they are becoming less and less successful in attracting them sooner and holding on to them longer."[1] Much of the synagogue's response to current needs is to invent more and more programs, each one tailored to fit a specific constituency. The problem with this is that it caters to the consumer mind-set of American culture. The single parent, the family new to the community, and the intermarried family come to the synagogue to consume the special program offered to meet their own, individual, special needs. But consumers just consume; they do not necessarily become a community. Since these consumers must meet their own individual needs, they are hungry for more and more synagogue programs that attempt to do just that. Synagogues are then faced with trying to meet individual needs *and* create community. Synagogue leaders, professional and voluntary, try to sustain this warehouse-sized market of programs and cannot.

Even more, synagogue programs should be only entry points into synagogue community life, not ends unto themselves. The question is how the structure of the synagogue, and the thinking of its leadership, can shape an organization that will transform a community of Jews into a Jewish community. The answer exists in transforming the American Reform synagogue into a learning organization supportive of change.

Transforming the American Reform Synagogue

The early thinking about learning organizations and organizational change comes from the work of Peter Senge.[2] His research in the world of business and industry shows that organizations cannot thrive without learning to adapt their attitudes and practices. The learning organization is one that learns about, and from, the external and internal challenges that confront it.

Senge talks about change, transformation, and profound change as the key concepts facing the business world today. He writes that the word *change* can mean many things and often seems contradictory. It can sometimes mean external changes, such as technology, customers, and the social environment. It can sometimes mean internal changes, such as how the organization adapts to change. The concern is whether the internal changes can keep pace with the external changes. *Transformation* is another key term that is used in the business world. Senge writes that it is often used to describe comprehensive organizational change initiatives. Transformational change really has come to mean large changes, not a singular episode of change.[3] For Senge *profound change* describes organizational change that "combines inner shifts in people's values, aspirations and behaviors with outer shifts in processes, strategies, practices and systems. In profound change the organization builds its capacity for doing things in a new way. It builds for ongoing change."[4]

The American Reform synagogue must transform itself so that it can undergo a profound change. Tobin states that "if synagogues continue to operate as they did in the past, the net result will be continued decline in synagogue affiliation and participation."[5] What was the nature of synagogue operation in the past? It included, among a number of things, top-down leadership, with either the rabbi or the board solely in charge. Congregants were far removed from decision making. It included a "business as usual" approach, so that maintaining the status quo became very important. It assumed that different arms of the synagogue did not have a real need to communicate with one another and to collaborate. It believed that the religious school's problems were somehow separate from the entire cradle-to-grave educational enterprise of the congregation. It included little or no leadership development, long-range planning, financial development, or marketing.

Six Characteristics of a Learning Organization

I want to propose six characteristics of a learning organization that American Reform synagogues must adopt if they are going to be supportive of, and affected by, profound change. They include (1) engaging congregants and professionals in shared learning about their synagogue, (2) a willingness and a capacity to challenge the assumptions and cultural regularities of the congregation, (3) the capacity for reflective thinking about problems and issues of the congregation . . . and the consideration of alternative understandings of the issues and the possible solutions, (4) the commitment of time by all those involved in this process of reflection and learning about the congregation, (5) the openness to thinking in new ways about the life and the functioning of the congregation, and (6) the application of process as a critical element of learning about the congregation and of creating a learning congregation.

Engaging Congregants and Professionals in Shared Learning about Their Congregation

The important word in this characteristic is *shared*. There is little history of congregational life where the professionals and the congregants actually share a task as equals. Stereotypically the professionals are the experts in the Judaic/Hebraic life of the congregation and the congregants know the more practical matters, such as finance and budget. Each defers to the other at the appropriate time, thereby holding on to some power by the special knowledge each possesses.

If the synagogue is to respond to future needs, then all who are involved in creating and maintaining that synagogue must be committed to learning together everything possible about their congregation. This means talking with congregants and professionals about all facets of the congregation, including past, present, and future programs. It means asking one another about hopes for the future. It means looking deeply into the past history of the congregation for insights into present, and possible future, functioning.

All of this work needs to be done by teams of congregants and professionals, who by working on these tasks together begin to model the type of engaged synagogue community they want to create. Sharing this work is energizing. Learning together about one's congregation is the first step toward profound change.

A Willingness and a Capacity to Challenge Assumptions and Cultural Regularities about the Congregation

In a congregation, underlying assumptions are those beliefs that the congregants hold and treat as facts. These are the givens in the congregation and are things the congregants usually do not want to change or cannot see being changed. These assumptions are usually unconscious and direct congregants how to perceive, think about, and feel about what happens in the congregation. They tell congregants what to pay attention to, what things mean, how to react emotionally to what is going on, and what actions to take in various situations.

Some would say that congregational assumptions are those things that are treated as nonnegotiable. For the congregation these assumptions provide comfort and stability.

Examples of underlying congregational assumptions could be: "Religious school is always Sunday morning, 9:30 A.M. to 12:00 P.M."; "The kids always hate Hebrew school"; "The rabbi is the only one who leads the service"; "This is not a singing congregation"; "Friday night services are exactly one hour long"; "The powerful board members are the wealthy ones"; "One has to give money in order to be recognized"; "The Sisterhood and the Brotherhood are the fundraising arms of the congregation"; "Adult couples without children will not join the congregation."

Joined with the congregational assumptions are the espoused values and the cultural artifacts of the congregation. Espoused values, which also include norms and rules of behavior, are seen in the congregation's mission statement and any texts that include the goals and the philosophies of the congregation.

The congregation's cultural artifacts are all those structures and processes that one sees, hears, and feels when encountering the congregation. Examples include the worship service, rituals, how people dress, stories congregants tell about the synagogue and its clergy, the building's architecture and decor, emotional displays and behavior of groups, ceremonies, and how congregational life is organized.

Leaders of a learning congregation have to make a deep examination of the congregation's assumptions and cultural regularities. The first step is spending the time to articulate all the assumptions and cultural artifacts and values that can be discovered. Because the leadership of the congregation lives in the midst of that culture, and in most ways is the transmitter of the congregation's culture, this is a difficult task, and one that the professional and voluntary leadership have to be willing to undertake.

Once a list of the assumptions and cultural regularities is made, the next step is to question which of the items on the list are limiting. This means asking which assumptions, when held on to by the congregation continuously, could limit the vision of the congregation. Of course, this will require the leadership to examine many cherished facets of the congregation. The goal is to be able to see which assumptions and cultural regularities limit future planning and which ones do not.

For example, by talking to a representative group of members, the congregational leadership may discover that there are a number of congregants who want to participate in leading a service and in singing during the service. To say "At our congregation the rabbi always leads the service, and we are not a singing congregation" could limit future planning.

In another example, the leadership examines the assumption that during worship services the congregation sits in pews. Given the fact that the sanctuary is built with permanent pews, this is an assumption that must be held as true, and it can be challenged only by mounting a building campaign. If the vision of the congregation includes a style of worship services where rows of pews are antithetical, then the leadership may indeed wish to challenge this assumption. The leadership of the congregation may look at the pews as well as other assumptions and cultural regularities related to worship (for example, the prayer book used, the use of an organ, when and how Torah is read, the length of the service, the time of day of the service) and challenge them all.

The American Reform synagogue cannot begin to become a community without the willingness and the capacity to challenge "business as usual" in the congregation. Examining the assumptions and the cultural regularities is a vital step.[6]

The Capacity for Reflective Thinking about the Problems and the Issues Facing the Congregation, and the Consideration of Alternative Understandings of the Issues and Possible Solutions

Synagogue leaders naturally do not like to dwell on the problems facing the congregation. This is common sense. Why deal with things that may be painful? The hope of the leadership is that the congregation is vibrant enough to have new members flocking to join. On the other hand, people do not want to be part of a congregation where there is a perception of difficulties. The result of this is that the congregation cannot learn from its problems and challenges if the leadership avoids thinking about them. On the contrary, the problems and challenges can be a source of data for future planning.

Synagogue professionals and voluntary leaders must be able to name the problems and issues facing their congregation. At the same time they must feel that doing so is part of their mandate as synagogue leaders and that it is safe to do so. They cannot feel that they will be branded as disloyal to the congregation when they participate in this process. Rather, they must feel validated in doing so.

Once problems and issues are named, the professionals and the voluntary leaders must try to understand them in the context of both internal and external concerns important to a Jewish organization. Externally the congregation exists as part of a larger Jewish community. The leaders have to reflect on the congregation's problems in light of trends within the larger Jewish community, whether that is the surrounding metropolitan area, the region, North America, or world Jewry. The leaders may also want to reflect on the congregation's problems and issues while assessing emerging needs in Jewish life. A consideration of a vision of Jewish communal life and the engaged contemporary Jew is another external concern that is important to consider.

Internally congregational problems and issues have to be considered in light of how the congregation is fulfilling its Jewish mission and serving its members. While this seems logical, frequently synagogue leaders do not take the time to revisit the congregation's mission and use it as a lens to look at current problems and issues.

The final step is the most difficult part of fulfilling this characteristic. The synagogue's leadership must consider alternative understandings of the congregation's problems and alternative solutions to these problems. The important concept is "alternative."

Synagogue boards, despite their stereotype of being combative, try very hard to be polite and agreeable. People want synagogue operations and governance to be smooth and cooperative. This is one reason that synagogue boards are not filled with divergent-thinking board members. Boards like to come to agreement as soon as possible.

However, one of the strengths of the learning organization/congregation is that it seeks to understand itself as deeply and fully as possible. Borrowing a phrase from business and industry, leaders should try to "think outside the box." In order to do that, the professionals and the voluntary leaders must push themselves to consider every way to understand the problems and the issues facing the congregation. They have to force themselves to think of every possible solution to the problems, even apparently outlandish ones.

The Commitment of Time by All Those Involved in This Process of Reflection and Learning about the Congregation

Time is the one resource that all humans get equally. It cannot be borrowed or given to someone else, and it cannot be saved. Time must be spent by the receiver or else it is lost to that person. Time is finite and therefore quite precious. Time is one of the major resources that we ask leaders to spend on behalf of the synagogue. In many ways it is a more major gift than any other they may give the congregation.

Living in this information age, many people are used to great amounts of speed in their lives. Information arrives via the Internet in seconds, and there is an expectation that responses to queries will be just as fast. Fast cars, fast planes, fast computers, cell phones and fax machines all lead to an expectation that one can cram more things into twenty-four hours than ever before. Along with these various forms of speed comes the rate of change in general. There is no doubt that changes—in society, institutions, organizations—are happening at an increasingly faster pace. This is not an age for contemplation and thinking, but that is exactly what synagogue leaders must do.

Edgar Schein writes, "As the rate of change itself increases, learning ability will not consist of one-time learning of a new system; perpetual learning and change will be the only constant."[7] Learning takes much time. Since synagogue leaders will be in a perpetual state of learning about their congregation, they will have to give even more time to the tasks of leading than ever before. The process of reflecting and learning about the congregation is the core activity needed in order to create the engaged religious community the congregation must become. It takes to time to get there.

The Openness to Think in New Ways about the Congregation

A recent article in the *Los Angeles Times* talks about "congregations freed from what some see as the ossified traditions of the East Coast."[8] Clearly there are some members of the Jewish community who are looking for new ways to conceptualize the synagogue. Congregations operating in familiar, normative ways may no longer be the ones that attract the most members. As the constituency dramatically changes, these new-type members will look for the synagogue to be different as well. There is the perception that the synagogue of the past (which is still operating in the present) is staid, closed, narrow, nonspiritual, hierarchical, and so on. Synagogue professionals and voluntary leaders must be open to reflecting on this indictment and its implications for their particular congregation.

In San Francisco Rabbi Stephen Pearce questions the status quo. The rabbi at Congregation Emanu-El, a more-than-150-year-old congregation of 1,660 households, Pearce says that his congregation on a Friday night is now a "synaplex." On any given Friday evening there are multiple religious services. There is the "traditional" Reform service led by a rabbi and a cantor in the sanctuary, a "Tot Shabbat," a "Family Sharing Shabbat," a "Service of Peace and Healing," and a "Shabbat LaAm," an informal worship experience with an emphasis on contemporary liturgy and music. There are also small *havurot* (small groups of Jews who come together for worship and celebration) who meet monthly at the synagogue.[9]

Why the multiple worship services? Pearce says, "The tradition at Emanu-El was, if you don't like the one service, go elsewhere. There was a feeling this shul was unresponsive." With multiple services there is now double and triple the total number of participants on a Friday night.[10]

Rabbi Pearce's comments are very revealing. He shows that he and his congregational leadership can learn about, and respond to, the challenges and issues facing a congregation. Emanu-El has the external Jewish pressure of a changed constituency with varied worship needs. The internal Jewish pressure includes the longtime members who are comfortable with the status quo. The "synaplex" is one creative way to respond to these pressures. What is especially compelling about the Emanu-El innovation is that it seeks to meet the needs of different members while still bringing everyone to the synagogue on a Friday night. Also there is the ability to gather together all the participants from each of the services if that is desired.

An openness to thinking about the congregation in new ways allows for the "synaplex," and Congregation Emanu-El, to operate successfully.

The Application of Process as a Critical Element of Learning about the Congregation and of Creating a Learning Congregation

The trouble with the word *process* is that for some people in organizational life it is too "touchy-feely," too amorphous. There is the point of view that "we have to get the job done," and so we must deal with content: concrete plans, policies, and programs. The reality is that an organization needs both good process and meaningful content issues to exist simultaneously for healthy decision making and learning. One without the other leads to either never making a decision or making decisions in which the members of the organization feel excluded and maybe not wedded to the decisions carried out.

The professionals and the voluntary leaders of the synagogue have to create a good process in order for the synagogue to become a learning congregation and be able to bring about profound change. Good process ideally includes all of the previous five characteristics of a learning congregation. The professionals and the voluntary leaders must be committed to the process itself, the process of becoming that learning congregation. In this case the process *is* the content! Engaging in shared learning, challenging assumptions and cultural regularities, thinking reflectively, considering alternatives, committing time, and being open to ways of thinking all combine to make up the process. There is no profound change without these. Together they facilitate the discovery of meaningful content areas for the change and growth of the synagogue. Together they are the critical elements for a congregation becoming transformed.

A Mission, a Vision

Temple Shir Chadash (Sing a New Song): We are an open and dynamic Reform congregation, a Jewish community that strives to inspire and deepen, nurture and enrich the lives of our members.

The American Reform synagogue must be able to articulate what is its purpose and where it wants to take its members. A statement of the congregation's mission, such as that of the hypothetical Temple Shir Chadash, answers the questions "Who are we?" "What are we?" "For whom are we?" and "To what end?" A vision is a statement of where the congregation is headed. Without a statement of mission and vision the professionals and the voluntary leaders have no guidance for planning and budgeting. The mission and the vision are vital for the setting of priorities.

Answering those previously stated four questions related to a mission is a wonderful exercise for synagogue leadership. "Who are we?" sends the leadership on a quest to find out about the congregation's name. Usually congregational names are related to some value that resonated with the founders. Rodef Shalom (pursuers of peace), Shir Chadash (a new song), Beth Am (house of the people)— all represent important values that the congregation wanted enshrined in its name. (A number of congregations that are breakaways from larger congregations take the word *shalom*, "peace," as part of their new congregation's name, perhaps as a way for them to deal with the bad feelings that frequently follow a breakaway.)

"What are we?" questions how the synagogue calls itself. Is it a temple, a congregation, a synagogue, a community, a family? Choosing one of these terms for a congregation's mission statement is done for a specific purpose. Leaders of synagogues spend hours upon hours writing the mission statement, weighing each word. For example, it is normative that Reform congregations use the term *temple*. Non-Reform congregations usually do not because they do not want to use a term that historically is associated with the Temple in Jerusalem. The usage of the term *temple* in the Reform world is a theological and political statement.

If a mission statement already exists, the present synagogue's leadership can discuss what term was chosen, why they think it was chosen, and what the meaning of the term is in relation to the value(s) embedded in that term.

"For whom are we?" tells which constituents are the center of attention in this congregation. Statements such as "We are for our members," "We are for all Jews," "We are for families," and "We are for the children," all reveal more of the core values of this congregation.

"To what end are we?" is, of course, the key question. When all is said and done, why do we exist? In some ways this question is directly related to, and cannot be antithetical to, the vision statement. Remember, the vision is a picture of some future state. Answering the "to what end" question forces the professionals and the voluntary leadership to say why this congregation is presently in business and should stay in business.

Analyzing the mission statement for its values is certainly a critical step in shared leadership as well as in questioning assumptions and cultural regularities. Here is a brief analysis of the hypothetical Temple Shir Chadash's mission statement.

> *Who are we?* We are Temple Shir Chadash. [Why is the congregation called "a new song"? Did the congregation offer something new to Jews in that area when it was founded? Does it still offer something new? Is it a breakaway?]

> *What are we?* We are a Temple. We are a dynamic Reform congregation. We are a Jewish community. [What values are revealed by each of these words and phrases?]

> *For whom are we?* We are for our members. [Is this still the value? Is it too narrow?]

> *To what end are we?* We exist to inspire and deepen, nurture and enrich the lives of our members. [What do these terms mean? How are they lived out in the life of the congregation?]

The Challenge Ahead

"Why have so few congregations been able to adapt to a changing environment and reach new generations of people . . . ?" writes Lyle Schaller.[11] Writing for a mostly Protestant clergy readership, Schaller says that Protestant churches are filled with leaders who feel obliged to perpetuate yesterday when the need is to create a new tomorrow. "Leaders were hopeful that the newcomers would adapt to fit the culture of the congregation."[12] But that does not happen. The changing society creates people who simply do not join those kinds of churches.

This lesson is clear for the American Reform synagogue. The synagogue will have to undergo profound change to meet the needs of its new members. To make these changes happen, the synagogue must have leaders with much more sophisticated skills, capacities, and abilities than ever were needed in the past. The instrumental skills of leadership—being able to write an agenda, delegating, chairing meetings, reading a budget—are far, far from enough. The interpersonal skills of leadership—listening, clearly communicating, responding to conflict, recognizing good work—are far, far from enough. It is those skills *plus* highly developed imaginal skills (to dream toward the synagogue's vision) and systemic skills (to see the interdependency and the dynamism of the various parts of the synagogue) that are required.

"It would take a genuine flight of fancy to . . . hold the view that change happens because great men 'drive' change from the top," writes Senge.[13] There is no possible way that one or two people can hold all the skills necessary for change and simultaneously deal with all the problems and challenges facing the Reform synagogue. The American Reform synagogue must create communities of leaders, professionals and voluntary, who together will have the skills, energy, and learning to make the necessary changes. Leadership is not simply a position in the hierarchy. "Leadership is the capacity of a human community to shape its future, and specifically to sustain the significant processes of change required to do."[14]

A Final Word . . . Hope

Hope, or optimism, is the hallmark of good leadership. Warren Bennis teaches that "exemplary leaders seem to expect success: they always anticipate positive outcomes. The glass for them is not simply full but brimming."[15] A study by the Center for Creative Leadership shows "that people in positions of leadership are consistently more optimistic . . . more hopeful."[16]

Hope combines with determination to achieve one's goals. When leaders share their optimism about their synagogue's future, it creates tremendous confidence in those around the leaders. That can build energy and commitment, which in turn influence outcomes. Bennis says that every exemplary leader he has met has what seems to be an unwarranted degree of optimism, which helps generate the energy and the commitment necessary to achieve results.[17]

The problems and the challenges facing the American Reform synagogue are tremendous. It will take talented leadership to articulate the vision and guide the changes needed in order to meet those challenges. There is no doubt that professional and voluntary leaders do exist in the American Reform community who are able to do this job. The American Reform synagogue needs these people to become that community of leaders.

Notes

1. Gary Tobin, "Restructuring the Contemporary Synagogue," *The National Association of Synagogue Administrators (NASA) Journal,* winter 1992, 3–7.
2. Peter Senge's foundational book is *The Fifth Discipline* (New York: Currency/Doubleday, 1990). See also his most recent book, *The Dance of Change* (New York: Currency/Doubleday, 1999).
3. Senge, *The Dance of Change,* 15.
4. Ibid.
5. Tobin, "Restructuring," 3.
6. For an in-depth understanding of the role of leadership and organizational culture, see Edgar H. Schein, *Organizational Culture and Leadership* (San Francisco: Jossey-Bass, 1992).
7. Edgar Schein, "Leadership and Organizational Culture," in *The Leader of the Future,* eds. F. Hesselbein, M. Goldsmith, and R. Beckhard (San Francisco: Jossey-Bass, 1996), 67.
8. Larry Stammer, "A Westward Shift for Jewish Spirituality," *Los Angeles Times,* May 16, 1999, B1.
9. E. J. Kessler, "Rabbis Bucking for Friday Nights at the 'Synaplex,'" *The Forward,* June 5, 1998.
10. Ibid.
11. Lyle E. Schaller, "Twenty-one Changes for the Twenty-first Century," *The Clergy Journal,* February 1995, 44.
12. Ibid., 44.
13. Senge, *The Dance of Change,* 565.
14. Ibid., 16.
15. Warren Bennis, "The Leadership Advantage," *Leader to Leader* 12 (1999), 20.
16. "Learning the Power of Hope," *Leader to Leader* 13 (1999), 53.
17. Bennis, "The Leadership Advantage," 22.

18

The Legitimacy of Reform Judaism

The Impact of Israel on the United States

EPHRAIM TABORY

The articles in this volume generally indicate the independence of American Reform Judaism as a religious movement. And though it may be called Liberal Judaism or Progressive Judaism in other countries, Reform Judaism is an international movement. For most American Jews, the transnational nature of the denomination does not really matter. For many persons, the success of the local synagogue or temple in meeting their religious, spiritual, or social needs constitutes the degree of their interest in their religious "movement." Macro-level questions concerning the national movement and the ideology and identity of the denomination in general may be irrelevant to many religious adherents.

The relationship of Reform Judaism to Israel, however, is different. First, Israel has been found to have an impact on the identity of American Jews.[1] More important for American Reform Jews is that the way the Reform movement is treated in Israel can impact on the perceived legitimacy of their own denomination as an authentic Jewish movement in the United States. While the personal identity of many Reform Jews on the micro level may not be affected by developments in Israel, Reform Judaism on a macro level is under attack. The purpose of this chapter is to analyze the manner in which the situation of the movement in Israel affects Reform Judaism and Reform Jewry in the United States.

A Historical Setting of the Stage

Some history is necessary in order to understand why Reform Judaism has had such a difficult time gaining a foothold in Israel and why the Israel Movement for Progressive Judaism faces such opposition from the political and rabbinical establishments.

Jewish law, halachah, has often functioned as a barrier isolating Jews from non-Jewish society and, indeed, traditionally observant Jews from nonobservant ones. The fate of the Jews was to be a "nation that dwelleth alone," even when the Jews lived in the midst of other nations. Surrounded by generally hostile populations, Judaism became a movement that virtually guaranteed an inward focus. The body of law that developed placed "fences around the Torah," guarding religious practice and sheltering the Jewish population from "contamination" by the Gentile environment. The dietary laws and Shabbat regulations prescribed by halachah ensured that Jews would find it difficult to conduct social relations with non-Jews.

It was political emancipation in Western and Central Europe in the eighteenth and nineteenth centuries that drastically changed the social and economic conditions of the Jews and had dramatic consequences for the religious development of Judaism.[2] The period of the Enlightenment led to increased social contact between Jews and non-Jews as equals. Many "enlightened" Jews, or *maskilim,* incorporated the values of their national societies into their own Jewish societies.[3] A feeling prevailed that traditional religious symbols, suitable for a closed, segregated subgroup that existed apart from and even on the fringes of mainstream society, had to be modified if the Jews were to become part of general society. Of particular relevance to us is the perception of some Jews that the nationalistic and peoplehood components of Judaism might support the accusation that the Jews owed political allegiance to an entity other than their countries of residence. This could serve as justification for denying Jews citizenship in their newly accepting nation-states.

Such was the feeling, then, for many nineteenth-century German Jews who were uncomfortable with their ambiguous status as Jews and as Germans, and with what they felt to be their ancient, and stagnant, religious laws. Publicly performed religious rituals were seen to be incongruous with the needs of persons aspiring to the status of full members of the German nation. The enlightened Jews of the upper classes preferred to deemphasize the national, cultural, and ethnic aspects of Judaism and to define Judaism only as a religion.

The development of the Reform movement in Germany in the nineteenth century thus involved a redefinition of the nature of Judaism as a religious collective.[4] By limiting the scope of Judaism to ritual, the movement that developed enabled its middle- and upper-class members to aspire to acceptance as equal citizens with non-Jews and yet to retain a Jewish identity as members of the Mosaic faith.[5] Detractors noted that Reform Judaism did not merely seek to introduce changes through religious reasoning or reinterpretation. The movement simply abolished the traditional halachic system by saying that it was no longer appropriate. In effect, Reform Judaism fundamentally negated the legitimacy of halachah and traditional Judaism, which came to be known as Orthodox Judaism. It is this perception that earned the ire of Orthodox leaders worldwide, and no more so than in the state of Israel, established in 1948.

The Attitude of Reform Judaism toward Zion

If Israelis perceive Reform Judaism as inauthentic because of its rejection of traditional Judaism, they perceive the movement as downright alien because of its past attitude toward Zionism and Zion. The attitude of Reform Judaism has undergone considerable change since the formation of the movement, but the effect of the initial orientation lingers on.

Prior to the first World Zionist Congress in 1897 the Central Conference of American Rabbis (CCAR) declared its total disapproval of any attempt at establishing a Jewish state. Such attempts were viewed as a misunderstanding of Judaism's mission, since the Jews were seen to constitute not a nation but rather a religious body. After having denied Jewish peoplehood in the Pittsburgh Platform of 1885, the Columbus Platform of 1937 referred to the rehabilitation of Palestine and its being built as a Jewish homeland. The Columbus Platform is also sympathetic to the idea of Jewish peoplehood, as it refers to the Jewish people as the body protecting the Jewish soul.[6] The 1976 Centenary Perspective openly refers to the Jews as constituting an "uncommon union of faith and peoplehood."

Serious thinking about Zionism in Reform, according to Reform leader Rabbi Eric Yoffie, is only two decades old.[7] Most symbolic of the change in the Reform movement is its affiliation with the World Zionist Organization in 1975. The Association of Reform Zionists of America (ARZA) held its first national assembly in 1978. The leaders of the Joint Commission of the Reform Movement, led by ARZA, formulated the Miami Platform, adopted by the CCAR in June 1997, which includes unprecedented support for Israel and the Israel Reform movement. The Miami Platform calls upon its members to make regular visits to Israel, and even encourages immigration to Israel, or aliyah.

Another indication of the changing stance of Reform toward Zionism is the outcome of the September 1997 election of American delegates to the 1997 World Zionist Congress. ARZA won the largest single bloc of votes (47.7 percent, up from 21.7 percent in 1987, when elections were last held). In fairness, though, it is to be noted that only 150,000 out of an estimated 5.5 million American Jews registered to take part in this election, and just 111,351 persons actually cast ballots. Newspaper reports of the campaign indicated that American Jews were barraged with mail and pleas from rabbis "to vote in an election for an organization that few even knew still existed"[8] An implied conclusion is that the Reform movement, as opposed to Reform Jews, has adopted a more positive orientation toward Zionism.

What Do We Care What They Think about Us?

Before turning to the actual manner in which Reform Judaism is treated, we need to ask why this question really matters to Reform Judaism abroad. As a religious denomination, American Reform Judaism should be able to shrug off criticism inasmuch as Reform Judaism has grown to be such a major Jewish denomination while Orthodox Judaism has declined considerably. If numbers are an indication of legitimacy, it is Orthodox Judaism that should be defensive. And yet the charges of being an inauthentic religious movement leveled against Reform by Orthodox leaders are not summarily dismissed even by all of Reform's own leaders and followers. For example, the executive director of the World Union for Progressive Judaism, Rabbi Richard Hirsch, has written that in the United States:

> Many Reform members belong to our synagogues because we offer the most palatable, the most aesthetic, and the easiest way to be a Jew. In other words, I suspect that the most influential factor in building American Reform Judaism has not been theology, but sociology.[9]

Since the social conditions that attracted Jews to Reform synagogues in the United States are so different in Israel, the success of Reform Judaism in Israel would be attributed to more religious factors. According to this perception, Israel serves as a testing ground for Reform Judaism as a religious movement:

> Israel offers a real test of our authenticity. For in Israel, there is no societal pressure or inner compulsion to join a synagogue in order to identify as a Jew. No Israeli Jew is subconsciously moved by the question "What will the gentiles say?" . . . The liberal Jew in America will never have a full and proper relationship to Israel until there is a liberal movement in Israel. Until then we shall always be considered as outsiders and therefore shall consider ourselves creations of the diaspora . . . an American sect practicing a way of life which can flourish only in a gentile soil, aliens and oddities foreign to the authentic Judaism of Eretz Yisrael.[10]

It is by succeeding in Israel, a society in which one need not affiliate with any religious or ethnic movement in order to maintain a Jewish identity, that the movement can most dramatically refute the charge of lack of authenticity and illegitimacy. Triumph in Israel strengthens Reform everywhere. Failure in Israel casts a shadow on the Reform denomination as a *religious* movement. We turn now to Reform Judaism in Israel to consider the developments that impact so greatly abroad.

The Apathetic and Hostile Environment of Reform Judaism in Israel

Early efforts to establish Reform, or liberal, Judaism in Palestine were not successful. The modern period of Reform Judaism in the country dates to the late 1960s. The Israel Movement for Progressive Judaism incorporated itself under

Israeli law in 1971.[11] Apparently Progressive Judaism was chosen as the name of the movement in order to symbolize a shared identity with the American Reform movement while at the same time placing some distance between the two movements, as well as between the Israeli movement and Classical Reform Judaism. The hope was that this would mitigate the negative connotations those associations might have for the Israeli population.

By any indicator the Israel Reform movement is small. No more than thirty congregations hold weekly services, and the membership attracts less than 0.5 percent of the Jewish population in Israel.[12] There is no real youth movement of which to speak. A relatively new forum for young (college-age) adults has thus far attracted fewer than two hundred persons nationwide who participate on a regular basis. Still, an increasing number of Israelis are exposed to the movement through attendance at bar and bat mitzvah ceremonies or weddings performed by movement rabbis. Several hundred wedding ceremonies are performed annually by Reform rabbis for non-Orthodox Israelis, but the majority of these persons do not maintain an affiliation with the movement. Reform weddings are not recognized in Israel. Those marrying through a Reform rabbi are required to undertake an additional civil ceremony abroad (which is then recognized by the Ministry of Interior but not by the Chief Rabbinate). Movement leaders estimate that as many as half of those who get married in this way do so in protest against the Orthodox establishment, as opposed to their expression of an adherence to Reform ideology.

The lack of authority for Reform rabbis to perform weddings that are recognized in Israel is just one aspect demonstrating the hostile environment in which Reform Judaism finds itself there. Pressure has been put on halls and schools to refuse permission for Reform services on their premises. Reform congregations have faced discrimination in obtaining land for the construction of synagogues and cultural centers. The Reform movement has continuously had to petition the High Court of Justice to receive funds that should be equitably allocated to religious institutions. Reform Jews are discriminated against with regard to their election and appointment to local religious councils, councils that are responsible for the administrative provision of religious services at the local level. Reform rabbis and the Reform establishment are regularly denigrated in Orthodox political party newspapers.

The constant charge is that Reform Judaism is not really a religious movement. Reform Judaism, it is said, permits rabbis and priests to conduct joint wedding ceremonies, and it sanctions intermarriage, same-sex unions, and assimilation. Reform Judaism, it is said, leads to the decline of Judaism and to the demise of the Jewish people. Pressure is exerted on political figures to refrain from activities that will grant recognition to Reform institutions. For example, an invitation to the newly elected prime minister, Ehud Barak, to attend a Reform service while on a visit to New York in July 1999 met with protest and pressure by Orthodox political parties in Israel. In the end the nonreligious prime minister spent Shabbat in his hotel and did not attend any religious service.

Some Reform leaders in Israel attribute the small size of the movement to its unequal treatment by religious and political authorities. The issue is more complex than that, however.[13] Persons who want to take part in Reform services can attend the Reform congregations that do exist, but many of the (rather small) halls are far from full. While rabbis are limited with regard to the state-authorized functions they can perform, they can minister to their congregations on a regular basis. To some extent the hostile environment is used as a scapegoat to explain general indifference and apathy on the part of the Israeli public. This was recognized early on by Ezra Spicehandler, the dean of Hebrew Union College in Jerusalem at the time, who wrote:

> Frustrated by the slow growth of liberal Judaism in Israel, some of us prefer to think that the fault lies in the disabilities imposed upon the Reform Rabbis of Israel. We delude ourselves that if only we were permitted to perform marriages and receive State funds . . . we would be free to rally thousands of Jews to the banner of Reform. This is a gross and pathetic fallacy. We will grow in Israel, not by gaining these privileges, but by offering a meaningful answer to the spiritual problems of modern man.[14]

Contemporary Reform leaders realize that more has to be done to identify the spiritual needs of Israeli Jews and to provide for them, a discussion that is beyond the scope of this paper.[15] What is relevant, though, is the conclusion that the Reform movement as it currently exists is indeed not attracting persons who, it is claimed, should be attracted to it. One occasionally hears Reform leaders say that Israeli Jews are Reform Jews but that they just do not know it. Reform Judaism, however, is clearly a Western religious movement. As such, it is basically closed off to Sephardim, who comprise half of the Jewish population in Israel. Furthermore, non-Orthodox Ashkenazim tend to reject the traditional synagogue structure as a means of religious expression. The fact that Reform leaders recognize this situation is important, but it does not in itself make the uphill struggle against apathy easier. The small size of the movement in Israel does not assuage the claim that Reform Judaism's attraction abroad is based on social factors and not on its religious message.

The Reform movement in Israel thus faces both an apathetic environment on a popular level and a hostile environment on the political and governmental levels. The impact of the limited size of the movement in Israel on the perceived legitimacy of Reform Judaism abroad pales compared with the direct effect of the most crucial question: the recognition of Reform conversions.

The Conversion Issue

Conversion has become a more pressing issue in Israel than it was in the past because of the large number of migrants from the former Soviet Union who are not considered Jewish by the standards of even Israeli Reform Judaism, let alone Orthodox Judaism: neither the father nor the mother of these persons is Jewish, and these migrants have not undergone any conversion process. It is estimated that between 200,000 and 300,000 of the over 800,000 migrants in the 1989–2000 period are not Jewish. In addition, about 200,000 non-Jewish foreign guest workers are in Israel. A substantial number of these persons might be interested in converting to Judaism in order to better fit into their new, Jewish environment. Some might wish to do so in order to marry Jewish Israelis. The Reform movement would like to take an active part in helping those who wish to convert, but Reform conversions performed in Israel are not recognized by state authorities. For our analysis recognition of Reform conversions goes to the heart of recognizing Reform Judaism as a legitimate religious movement.

The Israeli Reform movement has a Beit Din (religious court) that converts about 120 persons a year. Persons holding Israeli citizenship complete their conversion process in Israel. Foreign citizens who seek conversion by the Beit Din are told that a conversion procedure undertaken in Israel may not enable them to be registered as Jews under Israeli civil law. These persons study for their conversion process in Israel, but they undergo the actual Reform conversion procedure abroad (usually in London).

The foreign conversion used to be recognized by the civil authorities in Israel, but this was stopped when the Ministry of Interior was under control of the ultra-Orthodox Sephardi party, Shas. The ministry was transferred to the Russian party, Yisrael Be'aliya, following the 1999 elections, and a much more lenient position regarding the treatment of non-Jews in general has already been instituted by the cabinet minister, former refusenik and Jewish activist Natan Sharansky. In any case, the state rabbinate does not recognize any Reform conversion, no matter where it took place. That is to say that the rabbinate, which is responsible for administering the laws pertaining to personal status, does not recognize Reform converts to be Jews.

It is to be noted that the Reform movement's position in Israel regarding conversion is more traditional than that of the American movement. While the American Reform movement recognizes patrilineal descent as well as matrilineal descent for the transmission of Jewish identity, the movement in Israel (like the Reform movement in Europe and in other countries outside of the United States) retained the traditional Jewish view of recognizing only matrilineal descent. The reason for the Israeli decision was that recognition of patrilineal descent would be too far removed from what is acceptable to *klal Yisrael*, but, of course, this made no impression on the Orthodox rabbinate's decision not to accept Reform conversions.

The question of who is a Jew, with regard to conversion, is sometimes presented as really a question of who is a rabbi, meaning which rabbis are granted recognition as authentic and legitimate clergy.[16] But the question of who is a rabbi has a greater impact than merely determining the religious rights of religious functionaries. Lack of recognition and official standing for Reform rabbis affects the manner in which the movement is perceived by nonmembers and the extent to which the movement can be perceived as a religious and spiritual alternative to Orthodox Judaism. While the Orthodox may argue that they do not question the Jewish identity of Reform Jews born to Jewish parents, questioning the legitimacy of Reform rabbis means that a salient part of their Jewish identity— their identity as Reform Jews—is also questioned. Lack of recognition and official legitimacy for Reform rabbis has an impact on the perceived lack of authenticity of Reform Judaism and, by implication, Reform Jews.

In this case the message is really aimed at Jews outside of Israel, particularly in the United States. The message received, even if the senders claim that it is unintended and inaccurate, is that their religious belief and their religious identity are also not authentic. The message is even stronger than the insinuation that to be religious, one has to be Orthodox. The message is that if one wants to be part of the Jewish religion, one has to accept the premise of Orthodoxy as the yardstick of religious belief and practice.

American Reform Jews constitute the most sensitive audience for this message. According to the National Jewish Population Survey (NJPS) conducted in the United States in 1990, 24 percent of Reform synagogue members are converts to Judaism. Among married Jewish respondents some 63 percent of the converts to Judaism are married to adherents of Reform Judaism. The findings indicate that Reform Judaism is the usual denominational preference in marriages between a Jew and non-Jew in which the latter converts.[17] Furthermore, the data indicate that of all marriages entered into from 1971 to 1990 only 25 percent of the combined group of Reform and no-denominational-preference families will be formed by two Jewish-born spouses.[18]

The Conversion Bill

The Israeli government's policy, ever since 1970, has been to recognize non-Orthodox conversions abroad but only Orthodox conversions within Israel, for purposes of registration in the population registry. The Rabbinical Courts Jurisdiction Act (Marriage and Divorce) (Amendment) (Conversion)—which has come to be known as the Conversion Bill, was proposed in reaction to a 1995 decision by the Supreme Court, sitting as the High Court of Justice, in which a Brazilian woman converted by the Beit Din of the Council of Progressive Rabbis in Israel petitioned to be registered as a Jew and receive a visa as an immigrant.[19] In its decision the court drew a distinction between civil registration and matters relating to personal status. (Laws of personal status include laws pertaining to marriage, divorce, and conversion, which by legislation are under the authority of the respective religious communities, and in the case of the Jews, the Chief Rabbinate of Israel.) Issues relating to personal status, the court ruled in a 6–1 vote, must conform to the requirements of the Mandatory Religious Community (Change) Act, which means that Orthodox law applies to these issues. However, recognition of a conversion performed in Israel, as regards the Population Registry Law and the Law of Return, is not subject to the requirements of the Mandatory Act.

The reaction on the part of the Orthodox political parties was to press for legislation that would declare that the state of Israel recognizes only Orthodox conversions. The Conversion Bill, which passed the first reading (three readings, or votes, are required to adopt a law) in 1997 by a vote of 51–32 with seven abstentions, states that "the conversion of a person in Israel will be in accord with the 'Law of the Torah' (*Din Torah*), and that no conversion will be recognized without the approval of the President of the Supreme Rabbinical Court, that is, the chief rabbi of Israel. In principle the bill did not affect the right of Reform and Conservative Jews who undergo conversions abroad to have those conversions registered by the Minister of the Interior, but MK Rabbi Moshe Gafni (United Torah Judaism) stated in the Knesset that this is just an introductory bill for additional legislation that would extend the rejection of non-Orthodox conversions to those performed abroad.[20]

The proposed legislation threatened to cause a rift between the state of Israel and non-Orthodox Jews abroad. Rabbi Eric Yoffie, President of the Union of American Hebrew Congregations, said that the passing of the bill would constitute a declaration of war on American Jews. Speaking on Israeli radio, he said, "If the Reform rabbis in Israel are not rabbis and the conversions are not conversions, that means that our Judaism is not Judaism and we are second-rate Jews."[21] That, of course, is essentially the position of the Orthodox parties, although they are generally careful to point out that they accept Reform and Conservative Jews on an individual basis unless they were converted to Judaism by a non-Orthodox movement.

The leaders of the Reform and Conservative movements in the United States, following the passage of the first reading of the Conversion Bill, recommended that affiliate congregations ban visits by Knesset members who voted for the final bill. Some rabbis also called on the members of their congregations to channel their financial contributions to Israel specifically to Reform and Conservative institutions. In response, MK Rubi Rivlin (Likud) characterized the recommendation of the Reform movement as "contempt for the people of Israel and Israeli democracy," and he called on the speaker of the Knesset to forbid all Knesset members to take part in Reform movement events until the leaders retracted their threat and apologize.[22]

Eventually an agreement was reached to establish an official committee, chaired by Yaakov Ne'eman, an Orthodox Jew who had served as minister of justice and who would later be appointed minister of finance, to deal with the conversion issue. Rabbi Uri Regev, the executive director of the Reform movement's Israel Religious Action Center, served as one of the Reform movement's representatives to the committee and coordinated the movement's position in consultations with the chairman of the board and the executive director of the Israel Movement for Progressive Judaism, the heads of the Union of American Hebrew Congregations in the United States, the Central Conference of American Rabbis, the executive director of the World Union for Progressive Judaism, and the heads of the Association of Reform Zionists of America (ARZA), and Hebrew Union College.

The Ne'eman Committee never issued a signed report. The proposed agreement set forth by the committee was for the establishment of joint Reform, Conservative, and Orthodox conversion classes that would culminate in a conversion process undertaken by an Orthodox Beit Din. The proposal was placed before the chief rabbi of Israel, Yisrael Lau, but he refused to sign a resolution that would grant accreditation to any form of cooperation with the non-Orthodox. As a result, the committee members themselves refused to sign a document that would lead to a process that could eventually end in failure. The united conversion program was formulated anyway, despite the lack of official consensus on the part of the rabbinate. In fact, the first conversion classes have gotten under way in Jerusalem, and there are plans for additional conversion centers in various cities throughout Israel. The head of the Conversion Institute expects that the Orthodox Beit Din that will have to examine the conversion candidates in the year 2000 will not inquire too deeply into the nature of their commitment to observe a religious—Orthodox—life. The perception is that it was perhaps too much to expect the Orthodox rabbinate to accept a decision de jure that would recognize non-Orthodox Judaism.

Discussion

The conversion issue does not resolve the question of who is a rabbi or who is a Jew. In fact, the proposed solution offers a pragmatic way of dealing with a thorny issue without granting any degree of legitimacy to Reform rabbis or to Reform conversions. A bill to recognize only Orthodox conversions has already been tabled in the Fifteenth Knesset, following Ehud Barak's election as prime minister. With peace talks a primary issue on the Israeli agenda, and with the coalition government dependent on Orthodox religious parties, there is little likelihood in the immediate future of any substantial change regarding the nonrecognition of Reform rabbis or Reform conversions.

The threat of a rift with the American Jewish population over the conversion issue gave the movement a window of opportunity for substantial change. American Reform pressure was substantial. Bulletins, updates, and calls for action were issued by the Reform movement over the Internet almost daily. Israeli leaders were defensive. But the formation of the Ne'eman Committee reduced the pressure and eventually closed the window for a substantial period. The considerable decline of pressure leads us to differentiate between different publics affected by Israel's attitude toward Reform Judaism.

I have claimed that the question of the implications of the legitimacy of Reform Judaism in Israel for American Reform Jews is a moot one for many of those persons who care most about the spiritual, religious, and social benefits they obtain from their local congregations.[23] A key feature of Reform Judaism is that it facilitates the "privatization" of religion, the isolation of religious life from public practice. It enables Jews to take part in secular social life without undue restrictions. The religious identity of many Reform Jews as individuals is not challenged by what happens in Israel, a country that is both physically and psychologically remote. The fact that the Reform movement has "returned" to Zion does not necessarily mean that the average American Reform Jew cares about what happens in the Jewish state. In fact, a senior American Reform leader who is very much involved in ARZA lamented that the small number of Reform Jews who joined the Reform Zionist association (less than 5 percent of Reform Jews) was attributable to an apathetic orientation toward Israel. Elaborating, he said that Reform Jews do not even really care about Reform Judaism in the United States, so why should they care about Reform Judaism elsewhere? This is a sweeping generalization, but it apparently represents the perception of other movement leaders. One Israeli leader told me that the attempt to mobilize American Jewish opinion on the conversion issue had to be concentrated and it had to be fast, because once the momentum was lost, it would be hard to get American Jews to focus again on an Israeli issue.

We can note, in this connection, that some Reform leaders expressed reservations concerning efforts to mobilize American Jewry against Israeli religious policies on the conversion issue. Sensing that the attachment of Reform Jews to Israel is weak, they felt that hearing their leaders denounce Israel would further alienate them from Israel, and perhaps even from Judaism. Rabbi Richard Hirsch, past executive director of the World Union for Progressive Judaism, felt that Orthodox conversions should be the norm in order to ensure the continuity of *klal Yisrael* and to keep the Jewish state alive. Rabbi Hirsch explained that the Reform movement should be interested in ensuring that its conversions be in line with the requirements of all streams of Judaism and not seek to follow a procedure that will be rejected by others. "My position," he said in an interview, "is a minority position [within Reform], but it is that the Jewish state comes first, and Jewish rights come before human rights."

On the other hand, the professional and lay leaders of the Reform movement, including many rabbis, are very much sensitive to challenges to their leadership, authority, and, in the end, their legitimacy. Israeli Orthodox leaders often point out that they do not challenge the identity of Reform Jews. They want no quarrel with millions of Jews worldwide (as long as they are not the products of non-Orthodox conversions). It is "only" with Reform that they take exception. From an Israeli Orthodox perspective Reform Judaism negates traditional Judaism. Even many non-Orthodox Israelis do not understand the religious message of Reform Judaism, and they question its religious status. A common perception, whether accurate or not, is that Reform Judaism and, at the very least, many Reform Jews still negate Zion. Reform Judaism, many believe, legitimizes inter-marriage and in the end leads to and even sanctions assimilation and the decline of Judaism. Reform Judaism is therefore attacked by the Orthodox political estab-lishment in Israel and abroad.

The nature of the manner in which Reform Judaism is presented as a halfway movement that facilitates exit from Judaism leads many Israeli Jews, and appar-ently quite a number of Israeli politicians, to be sympathetic to Orthodox charges against Reform. It may seem paradoxical, but the widespread agreement with the Orthodox charges against Reform Judaism goes hand in hand with opposition to the religious coercion enacted by the Orthodox in Israel. Many nonreligious Jewish Israelis who identify and sympathize with the Reform movement do so primarily because of its fight against the religious establishment, and not neces-sarily because of their interest in a true religious alternative to Orthodox Judaism. The upshot of this situation is most problematic for Reform leaders, for on a macro level Reform leaders and rabbis represent Reform Judaism as a religious movement, not as an anti-Orthodox one, which in the Israeli context translates as an antireligious movement.[24]

The situation is fluid, and fraught with peril. Even if most American Reform Jews are apathetic about what happens in Israel, many are not. And even if there is general indifference toward Israel, this may not include a lackadaisical orien-tation about Israel's attitude toward converts. This is especially so for the large percentage of Reform synagogue members who are converts, or married to con-verts, or intermarried (with no conversion). There is also no assurance that greater numbers will not care in the future. Can the Jewish people tolerate the dif-ferent worlds of Judaism that seem to be developing in Israel and in the United States?[25] The focus of this article has been on the impact of Israel's attitude toward Reform Judaism on American Reform Judaism. We note, though, that

questions raised in Israel about the authenticity of Reform Judaism can potentially lead American Reform Jews to question the legitimacy of Israel as a Jewish
state representing the Jewish people.

Notes

1. Bernard Lazerwitz, J. Alan Winter, Arnold Dashefsky, and Ephraim Tabory, *Jewish Choices: American Jewish Denominationalism* (Albany: State University of New York Press, 1998).
2. Jacob Katz, *Tradition and Crisis: Jewish Society at the End of the Middle Ages* (New York: Schocken, 1961).
3. J. Milton Yinger, *The Scientific Study of Religion* (New York: Macmillan, 1970), 232–33.
4. David Philipson, *The Reform Movement in Judaism* (New York: KTAV, 1967).
5. Nathan Glazer, *American Judaism*, 2nd ed. (Chicago: University of Chicago Press, 1972).
6. Ammiel Hirsch, "Foreword," *Journal of Reform Zionism* 1, 2 (1993): 2.
7. Eric H. Yoffie, "Building a Reform Zionist Paradigm," *Journal of Reform Judaism* 1, 1 (1993): 19–21.
8. *New York Times* report, cited in *Jerusalem Post*, October 12, 1997, 12.
9. Richard G. Hirsch, *Reform Judaism and Israel* (New York: Commission on Israel, World Union for Progressive Judaism, 1972), 15–16.
10. Ibid., 19.
11. For the history of Reform Judaism in Palestine and Israel, see David Polish, *Renew Our Days: The Zionist Issue in Reform Judaism* (Jerusalem: World Zionist Organization, 1976); Ze'ev Harari, "Chapters in the History of the Movement for Progressive Judaism in Israel," incomplete thesis (in Hebrew) 1980, on file at Hebrew Union College Library, Jerusalem; Michael A. Meyer, *Response to Modernity* (New York: Oxford University Press, 1988); Shlomo Cohen, *Lo Lishlol Banu Ela Lislol* (Not to negate have we come, but rather to pave the way) (Ramat Gan: n.p., 1978); Meir Elk, "First Steps in the History of Our Movement in Israel," *Shalhevet* 1 (1969): 9–12.
12. Ephraim Tabory, "Reform and Conservative Judaism in Israel: A Social and Religious Profile," *American Jewish Yearbook* 83 (1983): 41–61; and *Reform Judaism in Israel: Progress and Prospects* (New York: Institute on American Jewish–Israel Relations; Ramat Gan: Argov Center of Bar Ilan University, 1998).
13. Stanley A. Ringler, "Reform Judaism in Israel—Why Is the Movement Marginal?" *CCAR Journal* 43, 1 (1996): 1–10; Stanley A. Ringler, "Reform Judaism in Israel: Debating the Future—A Response," *CCAR Journal* 43, 3 (1996): 85–92; Meir Azari, "Response: Let's Broaden the Horizons," *CCAR Journal* 43, 1 (1996): 17–21; Uri Regev, "Israel—The Real Challenge—A Response," *CCAR Journal* 43, 2 (1996): 1–17.
14. Ezra Spicehandler, "What Can We Say to Israel?" Central Conference of American Rabbis *Yearbook*, vol. 78 (1968): 227–36.
15. See Tabory, *Reform Judaism*.
16. Moshe Samet, "Who Is a Jew? (1958–1977)." *Jerusalem Quarterly* 36 (1985): 88–108; and "Who Is a Jew? (1978–1985)," *Jerusalem Quarterly* 37 (1986): 109–39.
17. Lazerwitz et al., 1998, *Jewish Choices*.

18. Bernard Lazerwitz, "Jewish-Christian Marriages and Conversions, 1971 and 1980," *Sociology of* Religion 56 (1995): 433–43.

19. For the Conversion Bill, see *Reshumot*, Legislative Bills, Hebrew, 2610, March 26, 1997. For the case, see HCJ 1031/93, Alian (Hava) Pessaro (Goldstein) and the Movement for Progressive Judaism in Israel v. the Minister of the Interior and the Director of the Population Registry, Judgments of the Supreme Court of Israel, Hebrew, 49 (4) *Piskei Din* 661.

20. *Yated Ne'eman,* April 1, 1997.

21. *Jerusalem Post,* April 1, 1997

22. *Ha'aretz,* April 4, 1997, A8; April 8, 1997, A3.

23. Ephraim Tabory, "The Identity Dilemma of Non-Orthodox Religious Movements: Reform and Conservative Judaism in Israel," in *Tradition, Innovation, Conflict: Jewishness and Judaism in Contemporary Israel,* ed. Z. Sobel and B. Beit-Hallahmi (Albany: State University of New York Press, 1991), 135–52.

24. Ibid.

25. Charles S. Liebman and Steven M. Cohen, *Two Worlds of Judaism: The Israeli and American Experiences* (New Haven and London: Yale University Press, 1990).

19

Reform Judaism of the New Millennium

A Challenge

ALFRED GOTTSCHALK

This is a time of great gestation in Reform Judaism. As a movement of modern Jewish religious expression, it is grappling with issues that transcend its Reform character, reaching into the very essence of Judaism's capacity to survive modernity and postmodernity. Modernity was an extension in time of a linear past. Its ideas reformed, reconstructed, or otherwise reshaped notions of the past. Postmodernity's New Age religious movements make no pretense of seeking past validation for contemporary ideas or beliefs. They are claimed to be new, as the age is claimed to be new, and their often bizarre ideas, or so they appear to be to traditionalists, are not validatable by any fact or experience of the past. Their validation is in their being and not by any context from which they seem to emerge.

The recent Pittsburgh Platform debacle was relatively untouched by New Age Jewish enthusiasts. Rather, it claimed its validation by what proceeded out of the past as Jewish tradition. Pittsburgh 1999 created a synthetic construct of venerable beliefs, emphasizing the importance of past customs, ceremonies, traditions, and core beliefs. Pittsburgh 1999 essentially looked backward for current authentication of Reform Judaism. It largely preferred rabbinic modalities to prophetic modalities, which was the emphasis of the 1885 Pittsburgh Platform. The current set of principles was accepted and voted on by less than half of the Central Conference of American Rabbis (CCAR) membership. The conversation among rabbis and laity since the Pittsburgh conference keeps centering on the question of how to solidify the authenticity of Reform Judaism for Reform Jews. Does the "new" reform of Pittsburgh, largely constructed out of a homiletic rather than a scholarly mode, adequately address the issue of Reform Jewish authenticity?

Reform Jewish Authenticity

The Reform Judaism of Europe and the Progressive Judaism of Israel, antecedent to Pittsburgh 1999, sought authenticity in the *Wissenschaft des Judenthums* approach. With that comes the conviction that the impartial study of Judaism in all its wide-ranging aspects, as it developed through the course of Jewish history, leads to a critical understanding of Judaism's spiritual and physical contours, which forms one of the sources for an individual's personal Jewish commitment. In that process of "Jewish learning" there was, and continually is, discovered what is Jewish essence and what is merely peripheral, what is true substance and what accretion, what is genuine and what artificial. And in that process of Jewish learning there is also revealed which *forms* of Jewish expression—mark, I am speaking of forms, not of content—have genuinely lent themselves to the expression of Jewish values, truth, and sentiment, and which forms have distorted them.

In my view this is the way Reform Judaism discovers Jewish authenticity. In fact, it is not merely Reform Judaism that bases its search for authentic Judaism on historical examination. Many have witnessed how in the past forty years a movement within Judaism, namely, Jewish mysticism, which for a long time had been subjected to extremes of hostile criticism and condemnation and marked as utterly alien to genuine Judaism, was restored to a prominent role in Jewish religious and intellectual life, reaching far beyond the boundaries of Reform Judaism. The late Professor Gershom Scholem, to whom we largely owe the rehabilitation of Jewish mysticism, described in an interview how the process started: "[T]he fact that I address myself to Kabbalah not merely as a chapter of history but from a dialectical distance—from identification and distance together—certainly stems from the fact that I had the feeling that Kabbalah had a living center; it expressed itself according to the time and that in another form it could, perhaps, have said something else in another generation."

I do not know of a better way to define Jewish authenticity than by adopting this term used by Scholem: a Jewish religious experience or practice is authentic by virtue of its "living center" and because of the fact that it expressed itself in accord with the genuine need of the time. Orthodox Judaism rejects this or any similar view. It asserts that these expressions of Judaism are *not* genuine, that somehow they are *merely* "copies" of the environment, issues *merely* of time and place, and not in consonance with the vast matrix of Torah handed down in its pristine form in a *shalshelet ha-Kabbalah*, an unbroken chain of tradition from Moses and Sinai to Joshua, and from him to the elders, and from the elders to the prophets, and from the prophets to the men of the great assembly,[1] and, as it is obviously presumed by the current Orthodox political establishment in Israel, from the men of the great assembly to the Israeli Chief Rabbinate.

It is difficult not to conclude that the notion of an orthodox Jewish canon, unerring and universally applicable, is often generated by those more concerned with authority and inerrancy in Jewish life than with authenticity. When the Jerusalem Chief Rabbinate last Rosh Hashanah again issued an *issur* or injunction, warning that those in Israel who heard the shofar blown in a Conservative synagogue or a Reform synagogue had not fulfilled the requirement of hearing the shofar blown, although they actually did hear it blown, and in Jerusalem of all places, it was concerned with authority and not authenticity. The halachah on where the shofar may be blown is so liberal that only a perverse reading of the text could have yielded such an outrageous, bigoted, and narrowly exclusivistic interpretation.

Rabbi Irving Greenberg, a foremost contemporary Orthodox rabbi, in an address delivered some years ago titled, "Does God Hear the Prayer of Conservative or Reform Jews?" concluded that the decision of the chief rabbis of Jerusalem was analogous to the cry of the Southern Baptist minister Dr. Bailey Smith in the early 1990s that "God does not hear the prayer of Jews." "To be sure," said Rabbi Greenberg, "we need a major investment in religious thought and dialogue to arrive at models showing us how to reconcile commanded truth with pluralism. Orthodox Jews or Christians cannot just drop their judgmental views or they will lose all their standards." Greenberg hoped that those who hold to canonicity in Judaism can recognize "God's capacity to love and command different people in different ways."[2] That is a sober statement in this period of Orthodox triumphalism, which questions both the authority and the derivative authenticity of that in Jewish life with which Orthodoxy cannot agree.

Rabbi Harold Schulweis, an eminent Conservative rabbi and theologian, observed, "Closer examination of the course of Jewish history and thought reveals the windings of a broad river with multiple branches running into the sea. Another's tributary is my mainstream and vice versa. Open to the rich diversity of Jewish ideas, ideals and practices, we observe that the streams of Jewish mysticism mingle with the waters of Jewish rationalism. Hasidism and Kabbala alongside Maimonides and the Haskalah, the analytic temper of the Vilna Gaon joined with the ecstatic passion of the Baal Shem Tov—that which yesterdays excommunicated as an aberration from Judaism is tomorrow celebrated as the vital undercurrent of Jewish faith."[3]

The late Professor Robert Gordis of the Jewish Theological Seminary, in a polemic with Professor Emanuel Rackman of Bar Ilan University in Israel, clarified this point by noting that "Conservative Judaism conceives of Jewish tradition as the product of an extensive historical development from ancient times to the present, for growth and change are the universal law of life. Rabbi Rackman avoided the term development and preferred to speak of interpretation, thus preserving the facade of monolithic immobility which is the hallmark of official orthodox dogma."[4]

The struggle for Reform and Conservative religious rights in Israel, a Jewish state with an Orthodox religious establishment, now reinforced by the recent

Israeli elections and the coalition required to exercise power, daily reminds us of this. A Judaism frozen at the shtetl level, starkly torn out of its historical habitat, points to our real problem—the crucial one, which we cannot escape. Jews in the Diaspora have been unable to escape it, and our brethren in Israel will be unable to escape it. How can Judaism survive and flourish in modernity? In Israel the problem has been shelved for now because of Prime Minister Ehud Barak's concentration on the peace process, in which he needs an unfragmented coalition. Its eventual resolution will be different from that achieved in the Diaspora. One need only glance at Chaim Potok's remarks to put a positive perspective on the problem. Potok asks us to "ponder the sort of creativity that will begin to take place sometime around the years 2010 and 2020 as those increasing numbers of children and grandchildren educated in the core of Jewish tradition begin to track their interaction with the core of secular humanism."[5] When these youngsters meet their peers in Israel, a new encounter will have begun. The outcome, I sense, will be positive and exciting.

A Delicate Balancing Act

It is clear from all we know that the founders of modern Judaism were not of one mind in their groping toward modernity. There were among them those who rejected too much of the core of Judaism for the purposes of assimilation and acculturation. There were some Reform and secular Jews who wanted so much to be part of the modern world that their Jewish identity became blurred. Indeed, some forgot what Ahad Ha-Am held in his unique Jewish mind to be the difference between Jewish and general assimilation. Jews, he argued, have historically assimilated around a core of their Jewishness compatible aspects of external culture they prized. They were not assimilated by them. A. B. Yehoshua recently reiterated Ahad Ha-Am's caution by noting, "Your life as Diaspora Jews has been totally organized so that you can protect your identity as Jews. You live for the preservation of your identity as Jews. You live for the preservation of your identity because your surroundings are not Jewish." And, he added, "It is a waste of energy when you could be doing the real thing by taking part in the great debate in which we are living," that is, by living in Israel.[6]

The delicate balancing act of Diaspora Jews from emancipation until today features the efforts of Reform and others, despite early and later mistakes, to live and exist as Jews not in isolation from but as part of the cultural and political worlds in which we find ourselves. The hazards are great and will increase. The choice, however, to remain part of the secular world and to interact with it as Jews or to live in isolation from it is the quandary for a sizable segment of modern Jewry.

There is a need for me to underscore a reading of Jewish history that argues that this has been a millennial problem for us. The interaction of biblical Israel with Canaan, Assyria, Babylonia, Persia, Greece, and Rome, and their worldviews, all testifies to our capacity to re-form, re-construct, conserve, and start the cycle again as the historical condition dictates. The vast body of Jewish religious and secular literature argues for the dynamics of reform, of restructuring, of making it possible for Jews to live and survive in changing environments. We have changed habitats, languages, customs, ceremonies, laws—we have stretched and shaped both halachah and Haggadah in order to exist. We have erred at times in judgment, but on balance history has smiled on our survival and on our capacity to assimilate while resisting, at least until the modern period, the pressure to lose our identity.

Freezing Judaism in some anachronistic time frame is not what is asked of us. Mordecai Kaplan stated that Judaism cannot be perpetuated merely by the replication of past beliefs, patterns, customs, and ceremonies: "The conditions which enabled Judaism to flourish in the past are irrevocably gone with the wind. Nothing less than original and creative thinking in terms of present-day realities and future possibilities can create anew the conditions which are indispensable to Jewish survival."

Thus, Reform is in principle opposed to Orthodoxy—as is Orthodoxy to Reform. They move from different premises in judging the central thrust of Judaism. I hold to the notion of progressive revelation in Judaism as one of Reform's essential premises. This functional view of the evolution of the Jewish religious spirit also allows us to judge when Reform itself has become "orthodox" in a particular cycle of Jewish history. So-called classical Reform falls into this category. It has been superseded in the last generation by a Progressive Judaism, which brought Zionism and peoplehood into mainstream Reform thinking and organizational life.

A new addendum has been made to recent Reform history that unquestionably will unfold further in the twenty-first century and beyond. I call this the "New Reform," because it focuses in a primary sense on the personal faith of the individual. Today in the ranks of Reform Judaism and in the ranks of its ideologists one finds traditionalists and meta-halachists on the right; mainstream religionists on the high center ground, characterized by the theological thrust of the new "gender-neutral" Gates of Prayer; and religious Zionists (Association of Reform Zionists of America), religious humanists, and loosely linked religious secularists on the left. What the "New Reform" offers, more strongly than anything before it, is personal autonomy within definable Reform conceptual and organizational boundaries.

Despite the risk that such diversity entails, I hail it, articulate it, and have vigorously encouraged it. We have through the Shoah lost more Jews than ever before, and therefore I plead for an inclusivistic rather than exclusivistic framework for modern religious Judaism. The messianic age is far in the horizon. The messianic formula is yet to be deciphered, Habad notwithstanding.

By permitting, in fact requiring, the personal autonomy of the individual, from which a personal religious decision can emerge, Reform Judaism will also be able to counterbalance a growing trend in Judaism working toward an increasing secularization of Jewishness. In the past decades Jewish consciousness and Jewish affiliation among caring Jews have become stronger. Yet the underlying reasons often were untouched by religious motivation. Jews became conscious, even conscientious Jews for political reasons, as members of an ethnic group, as contributors to philanthropic causes, for reasons of solidarity within a minority group, and so on. Without belittling these motivations, there is no doubt that they were often the first and the last in the Jewishness of those that were affected by them. Jews emerged as "corporate Jews," as joiners holding membership in Jewish organizations.

"An Ignoramus Cannot Be Pious"

What we need now is to open the windows and doors of our temples, synagogues, and institutions to individuals who choose to be Jewish in definable terms sacred to them and in consonance with the wide perimeters of diversity our religious tradition has placed over its millennial history. Our premise still is that "an ignoramus cannot be pious." Jewish learning is the bedrock in which Reform Judaism needs to continue to rest.

The traditional momentum in the movement manifests itself in a wider adherence to traditional religious practice such as *tallith* and *kippah*. *Kashrut*, liberalized or strictly adhered to, is becoming more common in Reform temples and synagogues. Bar and bat mitzvah ceremonies abound. Confirmation classes are large. Shabbat evening and morning services have grown in congregational importance. Hebraization is moving apace, and today Reform Jewish summer camps have whole encampments where Hebrew is taught and used in daily speech. Jewish liturgical music is flourishing, reaching from classical, organ-centered hymnology to hard-rock-style liturgies. New prayer books, reflecting a sensitively edited liturgy, aim at frequent and easy usage. A large number of life-cycle aids, guides, and programs are available for home use. New religious school curricula have been composed, and the first modern American liberal commentary to the Pentateuch, widely acclaimed for its excellence, is being used.

As we move into the secular new millennium, I see more liturgical creativity and study opportunity for the Reform Jewish laity. Living-room learning, study seminars, and *havurot* are in vogue and will grow. Of course, those phenomena exist in other contemporary Jewish religious movements as well, but what has remained unique to Reform has been the stress on the autonomy of individuals to study, practice, and shape Judaism to their own needs. Judaism has never solely thrived on dogmas or the pronouncements of rebbes or even chief rabbis. Ten shoemakers make up a minyan. Nine rabbis do not! Judaism's intellectual and spiritual dynamism thrives on disputation, the questioning of authority and minds contesting with one another, even uncomfortably so at times.

As we look further into the future, we are struck by problems that all of American Jewry will face together: the state of our country, the quality of our lives, the growing gap between rich and poor, racism, the still ominous threat of a thermonuclear accident, and many others. Specific Jewish problems will abound: a redefinition of roles between Israel and the Diaspora, assimilation, intermarriage, single-parent families, chemical addictions, zero population grown, and our growing Jewish gerontocracy. Clearly Reform faces these issues in concert with all Jews. Since, however, Reform has never insulated itself from societal problems, it moves onto them not uniformly or dogmatically but in a modus operandi born of its democratic structure and reflected in its historic social activism.

The last concrete example of a long process played out was the CCAR's position on the patrilineal descent issue. For our purpose, and because of the unique phenomenon of mixed marriages and the Jewish status of their offspring, children of Jewish fathers and Gentile mothers who are reared in a Jewish environment and who wish to identify with Judaism can claim a Jewish status equal to that of a child born of a Jewish mother. Equity and necessity were handmaidens in this historic decision. While Reform is currently castigated for enlarging on the traditional definition of who is a Jew, future generations will be in its debt, as has been the case with other modernizations initiated by Reform that are now taken for granted even by our Orthodox and Conservative coreligionists. There are pusillanimous Reform Jews who want to roll the clock back on the patrilineal descent decision. Alas, history's forces will defeat them.

Reform's "Celebration of Diversity"

Our movement's numerical growth will continue in the new millennium. Fifty-five percent of the fourth generation of American Jews now identify as Reform, and if Orthodox extremism continues trying to exact unity for the sake of sterile uniformity, Reform's growth will be even greater. No doubt there will be those who criticize Reform's liberal canopy because it takes the neatness out of halachic labeling. What Reform stands for may be even more varied than that to which we are now accustomed. Professor Jonathan Sarna of Brandeis University has called this phenomenon Reform's "celebration of diversity." It underscores Reform's historic insistence that "there are many ways to be Jewish."

This brings up the problem of converts, the increasing number of "Jews-by-choice," as they are called. The majority of such converts have proved not to be "Jews-by-convenience." They have studied, grappled with theological issues, and faced skeptical communities, and nevertheless decided to convert to Judaism. Converts to Judaism have been among the loudest voices in calling for more spirituality in Judaism. They have taken their new faith seriously. There will be more of them, and because Reform is the most hospitable movement for such converts, they welcome it. Our challenge will be to help them understand Jewish people-hood—for converts a most difficult, theological concept of our faith.

I should like to close this essay with another prediction for Reform Judaism in the early decades of the twenty-first century, a prediction that relates to Reform's status and growth in Israel. Long and hard has been the struggle for the recognition of rights for non-Orthodox Jewish religious denominations in Israel. It is well known that Conservative, Reconstructionist, and Reform rabbis and their congregations are still largely religiously disenfranchised despite several notable Israeli Supreme Court decisions in our favor. Yet nonestablishment Jewish religious movements will grow in Israel. The spiritual hunger for such religious expression is evident where one least expected it, namely, among the kibbutzim, in the army, among the new immigrants from the former Soviet Union, and in the growing middle-class sector of Israeli life, which is having increasing contact with Diaspora Judaism.

New, indigenous forms of Reform Jewish belief, ceremonies, and attitudes will appear in Israel. They will be different from what exists now. We have seen of late the moral strength of minority expressions in Israel in the form of demon-strations, protest rallies, new elections, and a new government oriented to a vital peace process. The current moral questioning in Israel will grow, and an increas-ing number of Jews, prompted by its momentum, will search for alternative Jewish religious life styles. The dynamics of Reform will manifest themselves there as accelerated evolution and not as a revolution.[7]

We need to commit ourselves to a new Zionism that indeed involves all of us in questions not of dual loyalties, of whether America or Israel is our first love, but of holding both in passionate embrace, refusing to have them separate. The Reform Judaism at the threshold of the new millennium needs to be courageous and not timorous. We are past the age of the hush-hush Jew, the apologist and the assimilationist. We are looking to the future with new hope and with a clarity of vision so that our revelation will not be frozen, a past-tense experience only, but can unfold progressively into the future.

Notes

1. Avot 1:1.
2. Irving Greenberg, "Does God Hear the Prayer of Conservative and Reform Jews?" *Kansas City Jewish Chronicle*, December 11, 1981.
3. Harold Schulweis, "The Single Mirror of Jewish Images: The Pluralistic Character of Jewish Ethics," *University Papers*, University of Judaism, 1982, 1.
4. Robert Gordis, *The Jewish American Examiner*, December 20, 1982, 32–33.

5. "Secular Humanism May Bring Third Great Jewish Period," *Jewish Post and Opinion*, April 30, 1982.

6. *Jewish Post and Opinion*, December 25, 1981.

7. Alfred Gottschalk, "Israel and Reform Judaism: A New Perspective" (in Hebrew), *Gesher* 109 (1977). Also "A Strategy for Non-Orthodox Judaism in Israel," response to Ephraim Tabory, "The Reform and Conservative Movements in Israel: Organizational Platform and Aims," *Judaism* 36, 4 (1982).

20

Transforming the Reform Jew

SHELDON ZIMMERMAN

In the year 2000 we celebrate the 125th anniversary of the Hebrew Union College–Jewish Institute of Religion (HUC-JIR). What an extraordinary moment it is! The College-Institute is the oldest institution of higher Jewish learning in North America and the Western Hemisphere. Its graduates, faculty, and administration have been leaders in the world of Jewish scholarship and in determining the vision, aspirations, dreams, and reality of Progressive/Reform/Liberal Judaism throughout the world. Modern Judaism and Jewish scholarship are interlinked with HUC-JIR. As we enter the period of maturity and continuing growth, it is time to take stock of Reform Judaism and its achievements, as well as look to the new challenges of the present and future. I address the following comments, based on my address to the Central Conference of American Rabbis in 1987, primarily to the community of rabbis of which I am a part.

Jews and Modernity

Almost more that any other comparable group, we Jews have bought into modernity. Part of the process of modernization in which Reform Judaism participated, both in Germany and in the United States, was the process initiated by Moses Mendelsohn: to take Jews at home in the medieval community in which Torah and Jewishness (for me *Torah* is the word for Judaism, and I will use the two words interchangeably) were the center of life and bring them into the modern world. In other words, our task was to take Jews and make them modern, helping them to live in both worlds.

We have succeeded beyond any legitimate expectations. Our people are at home with modernity. We Reform Jews today, for the most part:

- Are highly educated in secular areas
- Are affluent
- Are at home in both the professional and business worlds—in all areas of vocational possibilities
- Enjoy a family life that is not different from the family life of other contemporary Western peoples
- Have children who are highly programmed, from athletics to computers to camp and, yes, even to Hebrew school (although Jewish matters get a smaller and smaller share)
- Have few among us (although many are ethical) who see any connection between ethics and their Jewishness, for we feel that we gain our ethical insights from the world around us
- Think education is important, but do not place the importance of Jewish education on the same level as secular education
- Are very privatized, believing that our religion is our own affair and that no one can tell us what to do; we reject the power of the community over our lives, whom we love and marry and how we raise our children, if we have any at all
- Dress the same way, eat the same way, enjoy the same music, read the same books, and go to the same vacation spots as everyone else.

We have become—we are—thoroughly modern!

The old anchors, the things that rooted us, are no longer. For the most part we no longer live in intensively Jewish neighborhoods; our community institutions and philanthropy are totally voluntary; the extended family, living in one neighborhood or city, has all but disappeared; and the nuclear family has taken on a variety of forms. Our lives beat to the new rhythms of America and not to the old, calendrical beat of what was Jewish life. We are far distanced from immigrant memories and from the stories of our tradition that have shaped Jewish memory over the centuries. The tragedy of the Holocaust and the inspiring drama of the reborn state of Israel no longer fill the yearning hearts and spirits of Jews.

To respond to this new world, a new question arises—a question that by its very nature is different, a question which by its very nature reflects a new reality. We know that a question is often more important than its answer, for it sets the stage and structure for whatever answers we attempt. The question also reveals something of the new world out of which it arises.

First, however, what was the old question? The old question was "How can we change Judaism—if you will, reform it—so that the Jew, newly entered into the modern world, will not reject Judaism? How can I as a Jew live in the modern and Jewish worlds at the same time?" Of course, this question was concerned with creating Judaism or Torah. By creating Torah that was consonant with modern sensitivities, intellectual currents, and the modern aesthetic, we could save Torah for the Jew. The Jew was changing. Either Torah changed or the Jewish people would lose the emerging, modern Jew. So we reformed Judaism, and in the process created a form of Torah that not only helped the Jew become modern but helped Jews stay Jewish, loyal to God and the Jewish community. In our eagerness to respond to the new challenges of today, let us not ignore the great contributions of early Reform.

Then our people became thoroughly modern. Their sense of self, community, and God derived not from the ancient spring of faith, *ma-ayan hadorot,* but rather from the raging torrents of modernity.

Part one of our equation: we took Jews and helped them adapt to modernity.

For two centuries we in the West thought that modernity and its servants, reason, science and the idea of progress, would be sufficient for a contemporary faith—a faith in which *altglauben* (to stand Samson Raphael Hirsch's term on its head) would be done away with, a faith espoused in the dreams of the Conservative movement, for example, that they would be the new traditionalism as Orthodoxy withered on the vine.

But surprise of surprises! The fires of *altglauben* remain. Orthodoxy has not disappeared, and, more significantly for us, people still seek meaning, endowing the meaning they seek with religious symbols. A yearning is springing forth in the soul of the modern human for religion, or perhaps more accurately, for the realm of the religious quest. Not that we reject science and technology, but we have come to understand their limitations. As essential as reason is, it cannot of itself project us into the realm of the transcendent and the meaning of personhood. And progress—even General Electric has dropped progress as its central advertising logo.

Martin Marty, the noted Christian theologian, puts it thus as he reflects on the surprising ability of religion to survive:

> Why are people religious? Because they cannot tolerate a completely random and plotless existence. Because someone they trust beckons them to believe. Because they hear the call of God.
>
> Or, it may be that they need suprahuman instruments to cope with human tragedy. . . . And, just as likely people respond to the transcendent as they celebrate joys undeserved, births and marriages, boons and blessings. Still others are religious as they find belonging and purpose by congregating in sanctuaries.

Individuals keep on being religious . . . citizens do not have to sneak around during their spiritual searches. To use Peter Berger's phrase, they do not have to "smuggle in their Gods in plain brown wrappers." . . . The questions faith signals and the tentative answers it implies are too cogent to go unheeded. So say those returnees to the sanctuaries, those keepers of bedside vigils, those people of consciences formed by belief.

This brings us to the second part of our equation. After taking the Jews and making them modern—now what?

Part two, then—the question we are asking, the question which by its very nature reflects a new reality: How can we take these moderns who truly believe that what they are doing is as Jewish as they need to be, and whose Jewishness is often minimal, superficial, and irrelevant—how can we take them and their initial return to religious search, including those who have a yearning in their hearts, and enable them to grow Jewishly in that search, enable them to encounter Torah in its broadest sense, and be transformed in the encounter?

Perhaps crassly, and certainly oversimply, how do we take moderns who feel some sense of needing more and make them Jewish, transforming and reforming Jews instead of Judaism? Our task is to reform Jews, giving Torah its say, if you will. For we belong to a people who used to change the times, not merely who changed in response to the times.

The rabbis often pointed to Psalm 119, verse 126: "*Et la-asot l-Adonai heferu toratecha,* it is a time for acting for God, they have broken Your Torah."

In early Reform they relied on a rabbinic understanding of the verse that permitted temporary abrogations of Torah law to maintain the general integrity of the Torah. *Et la-asot l-Adonai,* it is a time for acting for God. Because of the challenges of modernity, Torah needed to be changed. Time dictated the need to transform Torah radically.

Therefore, *heferu toratecha,* in order to save Torah, they have broken Your Torah.

Today we start with *heferu toratecha;* Torah has become nearly obliterated in the lives of our people.

Therefore, *et la-asot l-Adonai*—we respond by transforming the Jew—that becomes the religious imperative for us.

La-asot l-Adonai, to be holy for God—to do God's work is to transform the Jew and renew the sense and imperatives of Torah.

Our starting point, then, is that the Reform Jew of the beginning of the twenty-first century needs to be transformed.

Transform means that we no longer accept what is as the final statement of what ought to be.

Transform means that we reject the current intellectual and emotional world as the primary criterion of what we need to become.

Transform means to question and challenge the times in which we live and the products of those times, accepting and rejecting at the same time.

Transform means to accept Torah (in the broadest sense, in all its aspects) as that starting point of the encounter, to accept *teshuvah* as the primary category for Jews in our time.

What our people need as community and as persons—what we need as rabbis, as communities, and as persons—will not be determined only by demographic studies of what our people claim they need and want to be, but by the vision, worldview, insights, challenges, and imperatives of our tradition. To believe in the need for transformation is to believe that we have to assist our people in learning what they need. This is not patronizing—as if we know all the answers. Rather, we have come to understand that that what is, is not enough, that it somehow fails the test for ongoing commitments, loyalties, and faith—and we need to enable our people and ourselves to discover their needs in personal and communal encounters with God, our texts, and communal institutions. Our people will discover these needs within themselves, without our telling them. Out of this encounter can come a setting of standards—a vision for what can be—for self-transformation and communal transformation. Growing and becoming, a kind of Jewish stretching, rather than an easy acceptance of what is, will become renewed operative categories of Jewishness. We shall move toward *kedushah,* the realm of the sacred. I believe in the transforming capacity of faith, mitzvah, and *teshuvah.* I have seen it work—in children and seniors, in recovering alcoholics and substance abusers.

How will we then be Reform? Shall we not become an aspect of neotraditionalism? We shall remain loyal to Reform (1) by how we face and encounter the tradition, and (2) by beginning with the person, in each individual's autonomy, by helping him or her grow from within. We know that we cannot transform by external edict, by a halachah imposed from without. The will must come from within.

In 1987 an article on the new Orthodox appeared in *New York Magazine.* What emerged was a picture of men and women still doing what they want. Even *they* do not accept external edict without internal warrant and acceptance. As Reform Jews, we shall insist always on an encounter between the autonomous individual and God, Torah, and community.

It is not that we have to make Judaism good for Jews. Rather, we start from the premise that Judaism in its fullness *is* good for Jews and can transform, enrich, and uplift their lives. Like the old song of the *chalutsim:* "Anu banu artsa livnot ulehibanot ba, we have come to the land to build and be rebuilt in it." For us, we have come back to an authentic encounter with Torah to build and be rebuilt, transformed, and renewed by it, to find *kedushah*—to renew the voyage set in place millennia ago—*kedoshim tihyu. Teshuvah* emerges again as the central need of our times.

We begin the return, and almost magically we feel embraced and drawn even closer. *Teshuvah* is for us, as it is classically, a combination of Hosea's call "*Shuva Yisrael*"—we begin with our return—and then the further call "*Hashivenu Adonai eleicha venashuva*" (Lamentations 5:21): "Bring us back, O God, as we return; meet us on the way so that our return can be complete." Not magic, but true! We have all seen it happen—even for ourselves. We are embraced and drawn closer.

Torah is in a conceptual sense a verb—to be Jewish is a constant becoming. We move toward *kedushah*. Often like Jacob, we find *kedushah* where we have been standing or sleeping all along: "*Achen yesh Adonai bamakom hazeh, ve-anochi lo yada-ti*, surely God is in this place, I did not know it." How, then, do we move to this old, yet new, understanding? Let us begin with Jewish professional leadership, rabbis, cantors, educators, communal service professionals—*kelei kodesh*, vessels and instruments of the process of consecration.

We need to train men and women who can lead our synagogues, schools, and communal institutions and be transformative agents, able and skilled in working with other professionals and lay leaders in the communities in which they live. These well-trained professionals will reshape the centers of learning and religious commitment that are essential for sustaining and renewing Jewish life. They will help young and old individuals and families embark on a journey of discovery in order to help them create personal and communal Jewish worlds for themselves and others. Their task will be not preparation for a Jewish life but creation of a Jewish life.

These *kelei kodesh* will be passionate, soulful, literate, learned, and observant Jews. Brimming over with their own commitment, they will share of their spirit, knowledge, and soulfulness. They will enlarge their people's vocabulary of possibilities for growth and encounter on all levels—study, *mitzvah*, and the doing. They will empower them to be *mamlechet kohanim vegoy kadosh*—to be a kingdom of priests and a holy people. What are the possibilities and realities of our search for *kedushah*? What kinds of *kedushah* are we talking about?

Kinds of Kedusha

Kedushat ha-Shem—God's holiness, that there is a realm, transcendent yet close, a paradigm for human endeavor, a source of our striving, that which calls us beyond where we are now to the realm we can only image in dreams of palaces and gates, a fiery mountain, an ancient text. Can we connect our people's yearning and striving for God's personal touch in their lives with institutions that are, of necessity, highly structured and at times unfortunately impersonal?

Kedushat ha-chayim—that life itself is sacred, that we are blessed each day with opportunities to touch and be touched, to form and be formed, to find and be found. That to be a Jew is to be high on life and its opportunities for service. That to be a Jew is to celebrate time's passage annually and in our journey through life. *Kedushat hamo-adim vehazemanim*—the sanctifying of times.

Kedushat hazeman—that time is not merely limiting, but expanding, that in time there are unfolding possibilities for meaning, that killing time is a sin and sanctifying time is a blessing, that, as Bertrand Russell (certainly no theist) asserted, no one else can fill your particular time and space, only you. For you are an absolute particular, and if you do not fill it fully, it is unfilled and empty forever, a jarring emptiness in the vastness of the universe.

Kedushat ha-adam—that persons and person-ness are sacred, that *kedushah* cannot be neutral to persons, that *kedushah* is both person and God-centered, that you also are a complete world that I must nurture and for which I must care, that internal piety and spiritual piety without love of one's neighbors are not genuine piety, that piety without ethics is contrary to Torah. We assert that part of *kedushat ha-adam*, the sanctity of persons, is *kiddushin*, the sanctity of human relationships, *kedushat hamishpacha vehabayit*, the centrality and holiness of family and home. Without the home, Torah is lost. Without loving, nurturing relationships, living becomes a burden, a battle against loneliness.

Kedushat ha-arets veha-olam—that the world is a workshop for the sacred, waiting to be pulled yet higher through human creative effort, yet to be guarded, preserved, and handled with care. For *tov,* the world is good. The land of Israel has a special place in this ordering of sanctity and need measure its efforts by the measure of a higher standard.

Kedushat ha-Shabbat—that Sabbath observance is a transforming and renewing experience, giving us a sense of our own worth as God's children *just as we are* and who we are, separate from the roles we play professionally or familialy, separate from how much we make. We are God's children, as we stop what we are doing and are renewed.

Kedushat hakehilla veha-am—that we know that we do not move to the sacred alone always. There are moments when, like Jacob, we dream alone at night of a meeting between heaven and earth, and there are moments when we stand together at Sinai, individuals yet essentially connected to each other. Together we are more than just an aggregate of individuals, we become Israel. To denigrate this, our people and our community, by unethical behavior is a sin—*chilul,* the antithesis of *kedushah,* for we are voyagers toward *kedushah.*

Kedushat ha-Torah—that reason and revelation are forever linked, that the use of the mind is sacred. Study is worship, and in the use of the mind we discover the ongoing voice of God, the divine address to which we respond.

We are voyagers on a journey. Our task is to be *ma-alim bi kedushah*—those who raise the imperfectly sacred to higher realms of sanctity.

Attaining Kedushah

Can we translate these concerns for *kedushah* to attainable levels through the tangible realities of liturgy, the synagogue, the home, the school, and the community?

There is a way. This is not the only way, but it is a way. This way is translated into a myriad of possibilities around the synagogue and communal world today. If Torah, liturgy, mitzvah, the synagogue, home, and community can make a difference in our people's lives, then the process of *kedushah* (not the finished product, but Kedushah), becoming holy and making holy, can be actualized in our world.

If our synagogues and schools become centers of caring and learning, humanizing institutions where people are not numbers but feel touched and blessed by human closeness, where healing can take place, then we are on the way to *kedushah*.

If our synagogues and schools are places where people do not feel powerless and insignificant, where we teach them of *kedushah* by letting them know and experience that they and their lives count, places where God-experiences and encounters are goals worked for in the school, in the auxiliaries, and at every level of synagogue life—then we are on the way to *kedushah*.

Our synagogues and schools can become places where Torah is not only something on view in the ark, but a hands-on experience every day. They can become places where *gemilut chasadim*, acts of loving concern, are part of the obligations of membership. They can be places that work together with our people to create homes that are centers for Jewish living and loving, places that work together to build a creative and mutually supportive partnership between home and synagogue.

The very existence of the synagogue is to teach people that they are unique and that their lives are significant. The test of a religious institution is how we treasure each and every person, no matter how smart, no matter how wealthy or poor. We need to teach people to find significance in their lives and in their relationships. Can we honestly say that the elderly, sick, or homebound are not relegated to the back pages, ignored or made to feel useless because they cannot get to the temple on Friday night or during the week for a luncheon? The very life meaning of the synagogue is to say, "Your life counts. You are important to us and to God, whom we serve in this institution." It is to teach that the world is open and not indifferent. It is to say, "When you are not here, we miss you. When you are here, we care for you."

Our liturgy can help us understand the wonder of the world, ourselves, and our place in it, affirming our lives and our special moments, restating our ideals and hopes and giving them spiritual shape, affording us the means by which to express thanks for the gifts undeservedly ours and for the greatest gift, life itself. Our lives become an act of gratitude, a continuous Shehecheyanu, helping us move closer to God and faith.

We can build communities that help our people trust enough that they can overcome the walls of privatism and individualism that the times have erected. Our synagogues, schools, communities, and homes can become the refuges so many are seeking. There is a new, magnificent obsession, a house in the country, or so the *New York Times Magazine* highlighted. A New Jersey Jewish lawyer felt he was on a merry-go-round. Stanley Golkin said, "My daughters were growing up. I started noticing my gray hair and I started worrying about mortality. You ask yourself, 'What is it all for?' So instead of having a midlife crisis, I bought a house in the country." The obsession of having a second home, a weekend retreat, is upon us. The leitmotif is escape. People are seeking escape from a city. People perceive their country weekends as a form of "therapy, enabling them to cope with urban living." Norman Jaffe, an architect, says, "The country craze is spawned by our inability to alter our state of consciousness in the place we are." Professor Wachtel of City University says, "For the people from the most privileged sector, the house is a retreat from the way of life they've created for themselves. The country house is where they can live as they should be living all week—that is, as human beings."

Our people have become spacebound. Torah offers us palaces in time, yet our people are trying to find those palaces in space. In so doing, they are killing (by intensity, by changing the environment) the thing they love.

Our synagogues, communities, schools, and homes can help our people find refuges in them—build palaces in time. Through new forms of Shabbat and festival observances, through new celebrations of life moments, through a life-enhancing partnership, we can become again the architects of *kedushah* for our people. Through the enhancing of every moment of every day, we can help our people change right where they are, helping them live all week, as they should, as human beings.

All of these we are taught by our people's yet incomplete voyage. Being a Jew and a part of the Jewish community makes a difference in the algebra and calculus of the universe.

To be leaders in this community-in-process requires personal integrity and a set of standards and values. The world of the ethical seems to be crumbling around us. Too many of our people are the featured subjects of the daily record of the disintegration of our moral fabric. Ethics must be the prerequisite of the life of the Jew. How much more so should we demand of those who are honored by us. "*Mechabedai achabed,* only those who honor Me shall I honor." If we want our people to overcome their sense of remoteness from our community, let us help them see our ideals in the character and actions of those whom we choose to honor.

Holding Ourselves to the Same Standards

But before we call other to this accounting, should we not expect the same standards for ourselves, our synagogue, and religious community? *Peahs* do not mean piousness, nor do neo-*peahs* guarantee morality. How do our own personal lives, professional lives, the College and Union measure up to Amos' plumb line of old? Yet we hear the words *tikkun olam* again and again. Our goal is not only *letaken olam,* but, as the phrase continues, *letaken olam bemalchut Shaddai,* ethics as the prerequisite on the road to holiness.

Belief, too, transforms. It helps me sense who I am, why I am here and how best I can serve. We are all *mevakeshei derech,* searching for God's hints and signals in every place and at every time. The joy, the agony, the celebration, and the doubts all are affirming of the One whose Name we long ago forgot how to pronounce.

God, too, transforms us. In all my work with Jewish alcoholics and substance abusers I have watched them struggle to let go and let God. They have taught us that we cannot always program it the right way. We cannot control it all. Often religious worship fails to lift us. Often our study ends in agonizing confusion and a myriad of interpretations. Often our attempts at helping others backfire in mutual resentment and antagonism. At times we feel the world will never change. We and our congregations fall short again and again. We can't always be in control and do it.

Sometimes we need to let go and let God. And at that moment we feel embraced, held, and uplifted. If you doubt this, then ask people of their faith. Talk to those who can teach us of God, of God's presence and love, of those moments when they encountered the divine in their lives. We need to create institutions that are open to the possibility of this encounter, an encounter that can take place in a moment of prayer, study, doing mitzvah, or even moving chairs. These are places in time or space where God has reached out, but we did not know or understand.

The world awaits. Our people await. Torah teaches that we are created in God's image, *betselem Elohim.* Many interpretations have been given of this concept, all helpful and important. Permit me to suggest another. What is the image of God in that first chapter in *Bereshit?* God is a *Borei,* a *Yotser,* a Creator. To be created in God's image is to be like God, a creator. Perhaps now we can understand the verse *"Ki vo shavat mikol melachto asher bara Elohim la-asot,* God rested on it [Shabbat] from all the work which God had created *la-asot,* to be done, for doing." By whom? By us. God created a world, a place where we can do God's work, *melachto.*

Et la-asot l-Adonai, back to the verse in Psalms, it is time for God's work, *la-asot,* to be done by us. We are God's workers on the journey toward the end of time itself—*yom shekulo Shabbat, yom shekulo kadosh*—a day that is totally Shabbat, totally sacred. This Jewish journey is the way of *kedushah*—becoming holy and making holy—*lehitkadesh ulekadesh.*

We are the sanctifiers-in-process, where we and our lives can make the ultimate difference in the journey to the fulfillment of the promise.

Bayom hahu yihyeh Adonai echad ushemo echad, finally, in that day God shall be One and God's name One—One and united forever.

Afterword

W. GUNTHER PLAUT

Writing an afterword to this impressive collection of essays is both easy and daunting. Easy, because there is a common streak that runs through most of the book, yet daunting because this very commonality hides a great variety of emphases, affirmations, and criticisms. The common streak lies in the issue-oriented nature of the articles: they invite discussion because they affirm one thing and criticize another, with the emphasis clearly on the latter. In fact, one might subtitle this volume "A Critique of Reform Judaism by Reform Jews and Some Others." This will not come as a surprise to members of the movement who consider self-criticism a quintessential element of Reform. For if change is its ineluctable context, as they will assert, such change is likely to take place, because Reform Judaism's performance will always call for improvement and even redirection. We change because we feel that our religious striving is more likely to be fulfilled if we admit that we have fallen short of our goal. By nature, Reform is always on the way.

I look at my own journey and know that redirection was its major theme as well. My home environment in pre-Nazi Germany was liberal, which in American terms might be likened to left-wing Conservatism. Regular synagogue attendance was a given and was supported by kashrut, the basic home rituals, and a magnificent library that had a large Jewish component. We owned no car, so that its use or nonuse on Shabbat was no issue. Walking was in any case our means of locomotion, and summer vacations consisted of organized hiking. Living in Berlin, I visited synagogues of all descriptions and listened to renowned preachers such as Leo Baeck, Joachim Prinz, Max Nussbaum, and Manfred Swarsensky.

I had my eye set on the legal profession, graduated from law school, and was promptly disenfranchised by the Nazis, who had come to power. An invitation by Hebrew Union College saved my life and set me on the way to the rabbinate. This sounds easier than it was, for there is nothing easy about being a refugee and trying to make another land, language, and culture one's own, aside from embracing a new profession.

I knew nothing about American Reform Judaism when I arrived in the middle of the Great Depression. A service with hatless rabbis and congregants was a shock, and the sparsity of Hebrew, combined with my own deficient knowledge of the English language, made me initially a stranger in the temple. Much later, and after a slow and often painful adjustment to my new environment, I would learn where the mid-1930s fitted into the flow of Reform history.

From the perspective of the new millennium I discern five distinct phases. The first encompasses the age of the German founders. They introduced their modest reforms only after answering the question "*Mah yomru ha-avot?* What would tradition say to this?" They studied halachic precedents and debated them vigorously at three conferences in the 1840s. Reformers of the first phase considered Judaism's halachic structure a given.

In America, Reform entered a new phase when Jews met a radically changed environment. For the first time in their lives immigrants experienced the wonder of civic equality and in short order ardently embraced the opportunity of full acceptance. Now the question was not "*Mah yomru ha-avot?*" but "*Mah yomru ha-goyim?*" The (first) Pittsburgh Platform reflected that concern, albeit hiding it behind the silver screen of modernity. Reform in the New World became nonhalachic.

The third phase began in the mid-1930s. It was a time when the impact of the new immigration, the dislocations of the First World War, and the threat of anti-Semitism on both sides of the Atlantic were fully felt. In addition, many Jews belonged to what was called later the "lost generation," who in their eagerness to meld into the American mainstream had changed their names and neglected their Judaism. That was the time when I arrived in the States. The question now was "*Mah yomru ha-banim?* How can we ensure Jewish survival?" World War II and Shoah made an effective answer to the question urgent, for the newborn state of Israel was too enmeshed in ensuring its own survival to be of assistance to us. We responded with an emphasis on Jewish education, and the creation of new congregations, new synagogues, and communal institutions; we enlisted our members in *tikkun olam,* the challenges of building a just community.

In the 1970s, when the baby boomers had grown up, they and their elders discovered the need for their own Jewish education and responded to a new question: "*Ma yomru chayai?* How can I make my own life Jewishly more meaningful?" That was the age when we ordained women; acknowledged the rights of the homosexual community; wrote guides for Jewish living as well as a spate of prayer books; brought out commentaries on Torah, Haftarot, and Pirkei Avot; and established study classes and a healing community. Not the least of the changes then occurring has been our identification with Israel and its future. This is the time in which the book conceived by Dana Evan Kaplan is being published.

Or perhaps we have already entered a fifth phase. Many of the writers here assembled seem to take cognizance of the challenge it will pose. I see them in their various approaches trying to respond to a new question: "*Mah yomru bameromim?* What does God say to us today?" It is a question we must try to answer for our sake and for the sake of the multitudes who have been joining our ranks or are waiting to do so.

About the Contributors

Steven Bayme has been the national director of the Jewish Affairs Department of the American Jewish Committee Institute of Human Relations since 1987. Since 1992 he has also been director of the AJC's Institute on American Jewish–Israel Relations. A visiting professor at the Jewish Theological Seminary of America, he is the author of numerous journal articles and book chapters as well as four books, including *Understanding Jewish History: Texts and Commentaries* (KTAV, 1997).

Jay R. Brickman is rabbi emeritus at Congregation Sinai in Milwaukee, Wisconsin, where he has served since 1955. A graduate of Hebrew Union College–Jewish Institute of Religion, where he also received an honorary doctor of divinity degree, he holds an M.A. in Hebrew studies from the University of Wisconsin–Madison. He has studied Jungian psychology at institutes in Zurich, Switzerland, and Evanston, Illinois. Winner of the Frank Zeidler Interfaith Award, he is the author of *Reflections in a Pumpkin Field* and *Reflections on a Lily Pond*.

Richard Cimino is editor and publisher of *Religion Watch,* a newsletter monitoring trends in contemporary religion. He is the author of *Against the Stream: The Adoption of Traditional Christian Faiths by Young Adults* (1996) and coauthor (with Don Lattin) of *Shopping for Faith: Religion in the New Millennium* (1998). Cimino is currently writing a book on renewal and reform movements in American religion.

Hillel Cohn has served as rabbi of Congregation Emanu El in San Bernardino since 1963. A native of Germany, he was brought to the United States as an infant by his parents, who were refugees from Nazism. Rabbi Cohn received a B.A. in political science from the University of California, Los Angeles, in 1959. His rabbinical training was received at Hebrew Union College in Los Angeles and Cincinnati, where he was ordained as a rabbi in 1963 and received an M.A. degree. He earned a doctor of ministry degree from the School of Theology at Claremont in 1984, specializing in ethics and communications. In 1988 he was awarded an honorary doctor of divinity degree by Hebrew Union College. Rabbi Cohn is treasurer of the Central Conference of American Rabbis and is a past president of the San Bernardino Clergy Association, the interdenominational ministerial group of the area.

Denise L. Eger is the founding rabbi of Congregation Kol Ami in West Hollywood, California. She has served as the rabbi to the gay and lesbian community of Los Angeles since 1988. Rabbi Eger chairs the Task Force on Gays and Lesbians in the Rabbinate for the Central Conference of American Rabbis and is a cochair of the Gay and Lesbian Rabbinic Network. She is married to Karen Siteman, an attorney, and together they have a son, Benjamin.

Lewis A. Friedland is associate professor in the School of Journalism and Mass Communication at the University of Wisconsin–Madison. The author of a number of articles on community, public life, and the media, he is coauthor with Carmen Sirianni of *Civic Innovation in America* (forthcoming, University of California Press). With Sirianni he edits the *Civic Practices Network* (www.cpn.org). Friedland is an award-winning documentary producer and consults for a variety of newspapers and television organizations in the United States. A lifelong Reform Jew, this is his first publication in this field.

Karla Goldman was the first full-time woman faculty member on the Cincinnati campus of Hebrew Union College–Jewish Institute of Religion in Cincinnati. She is the author of *Beyond the Synagogue Gallery: Finding a Place for Women in American Judaism* (Harvard University Press, 2000).

Rabbi **Alfred Gottschalk**, Ph.D., is the chancellor of Hebrew Union College–Jewish Institute of Religion. He is also Distinguished Professor of Bible and Jewish Thought and the John and Marianne Slade Professor of Jewish Intellectual History at HUC–JIR, where he served as president from 1971 to 1995. Professor Gottschalk is the author of numerous books and publications. One of his major works is *Ahad Ha-Am and the Jewish National Spirit* (in Hebrew), published in Jerusalem in 1992. He has written, edited, and translated several books and over 150 essays, articles, and translations. He has won numerous honors and awards, including fifteen honorary degrees from distinguished colleges and universities. Professor Gottschalk has been an active member of the United States Holocaust Memorial Council, since his appointment by President Jimmy Carter in 1978 and his reappointments to the council by Presidents Reagan and Clinton.

Samuel K. Joseph is a professor of Jewish education and leadership development at the Hebrew Union College–Jewish Institute of Religion, Cincinnati, Ohio. He is an ordained rabbi and has a doctorate in education. He lectures to, consults for, and facilitates for synagogues and churches throughout the world, including Australia, New Zealand, Brazil, Argentina, Canada, the former Soviet Union, Hong Kong, China, and Israel.

Dana Evan Kaplan is Oppenstein Brothers Assistant Professor of Judaic and Religious Studies and Director of the Danciger Program in Jewish Studies, both in the Department of History at the University of Missouri–Kansas City. He has a Ph.D. in American Jewish History from Tel Aviv University, and he also has rabbinic ordination from Hebrew Union College–Jewish Institute of Religion in Jerusalem.

Bernard M. Lazerwitz teaches in the Department of Sociology and Anthropology at Bar Ilan University in Ramat Gan, Israel. His publications have centered on the areas of survey research, ethnicity and religious involvement, and religious affairs. He has had more than thirty years of experience in survey work, covering all of its aspects, from the design of complex samples to interview schedule construction, training and management of field forces, and complex statistical analysis.

Joel L. Levine is rabbi of Temple Judea in West Palm Beach, Florida. He has an A.B. in history from the University of Michigan and was ordained a rabbi in 1973 at the Hebrew Union College–Jewish Institute of Religion in Cincinnati, where he received a doctor of divinity degree in 1998. He is active in a variety of community activities, including the United Jewish Communities Rabbinic Cabinet and the Palm Beach County Board of Rabbis. Rabbi Levine has published numerous articles in the *Palm Beach Post* and the *Palm Beach Jewish Times.*

Martin E. Marty is the Fairfax M. Cone Distinguished Service Professor Emeritus at the University of Chicago and the George B. Caldwell Senior Scholar in Residence at the Park Ridge Center for the Study of Health, Faith, and Ethics. The author of over fifty books, most of them in the field of American religious history, Marty, a Lutheran minister, has been involved in interfaith relations for over forty years. He is author of the three-volume *Modern American Religion,* is a National Book Award winner, and is recipient of the National Humanities Medal and the Medal of the American Academy of Arts and Sciences. Among his sixty-four honorary degrees is one from Hebrew Union College.

Jacob Neusner holds the position of research professor of religion and theology at Bard College, Annandale-on-Hudson, New York. He has published numerous books on a wide range of topics in the history of Judaism. He holds nine honorary doctorates and fourteen academic medals.

W. Gunther Plaut is the Senior Scholar at Holy Blossom Temple in Toronto, Ontario, Canada, where he has served since 1961. Born in Germany, where he graduated from law school and received a doctor of laws degree, he fled from the Nazis and studied to be a rabbi at the Hebrew Union College in Cincinnati. He has published twenty-five books, including fiction. His best-known book is *The Torah—A Modern Commentary,* of which he was the editor and chief author. In addition to writing on theology, philosophy, and history, he has held major communal posts, including that of president of the Central Conference of American Rabbis.

Rabbi **Alexander M. Schindler**, the president of the Union of American Hebrew Congregations from 1973 to 1996, presently serves as president of the Memorial Foundation for Jewish Culture and vice president of the World Jewish Congress. In response to the increasing rate of intermarriage among American Jews, Rabbi Schindler devised the controversial Outreach program, which has been ongoing since 1978. Born in Germany in 1925, Rabbi Schindler fled the Nazis with his family, arriving in the United States when he was twelve. He earned a Purple Heart and Bronze Star for bravery in action as a ski trooper in Europe, and graduated from the College of the City of New York before studying for the rabbinate at Hebrew Union College, where he was ordained in 1953. He has received honorary doctorates from several American colleges and universities.

Hinda Seif is a doctoral student in anthropology at the University of California, Davis, and a member of the advisory board of *Bridges: A Journal for Jewish Feminists and Our Friends*. She thanks Alina, Jim, Susie, and Naomi for providing invaluable help in organizing this project, and thanks also the Women's Studies Department of the University of Arizona, Myra Dinnerstein, Janet Jakobsen, Susan Philips, Clare Kinberg, Marla Brettschneider, and the Charles and Gertrude Gordon Foundation.

Dr. **Harold S. Silver** is rabbi emeritus of Congregation Beth Israel in West Hartford, Connecticut. He retired in June 1993 after occupying that pulpit for twenty-five years. Before coming to New England, he served Temple Emanuel in Pittsburgh for thirteen years and before that began his career with Solomon Freehof at Rodef Shalom Temple. He is currently working on his memoirs, *Confession of a Reform Rabbi*, to be published during 2001.

Aryeh Spero has served Orthodox congregations in both Canton, Ohio, and New York City. His articles have been published in *Tradition, Judaism, Sh'ma, Midstream, Jewish Spectator, Response, New York Jewish Week, Post and Opinion, Policy Review, Washington Times, Wall Street Journal*, and other magazines and journals. He appears often on television and radio and has testified before the House Judiciary Committee.

Ephraim Tabory is head of the graduate studies program in the Department of Sociology and Anthropology at Bar Ilan University, Israel, and director of the department's graduate program in social psychology. His research focuses on intergroup relations in Israel, especially between Orthodox and nonreligious Jews, and on Israeli liberal Jewish denominations. He is a member of the Scientific Advisory Committee of the World Jewish Congress for its International Survey of Jewish Communities (1999–2001).

Arnold Jacob Wolf, rabbi emeritus of the Midwest's oldest congregation, Kam Isaiah Israel, is responsible for six books, including *Unfinished Rabbi,* a collection of his essays and reviews (1998). He has taught at Hebrew Union College–Jewish Institute of Religion (in New York and Los Angeles), Yale, the University of Chicago Divinity School, and Loyola-Marymount University. He is a founding editor of *Shima,* theological editor of *Judaism,* and an activist with many human rights organizations.

Rabbi **Eric H. Yoffie** is president of the Union of American Hebrew Congregations. Since becoming president in June 1996, Rabbi Yoffie has made a return to Torah and the need for increased Jewish literacy his major messages. A staunch fighter for the rights of all Jews in Israel, he is also a leading spokesperson in the struggle for recognition of the rights of Reform Jews in Israel. Rabbi Yoffie, a native of Worcester, Massachusetts, is a Phi Beta Kappa, magna cum laude graduate of Brandeis University. Ordained at Hebrew Union College–Jewish Institute of Religion in New York in 1974, Rabbi Yoffie served congregations in Lynbrook, New York, and Durham, North Carolina, before joining the UAHC as director of the Midwest Council of the UAHC in 1980. In 1983 Rabbi Yoffie was named executive director of the Association of Reform Zionists of America and served as executive editor of *Reform Judaism* magazine. Rabbi Yoffie's articles have appeared in *Reform Judaism, CCAR Journal, Commentary, Tikkun, Jerusalem Post, The Forward, Jewish Spectator, Jewish Frontier, Sh'ma,* and *Hadoar.* He serves on the board of directors of many Jewish organizations, including MAXON: A Jewish Response to Hunger and the Jewish Agency for Israel.

Rabbi **Sheldon Zimmerman** is president of Hebrew Union College–Jewish Institute of Religion. He has served as rabbi of Central Synagogue, New York City, and Temple Emanu-El, Dallas. From 1993 to 1995 he served as president of the Central Conference of American Rabbis. He has served as adjunct faculty at Hunter College, Fordham University, and Perkins Seminary at Southern Methodist University.

Index